SIMONE WEIL:
SEVENTY LETTERS

SIMONE WEIL
Seventy Letters

Personal and Intellectual Windows on a Thinker

Translated and arranged by
RICHARD REES

WIPF & STOCK · Eugene, Oregon

Wipf and Stock Publishers
199 W 8th Ave, Suite 3
Eugene, OR 97401

Seventy Letters
Personal and Intellectual Windows on a Thinker
By Weil, Simone and Rees, Richard
Copyright©1965 Peters, Fraser, & Dunlop
ISBN 13: 978-1-4982-3920-2
Publication date 12/18/2015
Previously published as Seventy Letters:
Some Hitherto Untranslated Texts from Published
and Unpublished Sources by Oxford University Press, 1965

SERIES FOREWORD
SIMONE WEIL: SELECTED WORKS

SIMONE WEIL IS A thinker who is eminently quotable, one who could write in Pascal-like aphorisms. She also led a striking and distinctive life. What is therefore most readily known about her are a few of the facts of that life, and a few of her dazzling and often puzzling sayings. But she was so much deeper than that. Her essays, notebooks, and her letters together comprise a remarkable *oeuvre*, and all of them bear close study. They require attention, and they also require comparison across their various topics and genres in order for anyone to get a holistic sense of Weil as a thinker, indeed, as one of the most original and intellectually and spiritually profound thinkers of the twentieth century. Without question, Weil was somebody who could bring insights together from what to us are often seen as disparate subject matters, and she could then make these insights bear on our present states of affairs. But to see this profound integration, one has to first see all the different subject matters that Weil treated. Unfortunately, over the years that has become increasingly difficult for English speakers due to the limited availability of her complete body of writings.

At the time that Richard Rees published his translations of so many of Weil's writings in the 1960s, what was available to English speaking readers was the object of most of the world's envy. As those books went out of print, they were never adequately replaced, although there have been and currently are some decent smaller collections, especially on Weil's religious thinking. It will therefore be a matter of great help to those who would know Simone Weil in depth to have in these three volumes the republication of three of Rees' original volumes: the essays of *Selected Essays:1934-43*; complete notebooks, not just excerpted fragments, in *The First and Last Notebooks*; and thirdly, something that even French readers did not have until very recently, namely a number of Weil's letters in *Seventy Letters*. With new subtitles, the present trilogy of Selected Works printed by Wipf and Stock Publishers consists of:

1. First and Last Notebooks: Supernatural Knowledge
2. Seventy Letters: Personal and Intellectual Windows on a Thinker
3. Selected Essays, 1934-1943: Historical, Political and Moral Writings

Since the initial publication of her many writings, which began shortly after her death, Weil has continued to be an important figure for several successive generations, each finding something new and inspiring in her, whether it has been political, moral, or religious. Now, in an age that looks for a center while eschewing all authoritarianisms, it appears that Weil, the outsider who is also the fully committed witness, once more has something striking to say. Here, now, is full access to her voice.

Eric Springsted
March 2015
Co-founder and President of The American Weil Society 1981-2014.

CONTENTS

Series Foreword   iv
Foreword   ix

Part I   1931-1937

1 To a colleague, 1931 or 1932	1
2 To Émile Auguste Chartier, 1933(?)	3
3 To X, 1933 or 1934 (C.O.)	6
4 To a pupil, 1934	7
5 To a pupil, 1935 (C.O.)	10
6 To Albertine Thévenon, 1935 (C.O.)	14
7 To Boris Souvarine, 1935 (C.O.)	17
8-9 To Albertine Thévenon, 1935 (C.O.)	19
10-20 To B., 1936 (C.O.)	23
21 From B. to S.W., 1936 (C.O.)	53
22 To B., 1936 (C.O.)	53
23-25 To Auguste Detœuf, 1936-7 (C.O.)	55
26 From Auguste Detœuf to S.W., 1937 (C.O.)	64

Part II   1937-1942

27-28 To Jean Posternak, 1937	72
29 To her mother, 1937	79
30-32 To Jean Posternak, 1937-8	82
33 To Gaston Bergery, 1938 (E.H.P.)	96
34 To an Oxford poet, 1938	102
35 To Georges Bernanos, 1938 (E.H.P.)	105
36 To Jean Giraudoux, 1939 or 1940 (E.H.P.)	110
37-39 To A.W., 1940	112
40 To Edoardo Volterra, 1940	127

41 To Déodat Roché, 1941 (P.S.O.)	129
42 To Admiral Leahy, 1941	132
43 To A.W. (1941-2)	133
44 To Joë Bousquet, 1942 (P.S.O.)	136

Part III 1942-1943

45-47 To Maurice Schumann, 1942 (E.L.)	144
48 To Jean Wahl, 1942	157
49-52 To her parents, 1942-3 (E.L.)	161
53 To Maurice Schumann, 1943 (E.L.)	169
54-56 To her parents, 1943 (E.L.)	179
57 To André Weil, 1943 (E.L.)	184
58-69 To her parents, 1943 (E.L.)	185
Index	203

Published sources are indicated as follows:

C.O.: *La Condition ouvrière* © 1951 Éditions Gallimard
E.H.P.: *Écrits historiques et politiques* © 1960 Éditions Gallimard
P.S.O.: *Pensées sans ordre concernant l'amour de Dieu* © 1962 Éditions Gallimard
E.L.: *Écrits de Londres* © 1957 Éditions Gallimard

[Although not hitherto collected in a book, the following letters have appeared in magazines: Nos. 27, 28, and 30-32 in *Nuovi Argomenti* (Rome), No. 40 in *Letteratura* (Rome) and No. 48 in *Deucalion* (Paris)]

ILLUSTRATIONS

Plate *facing page*
I *a*. Simone Weil with her father in 1915 . . 18
  b. On holiday at Le Loote, 1922 or 1923 . . 18
  c. Portrait photograph of about 1926 . . . 18

II *a*. Simone Weil during her time with the C.N.T., at Barcelona, 1936 19
  b. In Marseilles, 1942 19
  c. In New York, 1942 19

III/IV Portions of her letter to her parents, 4 August 1943 (No. 68 in this book) *between pages* 194/5

FOREWORD

A good many of Simone Weil's letters have appeared in books by or about her, but no comprehensive collection of them has yet been published. The purpose of this volume is the limited one of making available as many as possible of those letters which have been published in France or elsewhere but not yet translated into English.[1] I have however, through the kindness of her executors and her correspondents, been able to include also a number of letters which have not hitherto been published anywhere.

I have seen the originals of some of the letters but all the translation has been done from typescript copies provided by Simone Weil's scrupulous French editor or from the published versions. As will be seen from the specimens between pages 194 and 195 her handwriting was exceptionally clear, so mistaken readings are likely to be few. The complete collection of her letters which will no doubt be made one day will be a very large book, but there are a sufficient number here to give a varied and impressive picture of her intellectual and practical activities during the last ten years of her life. I have arranged them so far as possible in chronological order, but some of them are undated drafts or copies (Simone Weil appears very often to have kept careful drafts of her letters). I have put conjectured dates and addresses in italics between square brackets.

In translating letters from the French one is faced immediately with the problem of modes of address. You can begin a letter in French with the single word 'Mademoiselle', but not in English with the single word 'Miss'; and 'Monsieur' is not such a cold and distant approach in French as 'Sir' in English. Nor is 'Cher ami' at all the same as 'Dear Friend'. So where the commencement of a letter seems to me untranslatable I have left it in French. Another problem is the number of English words used by Simone Weil. I have used the symbol ° to indicate words which are in English in the original text; but in the letters from London in 1942-3 the words *darling, Public Library, cockney, girl,*

[1] Letters or fragments of letters already translated into English will be found in Simone Weil's *Selected Essays* (Oxford), in the introduction to *Gravity and Grace*, in the *Letter to a Priest* and *Waiting on God*, and in *Simone Weil as we knew her* by J-M. Perrin and G. Thibon (all published by Routledge, Kegan Paul), and in Jacques Cabaud's *Simone Weil* (Harvill Press).

boy, pub and others occur so often that I have used the symbol only the first time they appear. Simone Weil often quoted Greek and Latin texts from memory. I have given the reference for every quotation and the reader who looks them up will find that she was not always word-perfect. But as the inaccuracies are trivial I have not indicated them. Dots between brackets indicate omissions; the others are Simone Weil's.

Without the untiring help of Simone Weil's mother, Madame Bernard Weil, it would have been impossible to produce this book; and among others who have allowed me to pester them for information on every subject from armature-winding to the *École Normale* and from Horace to incommensurables are Professor A. Weil, Mrs. Degras, Dr. A. S. F. Gow, Mr. M. St. C. Oakes, Professor J. Posternak, Professor E. Volterra, Mr. and Mrs. L. Whitaker, and Mr. L. L. Whyte. I have divided the letters chronologically into three groups and before each group I have added some biographical data to give the background. Her stay in the south of France, 1940-2, is well documented by Father Perrin and Monsieur Thibon; but concerning her Spanish civil war experience there is nothing in print, so far as I know, except the letter to Bernanos (no. 35 below)[1] and the brief 'Journal d'Espagne' in *Écrits historiques et politiques*.

* * *

The range of subjects covered by these letters is extremely wide – from the history of science to labour relations, from power politics to religion, from music to sabotage in war. Some of the letters are not easy reading, but the reader who picks and chooses is sure to miss something important. The letters of 1936 to B., for example, are oppressive to read through and it is easy to understand B.'s final outburst of irritation. But not to feel the oppressiveness and the irritation is to miss Simone Weil's unique insight into the psychology of manual labour. What she is writing about is what D. H. Lawrence called 'organic disintegration', the effect of rationalization upon the worker; and it would not be too much to say that oppressiveness and irritation are precisely the subject of those letters. It is significant that B. and Detœuf, the two long-suffering industrialists to whom she wrote in this vein, do not ever seem to have contradicted her with much conviction on this aspect of industrial organization.

[1] Translation reprinted from Simone Weil, *Selected Essays* (O.U.P. 1962).

Foreword

But her *Journal d'usine*, the diary she kept while working in factories, gives the flavour of the experience in a way that her painstaking letters to the two employers hardly succeed in doing. In this diary a machine-setter is called a 'young swine' (*jeune salaud*) and one of the foremen is very nice, 'with a positive kindness (whereas that of Leclerc, my own foreman, comes more from his being easy-going and not giving a damn) [. . . .] One day he glanced at me in passing, while I was miserably decanting some heavy bolts, with my hands, into an empty crate. . . . I must never forget that man.' (*La Condition ouvrière*, page 87.) Nevertheless, and for all her perceptiveness about her fellow workers, the suspicion remains that she sometimes forgot that many of them were constitutionally unsusceptible to the kind of intense irritation she herself felt at the monotony and automatism of the work.

The series of letters from Italy in 1937 makes a pleasing contrast and at the same time completely refutes the criticism that Simone Weil was unable to enjoy life and was exclusively obsessed with suffering. Not only did she know how to enjoy life but she continually recommended her friends to do the same and consistently maintained that joy as well as sorrow can be a road to wisdom. ('Joy is an indispensable ingredient of human life, for the health of the mind; so that a complete absence of joy would be equivalent to madness.') But it remains true, of course, that on the whole and most often she chose the more painful way for herself. And yet – it is surely not a fundamentally sorrowful woman who can write, as she does after reading Giraudoux's *Électre*: 'Why have I not the *n* existences I need, in order to be able to devote one of them to the theatre!'

One could comment indefinitely on the extraordinary glimpses these letters offer of a mind which could combine idealism with realism and extremism with moderation. When she is arguing the pacifist case, as in letter no. 33, she is under no illusion about the drawbacks of her policy. She offers it merely as the lesser evil. Herself a Jewess and indistinguishable, in Nazi eyes, from a Communist, she concedes that her pacifist policy would involve discrimination against Jews and Communists in France. This kind of honesty in political argument is so rare as to be almost unique.

Later, when events have converted her to militancy, she puts forward a scheme for getting women to the most dangerous parts of the front, which is remarkable in two ways. First, it was sufficiently practicable to be taken seriously by the military authorities; and second, it is the only scheme I have ever heard of which might conceivably, if put into practice, make war in the end impossible. What a contrast between the Russian and Spanish Amazons with rifles and Simone Weil's unarmed women facing certain death in the attempt to administer summary first aid against shock, exposure, and loss of blood. . . . Her frontline nurses might have made an even greater impression than she foresaw. They might have produced a situation not unlike the Christmas day fraternization across the trenches in the First World War.

And in fascist Italy how coolly she distinguishes between the good and the bad features of the State organization, and how clearly she recognizes the real Italy behind the Mussolinian façade: 'Thank heaven, the people who are obsessed by all these myths are not the only people in this country; there are also men and women of the people, and young fellows in blue overalls, whose faces and manners have visibly been moulded only by daily contact with problems of real life.' Which can be placed alongside her advice to the Oxford poet: 'Genius is distinct from talent, to my mind, by its deep regard for the common life of common people [. . . .] mankind can do very well without clever poetry [. . . .] the soul of genius is *caritas*.'

* * *

> *Wer Wissenschaft und Kunst besitzt*
> *hat auch Religion;*
> *wer jene beiden nicht besitzt,*
> *der habe Religion.*

(He who possesses art and science has also religion; he who possesses neither of these, let him have 'religion'.) But to Goethe art and science meant something very different from what they mean today; and so they did to Simone Weil. She, however, being separated from Goethe by a century of appalling history, saw from a different angle the interdependence of art and science and religion. She saw that where there is no real religion, but only 'religions', there can be no real art or science. She was one of the extremely, and increasingly, rare people who possess culture in Goethe's sense of the word; she did not keep art and science and religion (or politics either) in watertight compartments.

It is true, no doubt, that after the experiences beginning at Solesmes, which she describes in *Attente de Dieu*, she came nearer to orthodox

Christianity – but also to Catharism and several other religions, though this is often not remarked upon – than she had been before. But she wrote to Bernanos in the same year that 'nothing that is Catholic, nothing that is Christian has *ever* [my italics] seemed alien to me' (*ne m'ait jamais paru étranger*); and a year earlier, writing to Jean Posternak, she had found in Socrates, Plato, and the Gospel one and the same essential thought; and four years later, in a letter to Jean Wahl, she sees 'one identical thought', which is 'the truth', in a number of different religious and philosophical traditions, including Greek Stoicism, the Upanishads, Taoism, the dogmas of the Christian faith, and certain heresies, 'especially the Cathar and Manichaean tradition'. In the period covered by these letters, from 1931 or 1932 until her death in 1943, the subjects which engaged her attention varied from time to time, but I cannot detect any radical change in her attitude to life. She had certainly been a Stoic, and I believe also a Platonist, from the beginning.

Among the most valuable letters in this collection are those written to A.W. in 1940, about the foundations of Western science. They make a great deal of the contemporary controversy about two so-called cultures (scientific and literary) completely meaningless; and they make an essential corrective to the patronizing attitude so often adopted nowadays towards the Greeks who laid the foundations of our science. One finds this attitude even in writers like Russell, Popper, and Farrington. After giving the pre-Socratics a few pats on the head, they proceed to reprimand Plato for every crime in the twentieth-century liberal calendar, from historicism to paternalism, which they seem scarcely to distinguish from fascism. But the letters to A.W. do much more than expose the callowness of such an unhistorical judgement; they reveal the superficiality of nearly all modern thinking about religion and science and art.

> The [algebraic] work of Diophantus could have been written many centuries earlier than it was; but the Greeks attached no value to a method of reasoning for its own sake, they valued it in so far as it enabled concrete problems to be studied efficiently. And this was not because they were avid for technical applications but because their sole aim was to conceive more and more clearly an identity of structure between the human mind and the universe. Purity of soul was their one concern; to 'imitate God' was the secret of it [. . . .] It was for the Greeks that mathematics was really an art. It had the same purpose as their art,

to reveal palpably a kinship between the human mind and the universe, so that the world is seen as 'the city of all rational beings'.

* * *

This book contains one letter less than the title announces. The reader will perhaps agree, however, that the enclosures to letters Nos. 10 and 45 are more than long enough to count as an additional letter.

February, 1965   R. R.

PART I

1931–1937

In 1931, at the age of twenty-two, Simone Weil was appointed as teacher of philosophy at the *lycée* for girls at Le Puy. She was subsequently appointed to Auxerre (1932) and Roanne (1933). During all this period she took an active interest in left-wing trade union affairs in the Haute-Loire. In 1934 she took a year's leave of absence and, with the help of Auguste Detœuf (see pp. 55 and 91), got a job as an unskilled factory worker in Paris at the Alsthom electrical works, which was one of Detœuf's companies. From there she moved to the Forges de Basse-Indre, and thence to the Renault works, where she stayed until 31 July 1935. She then went back to teaching philosophy, at the *lycée* at Bourges. But as is indicated by her long correspondence with a local factory manager, Monsieur B., she still had thoughts of devoting herself permanently to factory work with a view to promoting co-operation between workers and managements.

1 To a Colleague

[1931 or 1932]

Dear Comrade,

As a reply to the Inquiry you have undertaken concerning the historical method of teaching science, I can only tell you about an experiment I made this year with my class (philosophy class at the Lycée for Girls at Le Puy).

My pupils, like most other pupils, regarded the various sciences as compilations of cut-and-dried knowledge, arranged in the manner indicated by the textbooks. They had *no idea* either of the connexion between the sciences or of the methods by which they were created.

In short, such knowledge as they possessed about the sciences could not be described as culture but the opposite. This made it very difficult for me to deal with that part of the philosophy syllabus entitled 'Method in the Sciences'.

I explained to them that the sciences were not ready-made knowledge set forth in textbooks for the use of the ignorant, but knowledge acquired in the course of ages by men who employed methods entirely different from those used to expound them in textbooks. I offered to give a few supplementary lectures on the history of science. They agreed, and all of them attended the lectures voluntarily.

I gave them a rapid sketch of the development of mathematics, taking as central theme the duality: continuous-discontinuous, and describing it as the attempt to deal with the continuous by means of the discontinuous, measurement itself being the first step. I told them the history of Greek science: similar triangles (Thales and the pyramids) – Pythagoras' theorem – discovery of incommensurables and the crisis it provoked – solution of the crisis by Eudoxus' theory of proportions – discovery of conics, as sections of the cone – method of exhaustion – and of the geometry of early modern times (algebra – analytic geometry – principle of the differential and integral calculus). I explained to them – as no one had troubled to do – how the infinitesimal calculus was the condition for the application of mathematics to physics, and consequently for the contemporary efflorescence of physics. All this was followed by all of them, even those most ignorant in science, with passionate interest and was very easily fitted into six or seven extra hours.

Lack of time and my own insufficient knowledge prevented me from doing the same for mechanics and physics; all I could do was to tell them some fragments of the history of those sciences. They would have liked to have more.

At the end of the series I read them the terms of your Inquiry into the historical method of teaching science and they all enthusiastically approved the principle of such a method. They said it was the only method which could make pupils see science as something human, instead of a kind of dogma which you have to believe without ever really knowing why.

So this experiment completely confirms your idea, from every point of view.

Simone Weil,
Lecturer in philosophy at the Lycée for Girls, Le Puy.

2 To Emile Auguste Chartier (Alain)

Simone Weil had been a pupil of Alain at the Lycée Henri IV.

[*1933*(?)]

I didn't reply to your letter because it seemed easier to answer it verbally; but as the opportunity fails to present itself I will try nevertheless to tell you very briefly how I am attempting to orient my mind. It appears to me that one might, if one wished, sum up the whole development of the last three centuries by saying that Descartes' venture has turned out badly. That is to say, there is something lacking in the *Discourse of Method*. To compare the *Rules for the Direction of the Mind* with the *Geometry* is to feel that there is in fact a good deal lacking. For my part, this is the lacuna which I think I can see in it: Descartes never found a way to prevent order from becoming, as soon as it is conceived, a thing instead of an idea. Order becomes a thing, it seems to me, as soon as one treats a series as a reality distinct from the terms which compose it, by expressing it with a symbol; now algebra is just that, and has been since the beginning (since Vieta). It is only the use of analogy that offers a way of conceiving a series without separating it from its terms. (That is one of your ideas, is it not?) And it is only analogy that makes it possible for thought to be at the same time absolutely pure and absolutely concrete. Thought is only about particular objects; reasoning is only about the universal. Through the trick by which it has tried to resolve this contradiction, modern science has lost its soul; this trick consists in reasoning only about conventional symbols, which are particular objects by the fact that they are black marks on white paper, but which are universal by virtue of their definition. The other way to resolve this contradiction would be by analogy. And this suggests to me a new way of conceiving mathematics – as materialistically and, so to speak, cynically as possible – so that it consists purely and simply of combinations of symbols; but so that its theoretical and its practical value, which would no longer be distinct, would reside in analogies, clearly and definitely conceived, between these combinations and the concrete problems to which they are applied in the course of man's struggle with the universe. The symbols would thus be relegated back to their rank as mere instruments, the rank which Descartes attempted to assign them in the *Rules*; and their real function would be revealed, which is not to assist the understanding but the imagination. Scientific work would thus be seen to be in fact artistic work – namely, the training of the imagination. Concurrently, it would be necessary to foster and develop to the maximum the faculty of conceiving analogies without making use of algebraic symbols. And this is a question of perception. But the lazy perceptions of the man who lives comfortably with matter which other men have worked on to make it convenient for him are of little importance. What is interesting is the perception of the man at work; and this implies a thorough study of the instruments of labour, no longer from the technical point of view – in their relation to matter, that is – but from the point of view of their relation to man, to human thought. It would be necessary to clarify and arrange in series all the relationships implied in the manipulation of all the instruments of labour – whether perceived vaguely by those who manipulate them, or perceived clearly by a few privileged workers higher up in the labour hierarchy (in industry, perhaps two or three engineers in each firm) or, as must often happen, not perceived at all by anybody. Where these two series of critical studies meet there would be a true science of physics, or at least of that part of physics concerned with the phenomena which are the material of human labour. Alongside this physics and by analogy with it, though on quite a different plane, would need to be organized the study of those phenomena which are objects of contemplation only.

You will excuse, I hope, the confusion and disorder and also the audacity of these embryo ideas. If there is any value in them it is clear that they could only be developed in silence. But, nevertheless, their development unfortunately presupposes a collective effort, which I would envisage as follows: To begin with, a survey of the applications of mathematics, or rather the various forms of mathematical calculation, taken one by one; this schedule would relate (so far as possible, of course) not only to the present but to the historical development of science and technology for the last three or four centuries at least. Then, a series of monographs on the trades and crafts, all of them concerned with the same problem, namely: what is the precise activity of thought implied in the function of an unskilled machine operative – a skilled worker – a professional turner, cutter, etc. – a workshop overseer – a draftsman – a factory engineer – a factory manager – etc., etc., etc.; and the same for mining, building, agriculture, navigation and so

To Emile Auguste Chartier 1933(?)

on. Needless to say that in imagining this programme I have no illusions about its chance of being realized.

Finally, I would like to see some educational books which would begin at once to apply the analogical method of teaching which I have adumbrated. I have hardly had any time to think about it; but I have sometimes dreamed of a textbook of physics for elementary schools, in which natural phenomena would be presented exclusively by the method of a series of analogies, increasingly exact, and based on the idea of perception as a stage in scientific knowledge. Thus, to take the case of light, there would first be a list of all the cases in which light behaves like something analogous to motion, proceeding thence to the analogy with rectilinear motion, the analogy with waves .... But up to now I have not got beyond these vague dreams. However M. tells me that a physics textbook for elementary schools is one of your projects. I don't know what sort of thing you have in mind, but I expect I can form some idea from certain pages of *Entretiens au bord de la mer*. I regret extremely that it is still only a project.

There remain the social problems. For them too I would envisage first of all some monographs on the various social functions – conceived, of course, as functions in the struggle against nature – and their reciprocal relatedness, and their relation to social oppression. Here again what I would chiefly aim at would be the drawing up of surveys. For example, a study of everything which contemporary agriculture owes to industry, or in other words a survey setting forth all the losses that cultivation would suffer if heavy industry were abolished overnight. And a series of studies of the various existing forms of property, related to the idea that property consists, in reality, of the power to dispose of goods. And a lot of other things which at present are out of my mind.

You asked what my plan of work is, and all I have replied with has been hazy outlines and overweening ambitions. Whether anything real could come of them, such as a magazine, I don't know. What I would like would be to be able to issue an appeal to all those who actually know something or are doing something and who are not satisfied with knowing or doing but want to reflect upon what they know and do!

3 To X

This is a fragment of a letter to an unidentified correspondent, written before she went to work in the Alsthom factory in Paris and probably while she was teaching at the lycée at Roanne.

[1933 or 1934]

Monsieur,

I am late in replying, because the rendezvous has been difficult to arrange. I cannot get to Moulins until quite late on Monday afternoon (about 4 o'clock) and I would have to leave at 9. If you are free to give me an hour or two between those times I will come. In that case you have only to fix a definite meeting place, remembering that I don't know Moulins. I hope it will be possible, as I think it will be an advantage to talk rather than write.

So the thoughts which your letters have suggested to me can wait until we meet. I will mention only one doubt which already occurred to me when I heard your lecture.

You say: Every man is both a link in some automatic series and *also* an instigator of trains of events.

First of all, it seems to me one must distinguish the various degrees of activity and passivity in a man's relations with the trains of events which enter into his life. A man may originate trains of events (be an inventor . . .) – he may re-create them in thought – he may enact them without thinking them – he may be the occasion of trains of events thought or enacted by others – and so on. But that is something obvious.

What worries me a little is this. When you say that an assembly line worker, for example, as soon as he comes out of the factory is free from the domain of the automatic series, you are clearly right. But what do you conclude from this? If you conclude that every man, however oppressed, still has the opportunity every day to act as a man and therefore never entirely forgoes his human status, very well. But if you conclude that the life of a worker at a conveyor belt in Renault or Citroën is an acceptable one for a man who wants to preserve human dignity, I cannot follow you. I don't think that *is* what you mean – in fact I am sure it isn't – but I would like to get the point perfectly clear.

'Quantity changes into quality', as the Marxists say, following Hegel. Both automatic series *and* motivated trains of events occur in all human lives, of course; but the question of proportion enters in, and it can be said in a general way that automatic series cannot occupy more than a certain proportion of a man's life without degrading it.

But I think we are agreed about this. . . .

4 To a pupil

My dear child, [1934]

I was very glad to have news of you. I think, as you do, that we are going to have a dictatorship. Nevertheless the fascist exuberance in the Haute-Loire is a local phenomenon. In the country as a whole the groups of fascist tendency are remarkably quiet, while on the other hand the government is singularly indulgent towards Socialist and Communist agitation. And this is the reason: the Socialist-Communist 'united front', which coincided with Russia's entry into the League of Nations, is little more than the Russian State's propaganda in France and is the mainstay of the Franco-Russian military alliance.

The Socialists have completely forgotten all those cases of State oppression in Russia, which a few months ago they were still denouncing. And as for the struggle against French militarism, colonial oppression, etc., . . . it is being conducted with ever-increasing gentleness by both Socialists and Communists, preparatory to bringing it definitely to an end (they would still go on issuing slogans of a demagogic kind, but nothing serious). On the other hand, if war breaks out, Socialists and Communists will send us forth to die for 'the workers' fatherland', and we shall see once more those famous days of the sacred union.[1]

The fascist groups, on the contrary, would mostly be in favour of a military alliance with Germany against Russia. Every military alliance is odious, but an alliance with Germany would probably be a lesser evil; for in that case a war between Russia and Germany (with Japan participating too, no doubt) would remain comparatively localized; on the other hand, if France and Russia marched together against Germany and Japan it would be another conflagration which would spread to the whole of Europe and beyond – an incredible catastrophe. As you can imagine, these considerations do not make me a fascist. But I

---

[1] *Union sacrée*: i.e. suspending political disagreements in order to combine against an external danger.

refuse to play the game of the Russian general staff on the pretext of opposing fascism.

What a lot of young fellows will shed their blood in the coming months, believing it is for the sake of liberty, the proletariat, etc. . . . , when in reality it will be for the Franco-Russian military alliance, and consequently for war preparations.

Such being the situation, it is my firm decision to take no further part in *any* political or social activities, with two exceptions; anti-colonialism and the campaign against passive defence exercises.

Briefly, I foresee the future like this: we are entering upon a period of more centralized and more oppressive dictatorship than any known to us in history. But the very excess of centralization weakens the central power. One fine day (perhaps we shall live to see it, perhaps not) everything will collapse in anarchy and there will be a return to almost primitive forms of the struggle for existence.

At that moment, amidst the disorder, men who love liberty will be able to work for the foundation of a new and more humane order than our present one. We cannot foresee what it would be like (except that it must necessarily be decentralized, because centralization kills liberty) but we can do what lies in us towards preparing for that new civilization. So I think that although there is no possible action for us and although we are to a great extent reduced, as you say, to a negative ideal, we can and ought to do positive work.

The most important from this point of view, in my opinion, is the *popularization of knowledge*, and especially of scientific knowledge. Culture is a privilege which, in these days, gives power to the class which possesses it.

Let us try to undermine this privilege by relating complicated knowledge to the commonest knowledge. It is for this reason that you ought to study, and mathematics above all. Indeed, unless one has exercised one's mind seriously at the gymnastic of mathematics one is incapable of precise thought, which amounts to saying that one is good for nothing. Don't tell me you lack the gift; that is no obstacle, and I would almost say it is an advantage.

You said in your letter that you were impatient to escape from this unreal life and to find yourself at grips with the material necessities of existence. But, alas, there are not many people nowadays, especially in your generation, for whom it is possible to confront those 'necessities'.

To a pupil 1934

Because, apart from those whose bread is already buttered, the majority are in thrall to the misery of unemployment or to a degrading dependence which has no appearance of 'necessity' but only of a crushing fatality which one no longer even tries to resist. If you don't want to remain indefinitely on your parents' hands, you must have a profession. You ought to begin thinking about it now. In my opinion, instead of wasting your time at the *lycée* (which leads precisely *nowhere*, believe me, even if you get the *bachot*)[1] you would do better to work for the École Normale. You still have time, I think? But only just. Do you realize that it is good to be a teacher in some out of the way hole? It is even one of the best ways you have of making real contact with the people.

If you don't like that, look for something else. But get it well into your head, and if possible into your parents', that when you leave the *lycée* with the *bachot* in your pocket (and *a fortiori* without it) you are purely and simply on the pavement. There was a time when to be on the pavement might mean being obliged to use your wits, to come bravely to grips with material necessities. Today it is quite different. It means being obliged to rely on some form of charity (living at one's parents' expense when one is of an age to earn one's livelihood is a form of charity), and to use up all one's time in that empty, anxious, humiliating occupation which is called seeking a post.

For the rest, believe me that no one could understand better than I your aspiration for a real life, because I share it. But it is precisely the worst cruelty of our time that it makes it very difficult to give precise meaning to the words 'real life'.

Meanwhile, and no matter what you may do – even if you stay on at the *lycée* – remember always that the first rule is to do well whatever it is that you are doing. By which I don't mean, as you well know, that you should be a good little pupil.... But since you are given opportunities of learning, make full use of them, in your own way. It doesn't matter if you get good or bad reports. But don't incur the disgrace of leaving the *lycée* without having really assimilated some ideas in mathematics, physics, history. I say nothing of French, because I know you can be trusted for that. Don't take anyone's advice about style, imitate good models, and avoid 'literature'. Further, you should keep a critical attitude about history, too. Try to get the main facts clear in your head,

---

[1] Baccalaureate: certificate giving access to a university.

but as for the interpretation of the facts, the textbooks are full of lies; later on you will read with profit the works of real historians. The same with science, never allow yourself to be persuaded that you understand what you don't. . . .

Let me hear about your work, and your reading (without forgetting all the rest . . .). And about the class too. Is there still the same good spirit of comradeship? And in this connexion, did you decide to tell your comrades the truth about Russia? If so, it must have seriously lowered the morale of several.

I have taken a year's leave, in order to do a little work of my own and also to make a little contact with the famous 'real life'. Anyway, you can be sure that if the Ministry of Education continues on its present lines I shall never make old bones as a teacher. They have their eye on me. I shall almost certainly get the sack within two or three years, and perhaps sooner.

Write to me now and then. I shan't be able to reply every time, but it will be a pleasure to have your news.

Yours affectionately,
S.W.

5 To a pupil

[Paris, Spring, 1935]

My dear child,

I have wanted for a long time to write to you, but work in a factory is not conducive to letter-writing. How did you know what I was doing? From the Dérieu sisters, no doubt? Anyway, it doesn't matter, because I wanted to tell you. But please don't you tell anyone, not even Marinette, unless you already have. This is the 'contact with real life' about which I used to talk to you. I only achieved it through a favour; one of my best friends knows the managing director of the Company,[1] and told him what I wanted. And he understood, which shows a largeness of mind altogether exceptional in that sort of person. In these days it is almost impossible to get into a factory without credentials – especially when, like me, one is clumsy and slow and not very robust.

I will tell you at once – in case you should have the idea of doing something of the same sort – that although I am glad to have succeeded

[1] The Alsthom Electrical Engineering Works.

To a pupil 1935

in getting work in a factory, I am equally glad not to be compulsorily committed to it. I have simply obtained a year's leave for 'private study'. For a man, if he is very skilled, very intelligent, and very tough, there is just a chance, in the present conditions of French industry, of attaining to a factory job which offers interesting and humanly satisfying work; and even so, these opportunities are becoming fewer every day, thanks to the progress of rationalization. But as for the women, they are restricted to purely mechanical labour, in which nothing is required from them except speed. And when I say mechanical labour, don't imagine that it allows of day-dreaming, much less of reflection or thought. No, the tragedy is that although the work is too mechanical to engage the mind it nevertheless prevents one from thinking of anything else. If you think, you work more slowly; and there are rate-fixed times, laid down by pitiless bureaucrats, which must be observed – both to avoid getting the sack and in order to earn enough (payment being by piecework). I am still unable to achieve the required speeds, for many reasons: my unfamiliarity with the work, my inborn awkwardness, which is considerable, a certain natural slowness of movement, headaches, and a peculiar inveterate habit of thinking, which I can't shake off. . . . So I believe they would throw me out if I wasn't protected by influence. As for leisure, one has a good deal of it, theoretically, with the 8-hour day; but in practice one's leisure hours are swallowed up by a fatigue which often amounts to a dazed stupor. You must add, to complete the picture, that life in the factory involves a perpetual humiliating subordination, for ever at the orders of foremen. Naturally, all this is more painful or less according to one's character, one's physical stamina, etc.; but in the end the total effect is what I have described.

Nevertheless, and although I suffer from it all, I am more glad than I can say to be where I am. I have wanted it for I don't know how many years; but I am not sorry that I did not achieve it sooner, because it is only at my present age[1] that I can extract all the profit there is for me in the experience. Above all, I feel I have escaped from a world of abstractions, to find myself among real men – some good and some bad, but with a real goodness or badness. Goodness especially, when it exists in a factory, is something real; because the least act of kindness, from a mere smile to some little service, calls for a victory over fatigue

[1] Twenty-six.

and the obsession with pay and all the overwhelming influences which drive a man in upon himself. And thought, too, calls for an almost miraculous effort of rising above the conditions of one's life. Because it is not like at a university, where one is paid to think, or pretend to think. In a factory it would be truer to say that one is paid not to think. So if ever you recognize a gleam of intelligence you can be sure it is genuine. Apart from all that, I find the machines themselves highly attractive and interesting. I should add that I am in the factory chiefly to inform myself on a certain number of very definite points which I am concerned about, and which I cannot enumerate for you.

That's enough about me. Let's talk about you. Your letter dismayed me. If the knowledge of as many sensations as possible continues to be your main objective – as a passing phase it is normal at your age – you won't get far. I liked it much better when you said you aspired to contact with real life. You think it's the same thing, perhaps; but in fact it is just the opposite. There are people who have lived by and for nothing but sensations; André Gide is an example. What they really are is the dupes of life; and as they are confusedly aware of this they always fall into a profound melancholy which they can only assuage by lying miserably to themselves. For the reality of life is not sensation but activity – I mean activity both in thought and in action. People who live by sensations are parasites, both materially and morally, in relation to those who work and create – who alone are men. And the latter, who do not seek sensations, experience in fact much livelier, profounder, less artificial and truer ones than those who seek them. Finally, as far as I am concerned, the cultivation of sensations implies an egoism which revolts me. It clearly does not prevent love, but it leads one to consider the people one loves as mere occasions of joy or suffering and to forget completely that they exist in their own right. One lives among phantoms, dreaming instead of living.

As regards love, I have no advice to give you but at least I have some warnings. Love is a serious thing, and it often means pledging one's own life and also that of another human being, for ever. Indeed, it always means that, unless one of the two treats the other as a plaything; and in that case, which is a very common one, love is something odious. In the end, you see, the essential point in love is this: that one human being feels a vital need of another human being – a need which is or is not reciprocal and is or is not enduring, as the case may be. Consequently, the problem arises of reconciling this need with freedom, and it is a problem with which men have struggled from time immemorial. That is why the idea of seeking love to find out what it is, or to get some animation in a too dull life, seems to me dangerous and, above all, puerile. I can tell you that when, at your age, and later on too, I was tempted to try to get to know love, I decided not to – telling myself that it was better not to commit my life in a direction impossible to foresee until I was sufficiently mature to know what, in a general way, I wish from life and what I expect from it. I am not offering you that as an example; every life evolves by its own laws. But it may provide you with matter for reflection. I will add that love seems to me to involve an even more terrifying risk than that of blindly pledging one's own existence; I mean the risk, if one is the object of a profound love, of becoming the arbiter of another human existence. My conclusion (which I offer you solely for information) is not that one should avoid love, but that one should not seek it, and above all when one is very young. At that age it is much better not to meet it, I believe.

It seems to me you ought to be able to resist your surroundings. You have the boundless realm of books, which is far from being everything but is a lot, especially in the way of preparing you for a more concrete life. I would also like to see you take an interest in your class work, from which you can learn much more than you think. To begin with, it teaches you to work. Until one is capable of sustained work one is no good for anything. And then so as to form your mind. I will spare you a repetition of my praises of geometry. But as for physics, did I ever recommend the following exercise? Examine the textbook and the lectures to see how much of the reasoning is sound. You will be astonished at how much false reasoning you'll find. While playing this extremely instructive game, the lesson often fixes itself in your mind without your noticing. As regards history and geography, most of it is false through being schematized, but if you learn it well you acquire a solid base from which to discover later on for yourself some real notions about human society in time and space – which is indispensable for anyone concerned with the social problem. I say nothing about French; I am sure your style is forming itself.

I was very glad when you told me you had decided to work for the *École Normale*; it freed me from an anxious preoccupation. I am proportionately sorry that it no longer seems to be in your mind.

I think you have a character which condemns you to a great deal of suffering all your life. I am even sure of it. You are too eager and impetuous to be able ever to adapt yourself to the social life of our time. You are not the only one in that predicament. But suffering doesn't matter, so long as you also experience some vivid joys. What matters is not to bungle one's life. And for that, one must discipline oneself.

It is a great pity you are not allowed to go in for sport: that is what you need. Try once again to persuade your parents. I hope at least that joyful hiking in the mountains is not forbidden. Greet your mountains from me.

I have learnt in the factory how paralysing and humiliating it is to lack vigour, dexterity, sureness of eye. And in those respects, unfortunately for me, one can never make up for what one didn't acquire before the age of 20. I cannot too strongly recommend you to exercise your muscles, your hands, your eyes, as much as possible. For the lack of such exercise one feels singularly deficient.

Write to me, but expect answers only at long intervals. I find the effort of writing too painful. Write to 228 rue Lecourbe, Paris, XVe. I have taken a little room close to the factory.

Enjoy the spring, relish the air and the sun (if there is any), read some fine things.

$\chi\alpha\hat{\iota}\rho\epsilon$
S. Weil

6 To Mme Albertine Thévenon

> Mme Thévenon's husband was a prominent trade unionist at St. Étienne. The Thévenons were members of the group around the dissident communist review Révolution Prolétarienne.

[January 1935]

Dear Albertine,

I am obliged to rest because of a slight illness (a touch of inflammation of the ear – nothing serious) so I seize the opportunity for a little talk with you. In a normal working week it is difficult to make any effort beyond what I am compelled to make. But that's not the only reason I haven't written; it's also the number of things there are to tell and the impossibility of telling the essential. Perhaps later on I shall find the right words, but at present it seems to me that I should need a new language to convey what needs to be said. Although this experience is in many ways what I expected it to be, there is also an abysmal difference: it is reality and no longer imagination. It is not that it has changed one or the other of my ideas (on the contrary, it has confirmed many of them), but infinitely more – it has changed my whole view of things, even my very feeling about life. I shall know joy again in the future, but there is a certain lightness of heart which, it seems to me, will never again be possible. But that's enough about it: to try to express the inexpressible is to degrade it.

As regards the things that can be expressed, I have learnt quite a lot about the organization of a firm. It is inhuman; work broken down into small processes, and paid by the piece; relations between different units of the firm and different work processes organized in a purely bureaucratic way. One's attention has nothing worthy to engage it, but on the contrary is constrained to fix itself, second by second, upon the same trivial problem, with only such variants as speeding up your output from 6 minutes to 5 for 50 pieces, or something of that sort. Thank heaven, there are manual skills to be acquired, which from time to time lends some interest to this pursuit of speed. But what I ask myself is how can all this be humanized; because if the separate processes were not paid by the piece the boredom they engender would inhibit attention and slow down the work considerably, and produce a lot of spoiled pieces. And if the processes were not subdivided.... But I have no time to go into all this by letter. Only when I think that the great Bolshevik leaders proposed to create a *free* working class and that doubtless none of them – certainly not Trotsky, and I don't think Lenin either – had ever set foot inside a factory, so that they hadn't the faintest idea of the real conditions which make servitude or freedom for the workers – well, politics appears to me a sinister farce.

I must point out that all I have said refers to unskilled labour. About skilled labour I have almost everything still to learn. It will come, I hope.

To speak frankly, for me this life is pretty hard. And the more so because my headaches have not been obliging enough to withdraw so as to make things easier – and working among machines with a headache is painful. It is only on Saturday afternoon and Sunday that I can breathe, and find myself again, and recover the ability to turn over a few thoughts in my head. In a general way, the temptation to give up thinking altogether is the most difficult one to resist in a life like this:

one feels so clearly that it is the only way to stop suffering! First of all, to stop suffering morally. Because the situation itself automatically banishes rebellious feelings: to work with irritation would be to work badly and so condemn oneself to starvation; and leaving aside the work, there is no person to be a target for one's irritation. One dare not be insolent to the foremen and, moreover, they very often don't even make one want to be. So one is left with no possible feeling about one's own fate except sadness. And thus one is tempted to cease, purely and simply, from being conscious of anything except the sordid daily round of life. And physically too it is a great temptation to lapse into semi-somnolence outside working hours. I have the greatest respect for workmen who manage to educate themselves. It is true they are usually tough; but all the same it must require a lot of stamina. And it is becoming more and more unusual with the advance of rationalization. I wonder if it is the same with skilled workers.

I am sticking it, in spite of everything. And I don't for one moment regret having embarked on the experience. Quite the contrary, I am infinitely thankful whenever I think of it. But curiously enough I don't often think of it. My capacity for adaptation is almost unlimited, so that I am able to forget that I am a 'qualified lecturer' on tour in the working class, and to live my present life as though I had always been destined for it (which is true enough in a sense), and as though it would last for ever and was imposed on me by ineluctable necessity instead of my own free choice.

But I promise you that when I can't stick it any longer I'll go and rest somewhere – perhaps with you. [. . . .]

I perceive I haven't said anything about my fellow workers. It will be for another time. But once again, it is hard to express. . . . They are nice, very nice. But as for real fraternity, I have hardly felt any. With one exception: the storekeeper in the tool-shop, a skilled worker and extremely competent, whom I appeal to whenever I am in despair over a job which I cannot manage properly, because he is a hundred times nicer and more intelligent than the machine-setters (who are not skilled workers). There is a lot of jealousy among the women – who are indeed obliged by the organization of the factory to compete with one another. I only know 3 or 4 who are entirely sympathetic. As for the men, some of them seem to be very nice types. But there aren't many of them in the shop where I work, apart from the machine-setters, who

To Albertine Thévenon 1935

are not real comrades. I hope to be moved to another shop after a time, so as to enlarge my experience.

[. . . .]

Well, au revoir. Write soon.

S.W.

7 To Boris Souvarine

This letter appears to have been written the day after she started work at the Forges de Basse-Indre, the second of the three factories in which she worked.

[Paris, Friday, 12 April 1935]

Dear Boris,

I force myself to write you a few lines, because otherwise I should not have the courage to leave any written trace of the first impressions of my new experience. The self-styled sympathetic little establishment proved to be, in the first place, a fairly large establishment and then, above all, a foul, a very foul establishment. And in that foul establishment there is one particularly loathsome workshop: it is mine. I hasten to add, for your reassurance, that I was moved out at the end of the morning and put in a quiet little corner where I have a good chance of remaining all next week and where I am not on a machine.

Yesterday I was on the same job the whole day (stamping press). I worked until 4 o'clock at the rate of 400 pieces an hour (note that the job was by the hour, at 3 frs. an hour) and I felt I was working hard. At 4 o'clock the foreman came and said that if I didn't do 800 he would get rid of me: 'If you do 800 tomorrow, *perhaps I'll consent* to keep you.' They make a favour, you see, of allowing us to kill ourselves, and we have to say thank you. By straining my utmost I got up to 600 an hour. Nevertheless, they let me start again this morning (they are short of women because the place is so bad that the personnel are always leaving; and they have urgent orders for armaments). I was at the same job for an hour and by making even greater efforts I got up to just over 650. Then I was given various other jobs, always with the same instructions, namely, to go at full speed. For 9 hours a day (because the mid-day break ends at 1, not 1.15 as I told you) the women work like this, literally without a moment's respite. If you are changing from one job to another, or looking for a container, it is always at the double.

There is a conveyor-belt (the first time I've seen one and it hurt me to see it) at which they have *doubled* the production flow, so one of the women told me, in the last four years. And only today the foreman took the place of one of the women at this belt and kept her machine working full speed for 10 minutes (which is easy if you can rest afterwards) to prove to her that she should work even faster. You can imagine the state I was in when I left the factory last night (though luckily my pains in the head at least were in abeyance); in the cloak-room I was astonished to see that the women could still prattle away and did not seem to be consumed with the concentrated fury that I felt. However, a few of them (2 or 3) did express something of the sort to me. They were the ones who are ill, but have to go on working. As you know, the foot action required by a press is very bad for women; one of them told me that she had had salpingitis, but had been unable to get work anywhere except at the presses. Now at last she has a job away from the machines, but with her health definitely ruined.

On the other hand, a woman who works at the conveyor-belt told me on the way home in the tram that after a few years, or even a year, one no longer suffers, although one remains in a sort of stupor. This seems to me to be the lowest stage of degradation. She explained to me (what I already knew very well) how it was that she and her comrades let themselves in for this slavery. 5 or 6 years ago, she said, one could get 70 frs. a day, 'and for 70 frs. we'd have put up with anything, we'd have killed ourselves'. And still today there are some who don't absolutely need it who are glad to work in the line for 4 frs. an hour with bonus. Why did no one in the workers' movement, so called, have the courage to think and say during the high wages boom that the working class was being degraded and corrupted? It is certain that the workers have deserved what has happened to them; only the responsibility is collective, while the suffering is individual. Any man with proper feelings must weep tears of blood to find himself swept into this vortex.

As for me, you must wonder how I resist the temptation to back out, since no necessity compels me to suffer these things. I will explain: it is because I scarcely feel any temptation, even at the moments when I am really at the limit of my endurance. Because I don't feel the suffering as mine, I feel it as the workers' suffering; and whether I personally suffer it or not seems to me a detail of almost no importance. Thus the desire to know and understand easily prevails.

PLATE I

above: Simone Weil with her father 1915.

right, above: On holiday at Le Loote, 1922 or 1923; *below*, Portrait photograph of about 1926.

PLATE II

Above: Simone Weil during her time with the C.N.T., at Barcelona, 1936.

Right, above: in New York, 1942.
below, in Marseilles, 1942.

All the same, perhaps I should have given way if I had been kept in that infernal shop. Where I am now I am with workers who take things equably. I should never have believed there could be such differences between two corners of the same place.

Well, that's enough for today. I am almost sorry I've written. You have enough troubles without my telling you more sad stories.

Affectionately,
S.W.

8 To Mme Albertine Thévenon

[1935]

My dear Albertine,
    I seem to feel that you have misinterpreted my silence. You think, probably, that I am embarrassed to reply freely. No, not at all; it is simply that the effort of writing was too great. The effect of your long letter on me was to make me want to tell you that I am profoundly with you. All my instinct of loyalty in friendship puts me on your side.

[. . . .]

But all the same I understand certain things which perhaps you don't, because you are too different. You see, you live so much in the moment – and I love you for it – that you perhaps don't realize what it is to see one's whole life ahead and form a steady and fixed resolve to make something of it, to steer it from beginning to end by one's will and effort in a definite direction. If one is like that – and I am like that, so I can understand it – the worst thing in the world that anyone can do to you is to make you suffer in a way that breaks your vitality, and consequently your capacity for work.

[. . . .]

I know only too well (because of my headaches) what it is to experience that sort of death-in-life. To see the years stretching ahead, and to possess enough to fill them a thousand times, and yet to feel that physical weakness is going to oblige one to leave them empty and that merely to live through them day by day will be an overwhelming task.

[. . . .]

I would have liked to tell you a little about myself, but I have no more time. I suffered a lot from those months of slavery, but not for anything in the world would I have avoided them. They enabled me to test myself and to touch with my finger the things which I had previously been able only to imagine. I came out very different from what I was when I went in – physically worn out, but morally hardened (you'll understand how I mean the word).

Write to me at Paris. I have been appointed to Bourges. It's a long way. We shall hardly be able to meet.

[....]

        I embrace you.

          Simone

9 To the same

[1935]

Dear Albertine,

  It did me good to hear from you. There are some things, it seems to me, in which only you and I understand one another. You are still alive; you can't imagine how happy that makes me [....]

You certainly deserved to get free. Any progress in life is always dearly bought. Almost always at the price of intolerable pain [....]

Do you know, an idea has suddenly struck me. I see you and me, in the holidays, with some sous in our pockets and rucksacks on our backs, tramping the roads and paths and fields. We'd sleep in barns now and then. And sometimes we'd do some harvesting in exchange for a meal. [....] What do you say?

[....]

What you wrote about the factory went straight to my heart. I felt the same as you, ever since I was a child. That is why I had to go there in the end, and you can never know how it made me suffer before, until I went. But once you get there, how different it is! As a result, I now see the social problem in this way: What a factory ought to be is something like what you felt that day at Saint-Chamond, and what I have so often felt – a place where one makes a hard and painful, but nevertheless joyful, contact with real life. Not the gloomy place it is, where people only obey orders, and have all their humanity broken down, and become degraded lower than the machines.

On one occasion I experienced fully the thing that I had glimpsed, like you, from outside. It was at my first place. Imagine me in front of a great furnace which vomits flames and scorching heat full in my face. The fire comes from five or six openings at the bottom of the furnace.

To Albertine Thévenon 1935

I stand right in front of it to insert about thirty large metal bobbins,[1] which are made by an Italian woman with a brave and open countenance who is just alongside me. These bobbins are for the trams and metros. I have to take great care that they don't fall into the open holes, because they would melt. Therefore I must stand close up to the furnace and not make any clumsy movement, in spite of the scorching heat on my face and the fire on my arms (which still show the burns). I close the shutter and wait a few minutes; then I open it and draw the red-hot bobbins out with a hook. I must do it very quickly or else the last ones would begin to melt, and must take even greater care lest any of them fall into the open holes. And then I do it all over again. A welder with a serious expression and dark spectacles sits opposite me, working intently. Each time I wince from the furnace heat on my face, he looks at me with a sad smile of fraternal sympathy which does me untold good. On the other side, around some big tables, is a group of armature winders. They work together as a team, like brothers, carefully and without haste. They are highly skilled copper workers; they must calculate, and read very complicated drawings, and make use of descriptive geometry. Further on, a hefty youth is sledge-hammering some iron bars, raising a din to split your head. All this is going on in a corner at the far end of the workshop, where one feels at home, and where the overseer and foreman hardly ever come. I was there 4 times, for 2 or 3 hours (at 7 to 8 frs. an hour – which counts, you know!). The first time, after an hour and a half of the heat and effort and pain I lost control of my movements and couldn't close the shutter. One of the copper workers (all very nice types) immediately noticed and jumped to do it for me. I would go back to that little corner of the workshop this moment if I could (or at least as soon as I have recovered my strength). On those evenings I felt the joy of eating bread that one has earned.

But that experience stands out as unique in my factory life. What working in a factory meant for me personally was as follows. It meant that all the external reasons (which I had previously thought internal) upon which my sense of personal dignity, my self-respect, was based were radically destroyed within two or three weeks by the daily experience of brutal constraint. And don't imagine that this provoked in me any rebellious reaction. No, on the contrary; it produced the last

---

[1] *Bobine*: the metal part which holds the copper wire coils of the armature.

thing I expected from myself – docility. The resigned docility of a beast of burden. It seemed to me that I was born to wait for, and receive, and carry out orders – that I had never done and never would do anything else. I am not proud of that confession. It is the kind of suffering no worker talks about; it is too painful even to think of it. When I was kept away from work by illness I became fully aware of the degradation into which I was falling, and I swore to myself that I would go on enduring the life until the day when I was able to pull myself together in spite of it. And I kept my word. Slowly and painfully, in and through slavery, I reconquered the sense of my human dignity – a sense which relied, this time, upon nothing outside myself and was accompanied always by the knowledge that I possessed no right to anything, and that any moment free from humiliation and suffering should be accepted as a favour, as merely a lucky chance.

There are two factors in this slavery: the necessity for speed, and passive obedience to orders. Speed: in order to 'make the grade' one has to repeat movement after movement faster than one can think, so that not only reflection but even day-dreaming is impossible. In front of his machine, the worker has to annihilate his soul, his thought, his feelings, and everything, for eight hours a day. If he is irritated, or sad, or disgusted, he must swallow and completely suppress his irritation, sadness, or disgust; they would slow down his output. And the same with joy. Then orders: from the time he clocks in to the time he clocks out he may at any moment receive any order; and he must always obey without a word. The order may be an unpleasant or a dangerous or even an impracticable one; or two superiors may give contradictory orders; no matter, one submits in silence. To speak to a superior – even for something indispensable – is always to risk a snub, even though he may be a kindly man (the kindest men have spells of bad temper); and one must take the snub too in silence. As for one's own fits of irritation or bad humour, one must swallow them; they can have no outlet either in word or gesture. All one's movements are determined all the time by the work. In this situation, thought shrivels up and withdraws, as the flesh flinches from a lancet. One *cannot* be 'conscious'.

In all this I am speaking of unskilled work, of course (and especially the women's work).

And in the midst of it all a smile, a word of kindness, a moment of human contact, have more value than the most devoted friendships among the privileged, both great and small. It is only there that one knows what human brotherhood is. But there is little of it, very little. Most often, relations between comrades reflect the harshness which dominates everything there.

Now I have chattered enough. I could write volumes about it all.

I wanted also to say this: I feel that the change from that hard life to my present one is corrupting me, I know now what it's like when a worker gets a 'permanent billet'. But I try to resist. If I let myself go I should forget it all and settle down among my privileges without wishing to think of them as such. But don't worry, I'm not letting myself go. Moreover, I said farewell to my gaiety in that life; it has left an indelible bitterness in my heart. Yet all the same I am glad to have experienced it.

Keep this letter – perhaps I'll ask you for it one day, if I want to collect all my memories of that time. Not so as to publish something about it (at least I think not), but to prevent myself from forgetting. It is difficult not to forget when one changes one's way of life so radically.

S.W.

10 To Monsieur B.

> The recipient of the following series of letters was manager of a factory producing stoves, at R. near Bourges. Simone Weil, who was teaching at the Bourges *lycée*, collaborated in his factory magazine.

Bourges, 13 January 1936

Monsieur,

I cannot say I was surprised by your reply. I hoped for a different one, but without counting on it too much.

I won't try to defend the article[1] which you have refused. If you were a Catholic I could not resist the temptation to show that its spirit, which shocked you, is purely and simply the Christian spirit; I don't think it would be difficult. But there are no grounds for using that argument with you. And anyway I don't want to argue. You are the boss and cannot be called to account for your decisions.

I only want to say that I deliberately and with intention developed the 'tendency' which you found unacceptable. You told me – I repeat

[1] See appendix to this letter.

your own words – that it is very difficult to raise the workers. The first principle of education is that in order to 'raise' anyone, whether infant or adult, one must begin by raising him in his own eyes. And this is a hundred times truer still when the chief obstacle to his development is the humiliating conditions of his life.

For me, this fact is the point of departure for any useful action affecting the mass of people, and especially the factory workers. And I understand, of course, that it is precisely this point of departure that you don't admit. In the hope of bringing you to do so, and because you control the fate of eight hundred workmen, I forced myself to tell you without reticence the feelings which my own experience had impressed on me. It was a painful effort to tell you some of those things which one can hardly bear to tell one's equals and which it is intolerable to speak of to a superior. It seemed to me that you were touched. But no doubt it was a mistake to hope that an hour's interview can counteract the pressure of daily routine. To put themselves in the place of those who obey is not easy for those who command.

In my eyes, the essential point of my collaboration in your paper was this: that my experience last year may perhaps enable me to write in such a way as to alleviate a little the weight of humiliations which life inflicts every day upon the workers at R., as upon the workers in all modern factories. That is not the only purpose but it is, I am convinced, the essential condition for widening their horizon. Nothing is more paralysing to thought than the sense of inferiority which is necessarily induced by the daily assault of poverty, subordination, and dependence. The first thing to be done for them is to help them to recover or retain, as the case may be, their sense of dignity. I know too well how difficult it is, in such conditions, to retain that sense, and how precious any moral support can be. I hoped with all my heart that by collaborating in your paper I might be able to give a little support of this kind to the workers at R.

I don't think you have a clear idea of exactly what class feeling is. In my opinion, it can hardly be stimulated by mere words, whether spoken or written. It is determined by actual conditions of life. What stimulates it is the infliction of humiliation and suffering, and the fact of subordination; but it is continually repressed by the inexorable daily pressure of need, and often to the point where, in the weaker characters, it turns into servility. Apart from exceptional moments which, I

To B. 1936

think, can neither be induced nor prevented, nor even foreseen, the pressure of need is always more than strong enough to maintain order; for the relations of power are all too obvious. But from the point of view of the moral health of the workers, the continual repression of class feeling – which to some extent is always secretly smouldering – is almost everywhere being carried much too far. To give an occasional outlet to this feeling – without demagogy, of course – would not be to excite it but on the contrary to soften its bitterness. For the unfortunate, their social inferiority is infinitely harder to bear for the reason that they see it everywhere treated as something that goes without saying.

Above all, I don't see how an article like mine could have a bad effect when published in your own paper. In any other paper an article of that kind might just conceivably seem to be setting the poor against the rich, the rank and file against the leaders; but, appearing in a paper controlled by you, such an article can only give the workers the feeling that an approach is being made to them, that someone is trying to understand them. I think they would be grateful to you. I am convinced that if the workers at R. could find in your paper articles really conceived for them, in which their susceptibilities were scrupulously respected (for the unfortunate have keen susceptibilities, though mute), and which concentrated upon whatever can raise them in their own eyes, nothing but good would come of it, from every point of view.

On the other hand, what might exacerbate class feeling is the use of unfortunate expressions which by an effect of unconscious cruelty emphasize implicitly the social inferiority of the readers. There are many such unfortunate expressions in previous numbers of your paper. I will point them out if you like at our next meeting. Perhaps no one can possess tact in dealing with these people when he has been too long in a position too different from theirs.

Apart from all this, however, the reasons you give for rejecting my two suggestions may well be perfectly sound. And anyway it is a relatively minor question.

Thank you for sending the last numbers of the paper.

If you are still disposed to take me on as a worker, I won't come to see you at R., for the reason I gave. But I have grounds for thinking that your views have changed. To be successful, an arrangement of the kind requires a very high degree of mutual confidence and understanding.

If you are no longer disposed to take me on, or if Monsieur M.[1] is against it, I will certainly come to R., since you are good enough to authorize it, as soon as I have time. I will let you know in advance.

Sincerely yours,

S. Weil

AN APPEAL TO THE WORKERS AT R.[2]

Dear unknown friends who are toiling in the R. workshops, I have an appeal to make to you. I want to ask you to collaborate in *Entre Nous*.

We don't want any more work, you'll say; we have enough on our plates already.

Of course you are right. Nevertheless I am asking you, please, to take pen and paper and say something about your work.

Don't protest. I know quite well: at the end of eight hours you're fed up, you've had it right up to there – to use two expressions which have the merit of saying forcibly what they mean. All you ask is not to have to think about the factory until tomorrow morning. It is a perfectly natural state of mind, which it is right to indulge. In that state of mind, the best thing is to relax: talk with friends, read something light, have a drink and a card game, play with the children.

But aren't there also some days when you find it oppressive never to be able to say what you feel but always to keep it to yourself? It is to those who know that oppressive feeling that my appeal is made. Perhaps some of you have never felt it. But when you do feel it you really suffer.

In the factory, all you have to do is to obey orders, and produce work which conforms to prescribed standards, and collect your money on pay-day according to the piece-rates in force. But in addition to this you are men – you toil and suffer, and also have moments of happiness, and perhaps a pleasant hour or so; sometimes everything goes quite nicely, at other times the work is a painful effort; some of the time you are interested, at other times bored. But nobody around you can pay attention to all that; and you can't even let it make any difference to yourself. All you are asked for is work, all you get is the rate.

All this becomes depressing sometimes, doesn't it? One feels like a mere machine for turning out parts of stoves.

[1] The owner of the factory.
[2] This is the article referred to in the preceding letter.

To B. 1936

But such are the conditions of work in industry. It is nobody's fault. Perhaps some of you can adapt to it all quite easily. It depends on one's temperament. But there are people who find that sort of thing hard to take; and for people of that type the state of affairs is really too unpleasant.

I would like *Entre Nous* to be used for an attempt to improve the situation a bit, if you will consent to help me.

This is what I ask you to do. If it happens some evening, or some Sunday, that you suddenly feel you don't want to go on bottling up your feelings for ever, take a pen and some paper. Don't try for fine-sounding phrases. Use the first words that come. And say what you feel about your work.

Say if the work makes you suffer. Describe the suffering, moral as well as physical. Say if there are times when you can't bear it; if there are times when the monotony of the work sickens you; if you hate being always driven by the need to work fast; if you hate being always at the orders of the overseers.

And say also if you sometimes enjoy the work and feel pride in labour accomplished. And if you manage to take an interest in your job, and if there are days when you have the pleasant feeling of working fast and earning good money. Or if you are sometimes able to work for hours like a machine, almost unconsciously, thinking of other things and losing yourself in pleasant dreams. Or if you sometimes feel glad to have nothing to do except carry out the work you are given, without having to worry your head.

Say, in a general way, if you find time goes slowly in the factory or if it seems to fly. Perhaps it's different on different days. If so, try to decide exactly what makes the difference. Say if you are full of beans when you come to work, or if you start every morning with the thought: 'Roll on, Saturday!' Say if you're cheerful when you clock out, or if you're dead beat, worn out, stunned by the day's work.

And finally, say if you feel sustained in the factory by the cheerful feeling that you are among comrades, or if on the contrary you feel lonely.

Above all, say whatever comes into your mind, whatever is weighing on your heart.

And when you've finished writing, there's no need whatever to sign it. Try rather to do it so that no one can guess who you are.

Or even, since there may still be a risk, take a further precaution if you care to. Instead of sending what you write to *Entre Nous*, send it to me. I will copy your articles out again for *Entre Nous*, in such a way that nobody can be recognized in them. I will cut one article into several pieces, and sometimes put together pieces from different articles. As for any imprudent words, I will fix it so that no one can even tell from which workshop they come. And if there are any remarks which I feel it would be dangerous for you to publish even with all these precautions, I will leave them out. You can be sure I will be very careful. I know what the position of a worker in a factory is. I wouldn't for anything in the world be responsible for bringing trouble on any of you.

In this way you will be able to express yourselves freely, without needing to be careful what you say. You don't know me, but you feel, do you not, that my only wish is to be of use to you and that for nothing in the world would I bring harm on you? I have no connexion with the manufacture of stoves. My only interest is in the physical and moral well-being of those who manufacture them.

Be quite sincere. Don't minimize or exaggerate anything, whether good or bad. I believe you will find a certain relief in speaking the unadulterated truth.

Your comrades will read you. If they feel the same as you they will be glad to see in print some things which they may have felt in their hearts but been unable to express; or perhaps some things which they could have expressed but forced themselves not to. If they feel differently, they will write to explain what they do feel. Either way, you will get to know more about one another. This can only make for more comradeship, which is already a great gain.

The managers will also read you. Perhaps they won't always like what they read. That doesn't matter. It will do them no harm to hear some unpleasant truths.

They will understand you better after reading you. Very often a manager who is at bottom a good man appears hard, simply because he doesn't understand. Human nature is like that. Men never know how to see things from one another's point of view.

Perhaps they will find ways of remedying, at least partially, some of the troubles you have described. These managers of yours show a great deal of ingenuity in manufacturing stoves; who knows if they mightn't also show it in organizing more humane conditions of work? They

To B. 1936

certainly don't lack goodwill. The best proof of that is the appearance of these lines in *Entre Nous*.

Unfortunately, their goodwill does not suffice. The difficulties are enormous. To begin with, the ruthless law of profit weighs upon the managers as it does upon you; it weighs with inhuman force upon the whole life of industry. One can't get round it. So long as it exists, one can only submit. All one can do in the meantime is to attempt to get round difficulties by ingenuity, trying to find the most humane organization that is compatible with a given rate of profit.

But this is the big snag: you are the ones who suffer the burden of the industrial régime, but it is not you who can solve or even state the problems of organization. That is the responsibility of the managers. And the managers, like all men, see things from their own point of view, and not from yours. They don't really know how you live. They know nothing of your thoughts. Even those of them who were once workmen themselves have forgotten a great deal.

By the scheme I am proposing you might perhaps be able to make them understand what at present they don't; and you could do it without risk or loss of self-respect. And perhaps they in turn will make use of *Entre Nous* to reply. Perhaps they will explain the inevitable difficulties which the organization of industry imposes on them.

Large-scale industry is what it is. The least one can say is that it imposes harsh living conditions. But neither you nor the employers will be able to change it in the near future.

In the circumstances, this would be the ideal solution, as I see it. The managers should understand exactly what is the life of the men they employ as hands. And their chief concern should be, not to be always trying to increase profit to the maximum, but to organize the most humane conditions of work that are compatible with whatever rate of profit is essential for the factory's existence.

The workers, on the other hand, should know and understand the necessities which control the factory's existence and their life in it. They would then be in a position to judge and appreciate the managers' goodwill. They would lose the sense of being always at the mercy of arbitrary commands, and the inevitable hardships would perhaps become less bitter to endure.

Needless to say, this ideal is unrealizable. Day-to-day preoccupations weigh much too heavily on both sides. Moreover, the relation of chief to subordinate is one which does not facilitate mutual understanding. One never fully understands the people one gives orders to. One never fully understands the people from whom one gets them.

Nevertheless, it may be possible to approach a little nearer to this ideal. It depends on you now to make the attempt. Even if your little articles don't lead to any serious practical improvements, you will always have had the satisfaction of saying for once what you really think.

So that's agreed, isn't it? I hope I shall soon receive a great many articles.

I cannot end without sincerest thanks to M.B. for having been willing to publish this appeal.

11 To Monsieur B.

Monsieur,

Bourges, 31 January 1936

Your letter removes all the reasons which kept me from coming to R.; so I will come to see you, unless I hear to the contrary, on Friday 14 February after lunch.

You consider that I paint too dark a picture of the moral conditions of the workers' life. How can I answer except by repeating – painful though it is to confess – that I myself had the very greatest difficulty in retaining my self-respect? To be more candid, I practically lost it at the first shock of such a brutal change in my way of living, and I had laboriously to recover it. There came a day when I realized that a few weeks of that life had been almost enough to turn me into a docile beast of burden and that it was only on Sundays that I returned to something like a conscious life. I then asked myself with terror what I would become if it should ever happen that I was obliged to work in the same way seven days a week. I swore to myself that I would not give up until I had learned how to live a worker's life without losing my sense of human dignity. And I kept my word. But up to the last day I found it was necessary to renew the struggle every day to keep that sense, because the conditions of life never ceased to undermine it and to encourage a state of subhuman apathy.

It would be easy and pleasant to deceive myself a little and forget all that. It would have been easy not to feel it at all, if I had undertaken the experience as a sort of game, like an explorer who goes to live

To B. 1936

among remote tribes but without ever forgetting his difference from them. But I did the opposite. I systematically eliminated everything which could remind me that the experience was a sort of experiment.

You can point out that generalizations are suspect. I have done so myself. I have reflected that perhaps it was not the life that was too hard but my character that was too weak. But yet it wasn't altogether weak, because I was able to hold out until the date which I had fixed in advance.

It is true that I had far less physical stamina than most of the others – luckily for them. And factory life is much more oppressive when it weighs on the body for twenty-four hours out of twenty-four, as it often did with me, than when it is shaken off after eight hours, as it is by the toughest workers. But there were other circumstances which went far to cancel this disadvantage.

And, moreover, my impressions were more than once confirmed by confidences or semi-confidences from workers.

There remains the question of the difference between R. and the factories I knew. Apart from the proximity to the country, in what can it consist? In size? But my first factory had only 300 employees and the manager was under the impression that he really knew the personnel. In social welfare schemes? Whatever their material value I fear that morally they tend to increase the workers' dependence. In the frequent contacts between superiors and subordinates? I find it hard to picture them as a source of moral comfort for the subordinates. Is there anything else? I want to take everything into account.

What you told me about the last general meeting of the Co-operative, when nobody said a word, seems to confirm my suppositions all too clearly. You stayed away, for fear your presence might intimidate them – but even so, nobody dared say anything. The invariable results of the municipal elections seem to me to point the same way. And finally, I cannot forget the expressions on some of the moulders' faces when I walked round with the proprietor's son.

Your most telling argument with me, although it has absolutely nothing to do with the question, is that if you believed what I say it would deprive you of almost all incentive to work. Indeed, it is true that I can hardly see myself becoming head of a factory, even supposing I had the necessary ability. This consideration has no effect on my views, but it does greatly lessen my wish to make you share them. It is not just for fun, believe me, that I make myself say demoralizing things. But would it be right, in such a matter, not to tell you what I believe to be the truth?

You must forgive me if I use the word 'boss' rather too bitterly. It can hardly be otherwise when one has known a state of total subordination and cannot forget it. But it is perfectly true that you were careful to give me all your reasons for objecting to my article, and I had no right to answer in the way I did.

You exaggerate a little in thinking that I estimate your debit as overwhelming and your credit as nil. The debit side represents the function rather than the man; and on the credit side I know at least that there are good intentions. I gladly concede that there are also achievements; only I am convinced they are far fewer and far smaller than one might think if one judges from above. It is very difficult to judge from above, and it is very difficult to act from below. That, I believe, is in general one of the essential causes of human misery. And that is why I myself wanted to go right to the bottom, and will perhaps return there. And that is why I so much want to be able to collaborate in some business, from below, with the man who directs it. But no doubt it's a chimera.

I don't think our relationship will leave me with any personal bitterness – on the contrary. It is encouraging for me, who have chosen deliberately and almost without hope to adopt the point of view of those at the bottom, to be able to talk frankly with a man like you. It helps one not to despair of men, despite their institutions. Any bitterness I feel concerns only my unknown comrades in the R. workshops, for whom I have to give up trying to do anything. But I have only myself to blame, for having indulged unreasonable hopes.

As for you, I can only thank you for consenting to conversations which may or may not be of some use to you, but which are precious for me.

Yours very sincerely,
S. Weil

12 To the same

Bourges, 3 March, 1936

Monsieur,

I think it may be useful if we alternate between written and verbal discussions; the more so because I have the impression that I failed to make myself clear at our last interview.

To B. 1936

I was unable to give you any concrete example of a superior resenting a legitimate complaint by a workman. But how could I have risked the experiment? To submit in silence – as I should probably have done – if my complaint was badly received, would have been an even more painful humiliation than the subject of the complaint. To make an angry reply would probably have meant looking for a new job straight away. Admittedly, one cannot be sure beforehand that one's complaint will be resented, but one knows it is possible, and that possibility is enough. It is possible because the superior, like everyone else, has spells of bad temper. And anyway one has the feeling that it is not normal in a factory to expect any consideration at all. I told you how I was compelled by a foreman to work for two hours in a place where I was in danger of being knocked out by a swinging balance weight and thus made to feel for the first time how much I counted, i.e. not at all. A number of little things have occurred since to refresh my memory. For example: at another factory, one was not allowed in until the bell rang, ten minutes before the hour; but before the bell a little door forming part of the big entrance was opened and any chiefs who arrived early went through it. Meanwhile the women workers – with me among them more than once – waited patiently outside, before that open door, even in pouring rain. And so on. . . .

One can, of course, decide to stand up for oneself – at the risk of having to find a new job; but anyone who takes this line is all too likely to have to drop it before long; in which case it is better never to have taken it. In industry at the present time, unless you have high professional credentials, looking for a job is an experience to swallow up most of your pride – trailing from factory to factory, dreading the expense of metro tickets, waiting indefinitely to be hired, being turned away and coming back again day after day. I saw the dispiriting effects of all this upon others, and particularly upon myself. One may conclude, of course, that it was simply and solely because I lacked guts; which is what I told myself on more than one occasion.

Anyway, as a result of all this I find your communist worker's reply perfectly natural. I must admit that what you said about it rankles. The fact that you yourself in the past were bolder with your superiors gives you no right to judge. Not only was your economic position totally different, but also your moral position – if, at least, as I think I understood, you were at that time holding more or less responsible jobs. I myself, I think, would run equal or even greater risks in resisting my university superiors if necessary (supposing we had some authoritarian type of government) and with far more determination than I would show in a factory against the overseer or manager. And why? Doubtless for the same sort of reason that made it easier for a N.C.O. than a private soldier to be brave in the war – a fact familiar to old soldiers, and which I have often heard mentioned. In the university I have rights and dignity and a responsibility to defend. What have I to defend as a factory worker, when I have to renounce all rights every morning at the moment I clock in? All I have left to defend is my life. It would be too much to be expected to endure the subordination of a slave and at the same time to face dangers like a free man. To compel a man in that situation to choose between incurring a danger and fading away, as you put it, is to inflict a humiliation which it would be more humane to spare him.

What you told me about the meeting of the Co-operative – when you said, with a touch of contempt, I thought, that no one dared to speak – inspired similar reflections. Is it not a pitiful state of affairs? These people are defenceless at the mercy of a force completely disproportionate to their own, against which they can do nothing, and by which they are continually in danger of being crushed – and when, with bitter hearts, they have resigned themselves to submission and obedience, they are despised for lack of courage by the very men who control that force.

I cannot speak of these things without bitterness, but please don't think it is directed against you. The situation is a fact, and no doubt it would be, on the whole, unfair to make you any more responsible for it than myself or anyone else.

To return to the question of relations with superiors. My own behaviour was governed by a very firm principle. I conceive human relations solely on the plane of equality; therefore, so soon as someone begins to treat me as an inferior, human relations between us become impossible in my eyes. So I treat him in turn as a superior. By which I mean that I endure his power as I endure the frost and the rain. Perhaps I have an exceptionally difficult character; but nevertheless I have always observed that, whether from pride or timidity, or a mixture of the two, a glum silence is the general rule in a factory. I have known some striking examples of it.

To B, 1936

When I suggested that you might have a box for suggestions, not concerning output but concerning the workers' welfare, it was because the idea came to me when I was in the factory. Such a procedure would eliminate all risk of humiliation (I know you will say you always welcome workers who come with suggestions, but are you quite sure that you yourself never have moments of ill humour or tactless irony?); it would represent a formal invitation from the management; and moreover the mere sight of the box in the workshop would mitigate a little the impression that one counts for nothing.

To sum it up, my experience taught me two lessons. The first, the bitterest and most unexpected, is that oppression, beyond a certain degree of intensity, does not engender revolt but, on the contrary, an almost irresistible tendency to the most complete submission. I verified this in my own case – I, whose character, as you have guessed, is not a docile one. The second lesson is that humanity is divided into two categories – the people who count for something and the people who count for nothing. When one is in the second category one comes to find it quite natural to count for nothing – which is by no means to say that it isn't painful. I myself found it natural; in the same way that now, in spite of myself, I am beginning to find it almost natural to count for something. (I say in spite of myself, because I am trying to resist; I feel so ashamed to count for something in a social system which treads humanity down.) The question at present is whether, in the existing conditions, one can bring it about, within a factory, that the workers count, and have the feeling that they count, for something. For this purpose it is not enough that the manager should try to behave well to them; it needs something quite different.

The first desideratum, in my opinion, would be the frank recognition by manager and workers alike that the situation in which the latter, like so many others everywhere, count for nothing cannot be thought of as normal; that the present state of affairs is not acceptable. It is true of course that everybody does know this in his heart; but nobody on either side dares make the slightest allusion to it – and let me note, purely incidentally, that when an article does make allusion to it, the article is not printed.... It needs to be frankly recognized, too, that this state of affairs is the result of objective necessities, and an attempt should be made to elucidate them a little. The sort of inquiry I outlined was intended to include (I am not sure if I made this point in the paper you have) some account by you of the obstacles to the desired ameliorations (problems of organization, profit, etc.). In certain cases, it should include exposés of a more general character. The rule for these exchanges of opinion ought to be absolute equality between the participants, with complete frankness and clarity on both sides. If that point could be reached, it would be already an achievement, in my eyes. It seems to me that any suffering, no matter what, is less overwhelming and less likely to degrade a man if he understands the complex of necessities which cause it; and that it is a consolation to feel that it is understood and in a certain measure shared by those who are not exposed to it. Moreover, it might turn out to be possible to make some ameliorations.

Also, I am convinced that it is only here that one can hope to find an intellectual stimulus for the workers. To interest people, one must touch them. What feeling can one appeal to so as to touch men whose sensibility is affronted and trampled on every day by social serfdom? One must use, I believe, the very feeling they experience of this serfdom. I may be wrong, no doubt. But what confirms me in this opinion is that there are in general only two types of workmen who educate themselves on their own initiative: those who want promotion, and rebels. I hope you won't find this disquieting.

If, for example, it became generally recognized during these discussions that one of the obstacles to a more humane organization was the workers' ignorance, would not this be the only possible opening for a series of articles of genuine popularization? The search for a valid method of popularizing – a thing completely unknown up to now – is one of my imperative preoccupations, and from this point of view the experiment I am suggesting might be of infinite value for me.

It is true that there is a risk in all this. According to Retz it was the Parlement of Paris which provoked the Fronde, by lifting the veil which ought to cover the relation between the rights of kings and those of peoples – 'rights which are never so well harmonized as in silence'. The same formula can be applied to every kind of domination. If the experiment was only half successful the result would be that your workers would continue to count for nothing but would no longer find this natural; which would be a disadvantage all round. There is no doubt at all that you incur a grave responsibility in taking this risk.

To B. 1936

But it is also a grave responsibility to refuse to take it. Such are the penalties of power.

In my opinion, however, you exaggerate the risk. You seem to be afraid of altering the power-relations which keep the workers under your control. But that appears to me impossible. There are only two things which could alter those relations: either the return of such economic prosperity as to produce a shortage of labour, or else a revolutionary movement. Both are altogether improbable in any near future. And if a revolutionary movement should arise, it would be a tempest blowing from the great centres of industry, which would sweep everything away; a phenomenon on that scale is independent of anything you may or may not do at R. But so far as one can prophesy in such a matter, nothing of the kind will happen, unless perhaps after a disastrous war. For my part, I have a little inside knowledge both of the French working-class movement and of the working population of the Paris region; and I have acquired the conviction – a very sad one for me – that the capacity of the French working class not only for revolution but for any action at all is almost nil. I think it is only the bourgeois who could have any illusion in this matter. We will talk about this again if you like.

The experiment I am suggesting to you would proceed by stages; you would be in control and could at any moment call the whole thing off. The workers could only submit, though with a little extra bitterness in their hearts. What else would you have them do? But I recognize that this is already a sufficiently serious risk.

It is for you to consider whether the risk is worth running. It would seem to me absurd to rush into it blindly. One should first explore the ground, or take a number of soundings. As I saw it, the article you refused to print would have been one of these soundings. It would take too long in a letter to explain how.

As to the paper, I have a feeling that I explained very badly what it was that was wrong with the passages I blamed you for (accounts of comfortable meals, etc.).

I will make use of a comparison. There is nothing unpleasant in contemplating the walls of a room, even a poor and bare one; but if the room is a prison cell one cannot look at the walls without a pang. It is exactly the same with poverty, when it is combined with complete subordination and dependence. Slavery and freedom are simply ideas;

what causes suffering is actual things. Therefore what hurts is every detail of daily life which reflects the poverty to which one is condemned; and not because of the poverty but because of the slavery. The clanking of chains must have had this effect, I imagine, for convicts in the past. In the same way too every image of the well-being one lacks is painful if it presents itself in such a way as to recall the fact that one is deprived of it; because this well-being also implies freedom. The thought of a good meal in pleasant surroundings was as haunting for me, last year, as the thought of oceans and plains for a prisoner, and for the same reasons. I felt a yearning for luxury which I never felt before or since. You may suppose that this is because I now indulge it, up to a point. But no; because, confidentially between ourselves, I have not changed my way of life very much since last year. I saw no point in losing some habits which I shall almost certainly have to resume some day, either voluntarily or compulsorily, and which I can maintain without much effort. Last year, any privation, however insignificant in itself, always reminded me a little that I counted for nothing, that I was a second-class citizen, that I had no place in the world except as an obedient subordinate. That is why it is not true that the difference between your standard of life and the workers' is analogous to the difference between a millionaire's and yours; in the latter case it is a difference in degree, in the former a difference in kind. And that is why, when you happen to have 'a regular banquet', you should enjoy it without mentioning the fact.

It is true that a man of strong soul, if he is poor and dependent, has always the resource of courage and indifference to suffering and privation. It was the resource of Stoic slaves. But that resource is not available to the slaves of modern industry. The work they live by calls for such a mechanical sequence of gestures at such a rapid speed that there can be no incentive for it except fear and the lure of the pay packet. The Stoic who made himself proof against these incentives would make it impossible for himself to work at the required speed. The simplest way, therefore, to suffer as little as possible is to reduce one's soul to the level of these two incentives; but that is to degrade oneself. So if one wishes to retain human dignity in one's own eyes it means a daily struggle with oneself, a perpetual self-mutilation and sense of humiliation, and prolonged and exhausting moral suffering; for all the time one must be abasing oneself to satisfy the demands of

To B. 1936

industrial production and then reacting, so as not to lose one's self-respect, and so on indefinitely. That is the horror of the modern form of social oppression; and the kindness or brutality of one's superiors makes little difference. You will perceive clearly, I think, that what I have just described is applicable to *every* human being, whoever he is, when placed in such a situation.

Do you ask again: What can one do? I will repeat again my belief that to make these men feel one understands them would be, already, for the best among them a source of comfort. The problem is to find out whether among the men now working at R. there are some whose hearts and minds are of such a quality that they can be touched in the way I conceive. You, being related to them as a superior to his subordinates, have no way of finding this out. I believe that I might be able to, by the method of sounding which I spoke about. But for this purpose I should have to be allowed to use the paper....

I think I have said all I have to say. It is for you to reflect. You alone have the power, and the decision rests entirely with you. All I can do is to put myself at your disposal if need be; and you should note that I do so unreservedly, since I am prepared to expose myself once again body and soul, for an indefinite period, to the monstrous mechanism of industrial production. I should in fact be risking as much as you in the experiment; this ought to be a guarantee of my seriousness.

I have only one thing to add. Please be assured that if you categorically refuse to undertake anything on the lines I have suggested I shall understand very well and shall still remain entirely convinced of your goodwill. And I shall always be infinitely grateful to you for having consented to discuss freely with me as you have done.

I dare not speak of another interview, because I fear I abuse your kindness; and yet there are still a few questions I'd like to ask you, for my own personal instruction (especially about your first chemical studies and about your work on industrial tool conversion during the war). I hesitate once again, for the same reasons as before, to visit you at the factory. I leave the matter in your hands.

With best wishes,
S. Weil

P.S. I have no longer any right to be supplied with *Entre Nous*, but all the same I should much appreciate having it.

13 To the same

Bourges, 16 March 1936

Monsieur,
     I must apologize for deluging you with letters; I fear you are finding me more and more obnoxious.... But your factory obsesses me, and I would like to work through the obsession to the end.

It occurs to me that very possibly my position, somewhere between you and the working-class organizations, may appear to you ambiguous; and although you trust me in our discussions (as I feel convinced you do) you may afterwards be inclined to suspect me of all sorts of reservations or ulterior motives. If this is so, you would be wrong not to be brutally frank and question me about it. No real confidence or genuine friendliness is possible without a certain rather brutal frankness. In any case, I owe you an account of my social and political attitude.

I long with all my heart for the most radical possible transformation of the present régime, in the direction of a greater equality in the relations of power. I do not at all believe that what is called revolution nowadays can bring this about. After a so-called working-class revolution, just as much as before it, the workers at R. will go on obeying passively – so long as the system of production is based on passive obedience. Whether the manager at R. takes orders from a managing-director who represents a few capitalists or from a so-called Socialist 'State Trust' makes no difference, except that in the first case the factory is not in the same hands as the police, the army, the prisons, etc., and in the second case it is. The inequality in the relations of power is therefore not lessened but accentuated.

This consideration, however, does not put me *against* the parties described as revolutionary. Because every significant political group nowadays tends equally towards accentuating oppression and getting all the instruments of power into the hands of the State; some of them call this process working-class revolution, some call it fascism, and some call it the organization of national defence. Whatever the slogan, two factors always predominate: one of them is the subordination and dependence which are implied in modern forms of technique and economic organization; and the other is war. All those who favour the increase of 'rationalization', on the one hand, and preparation for war, on the other, are the same in my eyes; and they include everybody.

So far as factories are concerned, the problem as I see it, quite in-

To B. 1936

dependently of the political régime, is to progress from total subordination to a certain mixture of subordination and co-operation, with complete co-operation as the ideal.

When you returned my article, you reproached me for encouraging a spirit of class, as opposed to the spirit of collaboration which you hope to establish in the R. community. By class spirit I suppose you mean spirit of revolt. If so, I don't want to encourage anything of the kind. Let us be clear about it: when the victims of social oppression do in fact rebel, they have my sympathy, though unmixed with any hope; when a movement of revolt achieves some partial success, I am glad. Nevertheless, I have absolutely no desire to stir up a spirit of revolt – not so much because I am interested in preserving order as because I am concerned for the moral interests of the oppressed. I know too well that those who are in the toils of a too harsh necessity, if they rebel at one moment, will fall on their knees the moment after. The only way to preserve one's dignity under inevitable physical and moral sufferings is to accept them, to the precise extent that they are inevitable. But acceptance and submission are two very different things. The spirit I want to encourage is precisely that spirit of collaboration for which you argue in your criticism of my article. But a spirit of collaboration calls for real collaboration; and at present I can discern nothing of that kind at R., but on the contrary a complete subordination. That is why I composed the article – which I conceived as the first of a series – in a style which could give you the impression of a disguised incitement to revolt. To induce men to proceed from a state of total subordination towards a certain measure of collaboration one must surely begin, it seems to me, by encouraging them to hold up their heads.

I wonder if you realize the power you wield. It is more the power of a god than of a man. Have you ever reflected what it means for one of your workers if you sack him? In most cases, I suppose, he will have to leave the parish to look for work elsewhere. So he will move on to other parishes where he has no right to any relief. If he is unlucky – which is all too probable in present conditions – and has to wander from place to place without finding a vacancy, he will gradually decline, abandoned by God and man, and with absolutely no resources, not only towards a slow death but before that to a state of utter disintegration – unless finally some firm has the charity to give him a job; and against all this no amount of pride and courage and intelligence will avail him. You know very well, don't you, that I am not exaggerating? Such, if he happens to be unlucky, is the price a man may have to pay for the misfortune of being judged by you to be for some reason unsuitable at R.

As for those who live at R., almost all of them are unskilled workers. At the factory, therefore, they do not collaborate, they only obey; they do nothing but obey from the moment they clock in until they clock out again. Outside the factory they find themselves surrounded by things which have all been made for them, but they have all been made by you. Even their own Co-operative is not in fact controlled by them.

Far be it from me to reproach you for this power. It has been put into your hands and you use it, I am convinced, with the greatest generosity possible – at least after one has allowed, on the one hand, for the obsession with profit and, on the other, for a certain inevitable degree of misunderstanding. But this doesn't alter the fact that everywhere and all the time there is nothing but subordination.

Everything you do for the workers is done gratuitously, from generosity; so they are perpetually obliged to you. Whereas everything they do is done from necessity or for gain. All their actions are compelled; the only sphere in which they can contribute anything of their own is that of quantity, and the reward of their efforts in this sphere is only an extra quantity of cash. They never earn any moral reward, either from others or from themselves: no thanks, no praise, not even a feeling of self-congratulation. That is one of the worst moral features of modern industry; it depressed me every day, and I am sure that many others feel the same. (I will add this point in my questionnaire, if you decide to use it.)

Perhaps you are wondering what concrete idea for collaboration I have in mind. So far, I have only a few sketchy notions; but I am fairly confident that a concrete study of the question would give rise to some more definite ideas.

All I can do now is to leave you to your own thoughts. You have, so to speak, an unlimited time for thinking it over – provided always that we don't find ourselves at war one of these days, or under some 'totalitarian' dictatorship, and so lose nearly all our freedom to decide anything in any sphere. . . .

I feel a certain guilt about you, because in the event, which is after all a likely one – of our discussions coming to nothing, all I shall have

To B. 1936

done will be to pass on to you some painful preoccupations. This thought distresses me. You are a relatively happy man, and happiness in my eyes is something precious and worthy of respect. I do not want to spread around me to no purpose the indelible bitterness with which my experience has left me.

Believe me, with best wishes,

S. Weil

P.S. There is one point which I stupidly forgot at our last interview. I mention it now for fear it again slips out of my mind. I think I gathered, from a story you told, that conversation is prohibited in the factory, and punishable by fine. Is that really the case? If so, I could say a great deal about how heavily such a regulation weighs upon a man, and also, more generally, about the principle that not one minute must be wasted in the day.

14 To the same

Tuesday, 30 March [1936]

Monsieur,

Thank you for your invitation. Unfortunately, our interview will have to be postponed for 3 weeks. I cannot come to see you this week. I am physically quite exhausted and have scarcely the strength to take my classes. Then there is a fortnight's holiday, which I shall not spend at Bourges. But after that I hope to be comparatively in form. Shall we say, in principle and unless either of us has to cancel it, that I will come to see you on Monday, 20 April?

On the whole, it seems to me that the only serious obstacle to your taking me on as a worker is a certain lack of confidence. The material obstacles you have mentioned are all such as could be overcome. I would like to say this – you will easily believe that I don't regard the workers at R. as material for an experiment; I should be quite as much distressed as you if any attempt to improve their lot should end by aggravating it. If, therefore, while I was working at R. I felt a certain atmosphere of serenity, as you put it, which might be jeopardized by the carrying out of my projects, I would be the first to renounce them. On that point we see alike. The difficult point is to discriminate what the moral atmosphere really is.

On that point you would not trust my opinion. That is quite justifiable, and I understand it. I recognize, too, that I myself am to some extent responsible for your mistrust, because I have written to you very clumsily and expressed everything in the crudest way. But this was intentional. I am incapable of using guile, for any purpose whatever, with people I esteem.

If you are in Paris, don't miss the new Chaplin film.[1] There, at last, is something which expresses a part of what I felt.

Don't imagine that my social preoccupations destroy all my joie de vivre. At this time of year, above all, I never forget that 'Christ is risen'. (Metaphorically speaking, of course.) I hope it will be the same for all the inhabitants of R.

Very sincerely,
S. Weil

As we shall not see one another for a little time I would like to add one word – to say that, judging by your reply, the anecdotes and thoughts about factory life in my letters have given you a worse opinion of me than I deserve. Apparently it is impossible to make myself understood. Perhaps the Chaplin film will succeed better than anything I can say. If I, who am vaguely supposed to have learned to express myself, cannot make myself understood by you, in spite of your goodwill, one asks oneself how any understanding will ever be reached between the average worker and employer.

One word more, about your approval of the division of labour by which one man makes the parts and another man thinks how to put them together. That, I think, is the fundamental point, and it is the *only* point of essential disagreement. Among the uncultivated people I lived with I observed that elevation of thought – the faculty for understanding and forming general ideas – was always (without any exception, I believe) allied with generosity of heart. In other words, whatever degrades the intelligence degrades the whole man.

And one more remark, which I put in writing now for you to meditate on it. As a female worker I was in a doubly inferior position, liable to have my dignity hurt not only by superiors but also, as a woman, by the workmen. (And please note that I had no idiotic susceptibility about the traditional kind of jokes in factories.) It was my experience, not so much in the factory as while I was travelling about, looking for work – at which times I made it a rule never to refuse a chance of

[1] *Modern Times.*

entering into conversation – that it is nearly always the qualified skilled workers who know how to talk to a woman without offending her, and the ones who are inclined to treat her as a toy are the unskilled. I leave you to draw conclusions.

In my opinion, work should tend, *to the full extent that it is materially possible*, to be an education. And what would one think of a class in which there were radically different exercises for the good pupils and the bad?

There are natural inequalities. In my opinion, social organization can be called good, morally speaking, in so far as it tends to lessen them (by levelling up, and not down, of course), and bad in so far as it tends to accentuate them, and odious if it creates water-tight compartments.

15 To the same

[April 1936]

Monsieur,

I have thought again about what you said; and these are my conclusions. You will think that I am very vacillating, but it is simply that my mind is slow. I apologize for not having made a definite decision at once, as I ought to have done.

It's like this. Given the immediate and very extensive opportunity which you are good enough to offer me, of studying your factory, I should be unreasonable to sacrifice it for the sake of a perhaps impracticable scheme. The conditions would not be suitable for entering your factory as a worker unless there was a vacancy which nobody in R. wanted to fill – and that is most unlikely in the near future. Otherwise, even if you added my name to a list and I waited my turn the workers would find it peculiar that I should be taken on when there are women at R. who would like to be; they would guess that you know me; I would not be able to give any clear account of myself; and it would become extremely difficult to establish relations of comradely trust. Therefore, without completely abandoning my original plan, though consigning it to an indefinite future, I accept your proposal that I should devote a day to the factory. I will suggest a date in due course.

As for Monsieur M., I leave it to you to decide whether it is better to ask him now to say yes or no in principle, while making it clear to him that my plan depends upon conditions which make its execution unlikely, at least for the time being; or whether it would be better to say nothing about it until I have a definite possibility of being taken on by you. The advantage for me of knowing one way or the other would be that, if he refused, I should be free to investigate without reservations, whereas if he said yes I should make every effort not to let my visits to the factory be too noticeable. On the other hand, the plan is so indefinite that perhaps it is not worth talking about. So just do as you please. I apologize again for having been so undecided.

I would remind you again of my request that you say nothing to Mons. M., or to anyone else, about my experience in the Paris factories.

I have thought about what you told me of the principle on which men are laid off when you want to reduce staff. I am well aware that it is the only defensible one from the point of view of the business. But look at it for a moment from the other point of view – from below. Think of the power it gives your heads of department, to be responsible for choosing which Polish workers shall be laid off as the least useful! Not knowing them, I don't know how they use this power. But I can imagine the feelings of those Polish workers who, I think, suspect that you will be obliged one day to get rid of some of them, towards the departmental head whose job it will be to pick out one or another of them as less useful than his comrades. How they must tremble before him and dread getting into his bad books! Will you again think me hyper-sensitive if I tell you that I can imagine it very well and it hurts me? Imagine yourself in such a position, with wife and children to support, and ask yourself how much of your dignity you would be able to preserve.

Would it not be possible to establish – and make known, of course – some other criterion, fixed instead of arbitrary; according to seniority, or family responsibilities, or by drawing lots, or a combination of the three? Perhaps there would be great disadvantages, I cannot judge; but I beseech you to consider the moral advantage there would be for those unfortunates, who find themselves here in such miserable insecurity, by the fault of the French government.

You see, it is not subordination in itself that shocks me, but certain kinds of subordination involving intolerable moral consequences. For example, a subordination which involves not only the necessity of

To B. 1936

obedience but also a constant anxiety not to incur disfavour seems to me grievous to bear. – And another unacceptable kind of subordination is that in which all the intelligence, ingenuity, will, and professional conscience are in the instructions elaborated by the superior, while the executant has only to obey passively, with his mind and heart totally uninvolved. In such a situation the subordinate is almost like an inert object used as a tool by the intelligence of another; and that was my situation as a factory worker.

On the other hand, there are circumstances in which subordination is something fine and honourable – for example: when orders confer a responsibility upon the recipient; when they make demands upon those virtues of courage, will, conscience, and intelligence which are the definition of human value; when they imply a certain mutual confidence between superior and subordinate and only a small degree of arbitrary power in the hands of the former.

Be it said in passing that I would have been grateful if one day a superior had assigned me some task, even a dirty, dangerous, and ill-paid one, which implied on his part a certain confidence in me. On that day I would have obeyed with all my heart. And I am sure that many workers are the same. There is a moral asset here which is not exploited.

But that is enough about it. I will let you know as soon as I can which day I expect to come to R. I cannot tell you how grateful I am for the facilities you are providing me for learning what a factory is.

Very sincerely,
S. Weil

P.S. Could you have the issues of your magazine after no. 30 sent to me? My collection stops there. But I should be sorry if anyone got scolded about it. . . .

16 To the same

[April 1936]

Monsieur,

I had hoped to reply sooner, but up to now it has been impossible to fix a date. Will it suit you if I come to see you Thursday, 30 April at the usual time? If so, don't bother to reply. Your suggestion that I should spend a whole day at R., to see everything at close quarters, is exactly what I would like best; only I think an interview beforehand is necessary, to draw up a programme. I am infinitely grateful to you for giving me a chance to get a clearer picture, and there is nothing I want so much as to confront my ideas with facts. I assure you that intellectual honesty is always in my eyes the first of obligations.

In order not to waste time when we talk, I will say now that I hope you agree you misinterpreted some of my reactions. Systematic hostility to superiors, envy of the more favoured, hatred of discipline, continual discontent – all those mean sentiments are totally repugnant to me. I have to the highest degree a respect for discipline in work, and I feel contempt for people who don't know how to obey. I am well aware too that all organization implies the giving and receiving of orders. But there are orders and orders. As a factory worker I endured a discipline which I found intolerable, although I was always, or nearly always, strictly obedient and arrived painfully at a sort of resignation. I am not called upon to justify (as you put it) my feeling of intolerable suffering in that situation, but only to try to determine precisely its causes. All I can be reproached with, in this connexion, is to have mistaken those causes – which I may have done. On the other hand, I could never in any circumstances agree to consider appropriate for one of my fellows, whoever he may be, something that I judge to be morally intolerable for myself. For all the differences between men, my sense of human dignity remains identical, whether for myself or anyone else – even though in other respects there may be relations of superiority or inferiority between us. On this point nothing in the world will ever shake me, or so I hope. But in everything else my one desire is to get rid of every preconceived idea which could distort my judgement.

One thing you said gave me cause for prolonged reflection. I mean when you spoke of the possibility of arranging for closer contacts some day between the factory and myself. Did you have anything definite in mind when you said this? If so, I hope you'll tell me what. I ask myself whether you merely desire, out of pure generosity towards me, to afford me the means of learning, and of defining and correcting my too summary and doubtless partly false views on industrial organization; or whether you think that I might somehow be able to be useful in some other way than the one I suggested. Speaking for myself, I have no reason up to now for confidence in my own abilities. However, if you had in mind some way of trying them out in the interest of your workers – on the basis of some ideas previously agreed between us, in

To B. 1936

spite of divergences – then I should feel bound to consider it seriously.

We can speak of all this and many other things on Thursday, if you care to. If Friday suits you better, just let me know and I'll come then.

Very sincerely,

S. Weil

17 To the same

[April or May 1936]

Monsieur,

I am still not able to fix a date. But, in the meantime, I have been so touched by your generosity – receiving me and answering my questions, and opening your factory to me as you do – that I have resolved to write some copy for you, to repay at least a little of the time you spend on me.

But I feel anxious about how I shall manage to conform to the required approach, for clearly I must offer you only the best-behaved prose, so far as I am able. . . . Luckily I have remembered an old project which is very close to my heart, of making the masterpieces of Greek poetry (which I love passionately) accessible to the mass of people. I felt last year that the great poetry of Greece would be a hundred times closer to the people, if they could know it, than French literature both classical and modern. I have started with *Antigone*. If I have done what I intended it should be able to interest and touch everyone, from the manager to the last of the workers. And the latter should be able to enter into it with almost no difficulty and yet without the feeling that there has been any effort of condescension to bring it within his reach. That is how I understand popularization. But I don't know if I have succeeded.

Antigone is by no means a moral tale for model children; but all the same I hope you won't go so far as to find Sophocles subversive. . . .

If this article is appreciated – and if it isn't, it will be because I don't know how to write – I could do a whole series, from other tragedies of Sophocles and from the *Iliad*. There are ever so many poignant and profoundly human things in Homer and Sophocles, and it is only a question of expressing and presenting them in a way that makes them accessible to all.

It gives me some satisfaction to think that if I do these articles and they are read, the most illiterate operatives at R. will know more about Greek literature than 99% of college students – to say the least!

But I shan't have the leisure for it until towards the summer. Hoping to see you soon,

Very sincerely,
S. Weil

I hope you can manage to have the article printed in one instalment.

18 To the same

(A fragment of a letter)

[April or May 1936]

Monsieur,

In principle, I hope to come in a fortnight's time. I will write to confirm it.

As a *nom de plume* for the *Antigone* article you can put 'Cleanthes' (the name of a Greek who combined the study of Stoic philosophy with the profession of water-carrier). I would sign my name, were it not for the possibility of my coming to work in the factory.

If you believe it was against the grain that I presented *Antigone* in the way I have done, you ought not to thank me: one does not thank people for the strains one imposes on them. But in fact it was no strain, or very little. I think it is more beautiful to expose the drama in its nakedness. Perhaps some other texts will inspire me to add a few words suggesting their possible application to contemporary life; but I hope you won't find the applications unacceptable.

What was a strain however was the mere fact of writing with the thought in my mind: Will this be allowed? I have never done so before and there are very few considerations which could induce me to submit to it. The pen refuses that sort of constraint, once one has learned to use it as it should be used. But of course I will continue in spite of this.

I have a great ambition, though I scarcely dare think about it, so hard would it be to realize: I would like, after this series of articles, to do another – which should be intelligible and interesting to any unskilled labourer – about the creation of modern science by the Greeks; it is a marvellous story and not generally known even to cultivated people.

To B. 1936

You misunderstood me about the reductions of staff. It is not the arbitrariness in itself that I wanted to see controlled. In carrying out such a cruel measure (the reproach is not addressed to you) the choice itself seems to me to some extent a matter of indifference. What I find incompatible with human dignity is the fear of displeasing a superior which is engendered by the belief that his choice of whom to get rid of may be arbitrary. Any rule, however absurd in itself, but fixed, would be an improvement in this respect, or else some method of control which would enable the workers to satisfy themselves that the choice was not arbitrary. Obviously, however, you alone can judge of the possibilities. But how can I not regard men placed in that moral situation as victims of oppression? Which does not necessarily imply that you are an oppressor.

19 To the same

[May 1936]

Monsieur,

I have put off writing from day to day in the hope of being able to fix a date. It hasn't been possible until now, because I have not been at all well recently. And to spend a whole day visiting a factory is exhausting; it cannot be profitable unless one is able to remain alert and clear-headed all day.

Unless you hear to the contrary I will come on Friday, 12 June at 7.40 a.m. as arranged.

I will bring you a new article on another tragedy of Sophocles. But I won't leave it with you unless you can arrange for a better typographical lay-out. I have some rather serious complaints to make about the way *Antigone* was printed.

All things considered, I will not visit a worker's house. I cannot believe there is not a risk that such a visit would wound someone's susceptibilities; and it would require a very weighty consideration to make me risk hurting the feelings of people who, when they are hurt, must keep quiet and even smile.

But in fact, when I say there is a risk of wounding susceptibilities, I really mean I am convinced that those workers who have managed to retain some pride are effectively wounded by that sort of thing. Suppose that an exceptionally curious visitor wanted to see the living conditions not only of the workers but also of the manager, and that Mons. M. took him to visit your house. I can hardly believe you would find this quite natural. And between the two cases I recognize no difference at all.

I was pleased to see that there appears to have been some workers' collaboration in your magazine with regard to the *croissants*. I was particularly struck by the woman worker's article saying they should be discontinued. I hope you will give me some information about her.

Very sincerely,
S. Weil

P.S. I was also much interested by the response of the woman who wants articles on the organization of the factory.

20 To the same

Wednesday [10 June 1936]

Monsieur,

I find I am obliged to be in Paris tomorrow and the next day, to see some friends who are passing through. So my visit will have to be postponed again.

It's better so, in any case; because if I found myself among your workers at this moment I could not resist offering them warm congratulations. You will realize, I think, what feelings of unspeakable joy and relief this splendid campaign[1] has given me. The consequences will be what they will. But nothing can destroy the value of these lovely days of joy and fraternity, nor the relief the workers have felt at being for once given way to by those who dominate them.

I write like this so that we may not misunderstand one another. If I congratulated your workers on their victory you would doubtless consider I was abusing your hospitality. It is better to wait until things have settled down. Supposing always that you still consent to receive me, after these few lines. . . .

Very sincerely,
S. Weil

---

[1] The stay-in strikes which coincided with the formation of Léon Blum's Popular Front government in June 1936.

21 To Simone Weil, from Monsieur B.

13.6.36

Mademoiselle,
    If the events you rejoice over had developed in the opposite sense I believe, since my reactions are not one-way only, that I should not have experienced 'feelings of unspeakable joy and relief' at seeing the workers give way to the employers.

At any rate I am quite certain it would have been impossible for me to express those feelings to you.

I must ask you, Mademoiselle, to accept my regret at being unable without falsehood to close with any expressions beyond those of courtesy.

22 To Monsieur B.

[June 1936]

Monsieur,
    You write to me exactly as though I had committed the moral indelicacy of triumphing over the vanquished and oppressed. I assure you that if you were in prison, or on the pavement, or in exile, or anything of that sort, I would refrain from expressing joy or even feeling it. But I think you have not yet ceased to be manager at R.? And the workers are still working under your orders? Even with the new wage scales you still earn a little more than a moulder, I imagine? In the last analysis, there has been no essential change. As for the future, no one knows what it will bring, nor whether the present working-class victory will turn out in the end to have been a step towards a totalitarian communist régime, or a totalitarian fascist régime, or – as I hope but, alas, do not believe – a non-totalitarian régime.

Believe me, and above all believe that I speak without irony, the joy that the successful strikes have given me (a joy that was soon replaced by the anxiety I have felt ever since the distant day when I realized what disasters we are heading for) was a joy not only on behalf of the workers but also on behalf of the employers. I am not thinking now of their material interests – it may be that the results of the strike will be disastrous in the end for the material interests of both sides, one cannot tell – but of their moral interests, the good of their souls. I think it is good for the oppressed to have been able to assert their existence for a few days and lift their heads and impose their will and obtain some advantages which they do not owe to a condescending generosity. And I think it is equally good for the bosses – for the good of their souls – to have been obliged in their turn, for once in their lives, to give way to force and endure a humiliation. I am glad for them.

What ought I to have done? Not feel that gladness? But I think it legitimate. I never at any time had any illusion about the possible results of the strikes; I did nothing to promote or prolong them; but at least I could share the pure and profound joy that inspired my comrades in serfdom. Then ought I not to have expressed it to you? But just consider our respective positions. Cordial relations between you and me would involve the worst hypocrisy on my part if I left you to believe for a moment that they imply the slightest hint of approval for the oppressive power which you represent, and which you wield in your sphere as immediate delegate of the owner. It would be easy and advantageous for me to leave you in error on this subject. In expressing myself with a brutal frankness whose practical consequences can only be disadvantageous I show my esteem for you.

In short, it is for you to decide whether or not to renew the relations which existed between us before the present state of affairs. Whichever you do, I shall not forget that I owe to you, intellectually, a somewhat clearer view of certain of the problems which concern me.

S. Weil

P.S. I have one more request to make, which I hope you will grant in any case. I shall probably decide in the end to write something about industrial labour. Would you be so kind as to return to me all the letters in which I spoke about the condition of the workers? They include a number of facts and impressions and ideas, some of which I might not be able to recall. Thanks in advance.

For the rest, I hope that no change in your feelings towards me will make you forget your promise of absolute secrecy about my factory experiences.

23 To Auguste Detœuf

The recipient of this letter was a manager of electrical companies. It was he who arranged for Simone Weil to be taken on at the Alsthom works in December 1934. See also page 91 below.

[Summer, 1936]

Cher Monsieur,

    I am very upset that I cannot make myself clear to you, because it is entirely my fault. If my plan is to be carried out one day – the plan of being employed by you in a factory for an indefinite period, so as to co-operate with you in that capacity in some attempted reforms – then the fullest understanding must first be established between us.

    I was struck by what you said the other day – that dignity is something interior and is independent of external doings. It is perfectly true that one can bear a great many injustices, outrages, and arbitrary commands, in silence and unresistingly, and yet without one's dignity disappearing, quite the contrary. All that is needed is a strong soul. So if I tell you, for example, that the first shock of that life in the factory turned me for a time into a sort of beast of burden and that I only retrieved my sense of dignity gradually, at the price of daily struggles and heavy moral suffering, you have the right to conclude that it is I who lack firmness of soul. On the other hand, if I kept quiet about it, which I would much prefer, what would be the use of having had the experience?

    Equally I shall fail to make myself clear so long as you attribute to me, as you evidently do, a certain repugnance either for manual labour in itself or for discipline and obedience in themselves. On the contrary, I have always been strongly attracted to manual work (though it is true I am not gifted for it) and especially to the most laborious jobs: hay-making – harvesting – threshing – potato-lifting (from 7 a.m. to 10 p.m. . . .), and in spite of crushing fatigue I found some deep and pure joy in it. And I assure you too that I know how to submit to any discipline that is necessary for efficient work, so long as it is a humane discipline.

    I call any discipline humane which addresses itself largely to the goodwill and energy and intelligence of the subordinate. I entered the factory with a ridiculous amount of goodwill and discovered soon enough that nothing could be more out of place. Nothing was ever asked from me except what the most brutal constraint could extort.

The obedience I had to practise can be defined as follows. To begin with, it shrinks the time dimension down to a few seconds. In every human being the relation between body and mind is that the body lives in the present while the mind controls, surveys, and directs the flow of time. In the factory, such was the relation between myself and the foremen. My attention had to be constantly restricted to the movement I was performing. I did not have to coordinate it with other movements, but simply to go on repeating it until the moment when I received an order to perform a different one. It is a well-known fact that when the time-sense is restricted to waiting for a future over which one has no control one's courage dies. Secondly, it is an obedience to which one's entire being is committed. In your own sphere, obedience to an order means directing your activity in a certain way; but for me an order might overwhelm soul and body together because – like some of the others – I was almost continually at the limit of my strength. An order might catch me in a moment of exhaustion and compel me to force myself – and keep on forcing, to the point of desperation. A foreman can impose a method of working, or defective tools, or a rhythm of work, such as to produce an excess of fatigue which makes all one's hours outside the factory a blank. And a small difference in pay, too, can in certain conditions affect one's very life. In these circumstances one is so dependent upon the foremen that one cannot help fearing them and one is obliged to struggle continually – this is another painful admission – against falling into servility. In the third place, this discipline relies upon no incentives except the most sordid form of gain, on a paltry scale, and fear. To attribute an intrinsic importance to these incentives is to degrade oneself; and to reject them by schooling oneself to an indifference to half-pence and abuse is to become at the same time inapt for the required completely passive obedience and for repeating the required motion at the required speed; an inaptitude which is very soon punished by hunger. I have sometimes thought it would be better to be subdued to that sort of obedience by external compulsion, such as the whip, rather than have to subdue oneself to it by repressing all that is best in oneself.

In this situation, the greatness of soul which allows one to despise injustice and humiliation is almost impossible to exercise. So much so that, on the contrary, many apparently insignificant things – clocking in and out, and showing one's identity card (at Renault's), the pay procedure, any slight reprimand – are felt as profound humiliations because they remind one of one's situation and make it palpable. And the same is true of privations and hunger.

The only way not to suffer is to lapse into unconsciousness; and there are many who yield, in one way or another, to this temptation. I often did so myself. I do not say it is impossible to retain the lucidity, self-responsibility, and dignity appropriate to a human being; but it means condemning oneself to a renewed fight every day against despair. That at least was my experience.

The present wave of strikes is based on despair. That is why it cannot be reasonable. In spite of your good intentions you have not so far tried any way of releasing those who depend on you from that despair; so it is not for you to blame what is unreasonable in the movement. It was for this reason that I got rather heated in our discussion the other day – which I regretted afterwards – although I entirely agree with you about the possible serious dangers ahead. In my case too it is really despair which makes me feel an unmixed joy at seeing my comrades at last and for once lifting their heads high, without any thought for the possible consequences.

And yet I think that if things go well, that is to say, if the workers return to work fairly soon and with the feeling of having won a victory, the situation will be favourable in a little time for attempting some reforms in your factories. It would be necessary first to give them time to lose the sense of their passing moment of power, to lose the idea that they can be feared, and to resume their habits of submission and silence. After which you will perhaps be able to establish between yourself and them the direct relations of confidence without which no action is possible, by making them feel you understand them – assuming always that I am able to make you understand them, which evidently presupposes first of all that I am not mistaken in thinking I understand them myself.

As for the present situation, if the workers go back to work for wages not much higher than before, it can only happen in two ways. Either they will feel they have yielded to force and will resume their work in humiliation and despair; or else they will be offered some moral compensation, and there is only one that is possible – namely, the ability to satisfy themselves that their low wages are dictated by necessity and not by the employers' ill-will. I am well aware that this is almost impossible. In any case, if the employers are wise they will do all they can to give to any concessions they make the appearance of a victory for the workers. In their present mood they would find the sense of defeat intolerable.

I shall certainly return to Paris Wednesday evening. I would gladly come to you on Thursday or Friday before 9 a.m. if you are sure that would not be inconvenient and if you think a talk would be useful. I know myself; and I know that once this period of excitement has died down I shall no longer dare to call on you in this way, for fear of being a nuisance; and you on your side will perhaps become so submerged again in your daily preoccupations that you will postpone considering certain problems.

If I should be disturbing you the least little bit you have only to tell me, or else simply don't have me admitted. I know you have a lot more things to do than talk.

With kindest wishes,

S. Weil

P.S. I suppose you have seen *Modern Times*? The feeding-machine – that's the most perfect and truest symbol of the workers' position in the factory.

24 To the same

Friday [summer, 1936]

Cher Monsieur,

This morning I managed to get into the Renault works clandestinely, in spite of the strict control. I thought it might be useful to let you know my impressions.

(1) *The workers know nothing about the negotiations.* – No one tells them anything. They believe that Renault is refusing to accept the collective agreement. A woman worker said to me: 'Apparently the wages are settled, but he won't admit the collective agreement.' An unskilled workman said: 'I think we could have won our demands 3 days ago, but as the skilled grades stood by us it's our turn to stand by them.' Etc. – Alas, they find it quite natural to know nothing. They are so used to it. . . .

(2) They are definitely beginning to have had enough. Some of them, although keen and loyal, openly admit it.

(3) There is an extraordinary atmosphere of distrust and suspicion. And they have a weird ceremonial: those who leave the factory and don't come back, or are absent without authorization, are held up to infamy by the publishing of their names on a placard in one of the workshops (a Russian custom), and by hanging them in effigy and giving them a burlesque funeral. Almost certainly, when work starts again, their dismissal will be one of the conditions. In general, there is not much camaraderie in the air. Silence everywhere.

(4) Three days ago (I think) a 'professional' trade union of skilled grades (down to – and *including* – machine-setters!) was formed, on the initiative of the Croix de Feu[1] it is said. The workers claim that it was dissolved the next day and that 97% of the skilled craftsmen and technical personnel have joined the C.G.T. However, the Renault insurance office – which occupies premises in the factory area and is a part of the organization, and which is on strike, though without banners over the door – exhibits two copies of a paper denying the dissolution of the union, claiming that it has 3,500 members and that similar branches have been formed at Citroën, Fiat, etc., and announcing an immediate campaign for membership. And this only a few yards away from buildings flying the red flag. No one seems to want to destroy the papers or even to contradict what they say.

My conclusion is that there is certainly some manoeuvre going on now. But by whom? Maurice Thorez has made a speech which is a clear invitation to end the strike.

This makes me wonder if the lower levels of the Communist Party have escaped from the Party's control and fallen under some unidentified influence. Because it is clear enough that everything is still being done in the name of the Communist Party (hammers and sickles, banners, the *Internationale*, etc., everywhere), and yet one hears rumours that Costes got a bad reception.

I still stick to my idea, which may be utopian but so far as I can see it is the only alternative to the totalitarian State. If the working class imposes its power with such crude force it must assume the corresponding responsibilities. It is inadmissible and in the last resort impossible that one irresponsible social category should impose its wishes by force and that the employers, who bear the whole responsibility, should be obliged to yield. There must be either a certain joint re-

---

[1] A war veterans' organization, which later tended towards fascism.

sponsibility or else a ruthless re-establishment of hierarchy, which would no doubt involve bloodshed no matter how it was effected.

When work is resumed, after some sort of provisional solution of the crisis, I can very well imagine the head of a business saying something like this to his workers: As a result of your action we have entered a new era. You wanted to put an end to the suffering which has been imposed on you for years by the necessities of industrial production. You decided to demonstrate your strength. Very good. But this has created a situation without precedent, which calls for new forms of organization. Since you intend to compel industrial enterprises to acknowledge the force of your claims, you must be able to face the responsibilities of the new situation which you have brought about. We want to facilitate the adaptation of the business to this new relation of forces. To this end we will encourage the formation of technical, economic, and social study groups in the factory. We will provide accommodation for these groups and will authorize them to call upon the factory's technicians for lectures, and also upon the technicians and economists of trade union organizations. We will arrange for tours of the factory, with technical explanations; and we will encourage the production of bulletins explaining the technical problems in simple language. All this with a view to enabling the workers, and more particularly their delegates, to understand the organization and management of an industrial concern.

It is a bold idea, no doubt, and perhaps risky. But what is not risky at the present moment? The present enthusiastic mood of the workers might make it practicable. Anyway, I urgently beg you to consider it.

This is how I conceive the question of authority, on the purely theoretical level: on the one hand, the managers should give orders, of course, and the subordinates should obey; but on the other hand the subordinates ought not to feel themselves delivered body and soul to an arbitrary domination – which does not at all mean that they ought to collaborate in framing the orders, but that they ought to be in a position to judge how far the orders correspond to some necessity.

However, all that is in the future. The present situation amounts to this:

(1) The employers have made some unquestionably satisfactory concessions; indeed, your own workers have already been satisfied with less.

(2) The Communist Party has come out officially (though with circumlocutions) in favour of a resumption of work; and moreover I have it from a reliable source that in certain unions (e.g. in the public services) the Communist Party members worked effectively to prevent a strike.

(3) The workers at Renault, and doubtless at other factories, know nothing about the negotiations in progress. Therefore it is not they who are obstructing an agreement.

I have written to Roy (who is away from Paris today) to give him this information and have also conveyed it to a responsible and serious comrade in the Seine federation of trade unions, who has given it due attention.

Everything I have been saying refers to the situation as it is now; because the rejection of the agreement between the employers and the C.G.T. (15% and 7%)[1] seems, on the contrary, to have been quite spontaneous.

With kindest regards,
S. Weil

I shall no doubt come back to Paris tomorrow for 24 hours. It is extremely trying and nerve-racking to be kept in the provinces at a time like this.

25 To the same

This letter was published, with Detœuf's reply, which follows, in Nouveaux Cahiers *of 15 December 1937.*

[1937]

Cher ami,

I heard a conversation in the train between two employers, apparently of middling status (travelling second class, Legion of Honour ribbons); one of them seemed to be provincial, the other working between the provinces and the Paris region; the first in textiles, the second in textiles and metals; white-haired, rather corpulent, very respectable; the second fairly prominent in employers' organizations of the Paris metallurgical industries. Their observations seemed to me

[1] Wage increases agreed by the *Accords Matignon*, 7 June 1936.

so remarkable that I made a note of them when I got home. I have copied them for you, adding a few comments.

[. . . .]

'Now there's more talk of controlling the engagement and laying-off of personnel. In the mines they have to have joint committees – yes, with workers' representatives alongside the employer. Do you realize? It means you won't be able to hire or fire whom you please.' – 'Oh! It's a gross infringement of liberty.' – 'It's the last straw!' – 'You're quite right. As you said just now, the way they go on simply makes one sick, *so sick that one doesn't bother to get business, even if there is any.*' – 'Precisely.' – 'What we did, we passed a practically unanimous resolution that we didn't want any control, we'd rather close down the factories. If everyone did the same, they'd have to give in.' – 'Yes indeed, if that law is passed, there'd be nothing to do but close down everywhere.' – 'Quite. We've nothing left to lose. . . .'

Parenthesis: It is odd that men who are well fed, well dressed, and warm, and who are travelling comfortably second class, should think they have nothing to lose. If their policy, which is the same as the Russian employers' in 1917, should produce a social upheaval which sent them wandering in foreign lands without money or passport or work-permit, they would perceive at last that they had a good deal to lose. They could begin to inform themselves now by consulting the men who held similar positions to theirs in Russia and who are still toiling miserably, twenty years later, as unskilled hands at Renault's.

'. . . nothing left to lose!' – 'Absolutely.' – 'And anyway, one would be like a ship's captain without authority, just sitting in his cabin while the crew ran the ship.'

[. . . .]

'. . . The employer is the most hated man. Hated by everybody. And yet he's the one who gives everybody a living. What monstrous injustice. But yes, everyone hates him.' – 'At one time, at least there used to be some respect. I remember, when I was young . . . .' – 'That's all finished now.' – 'Yes, and even where the skilled men are good . . . .' 'Oh, the swine! They've done everything possible to ruin the show. *But they'll pay for it.*'

These last words in a tone of concentrated venom. Without wishing to be alarmist, one must recognize that the atmosphere in which conversations like this can take place cannot be described as social peace.

'... No one realizes it, but the whole stream of social life is fed from the employer's funds. If they all closed down at the same time, who would be able to do anything? It'll come to that in the end, and then people will understand. The employers were wrong to be afraid. All they needed was to say: The master switch is in our hands. And they'd have got their way.'

They would have been very surprised to be told that their tactic is the employers' equivalent of the general strike, for which no doubt they lack words to express their horror. If the employers can legitimately call such a strike in defence of their right to hire or fire whom they please, why should not the workers do so in defence of their right not to be arbitrarily refused work or fired? And the workers really did have very little to lose in those sombre years of 1934-5.

Moreover, these two worthy gentlemen didn't seem to have a notion that if the employers all closed down together and locked their factories they wouldn't even be asked for the keys; the factories would be reopened and run without them. The Russian example doesn't suggest that the ensuing years would be pleasant for anybody; but least of all for the former employers.

'... Yes, after all, there's nothing more to lose.' – 'Absolutely nothing at all; one might as well give up.' – 'And if it's the end anyway, why not end with a bang!' – 'It seems to me it's the employers' Battle of the Marne. They're right up against the wall, and now....'

At this point the train stopped, and put an end to the conversation. The reference to the Marne once again suggested civil war rather than ordinary social conflicts. These military memories, and expressions like 'end with a bang' and 'nothing to lose', repeated over and over again, sounded quite comic in the mouths of two correct, well-nourished, and portly gentlemen whose whole aspect was a perfect example of the comfortable, peaceful, reassuring type of middle-class Frenchman.

Of course, this is only one conversation. But I think a conversation in a more or less public place between two people not remarkable for originality – as was obvious in this case – must reflect a pretty general atmosphere; so that a single conversation can be conclusive. This one, I think, could appropriately be included among the comments on Detœuf's article, 'Employer's sabotage and workers' sabotage'. I agreed, on the whole, with that article; I think Detœuf was right, but more so for the immediate past than for the present moment. Or rather, so as not to exaggerate, I think the situation is evolving in such a way as to make him a little less right every day. In any case, what must be recognized is that ideas of sabotage are in the air; and that in some minds disgust has engendered a mood which is the employers' equivalent of a stay-in strike. That, at least, is what I heard stated in so many words, and I guarantee the accuracy of the words I have reported.

You may publish this letter in *Nouveaux Cahiers*. (In fact, I wrote it with that in mind.)

With best wishes,
S. Weil

P.S. This is the chief paradox of the situation. The employers, because they *think* they have no more to lose, are adopting a revolutionary language and attitude; and the workers, because they *think* they have something quite important to lose, are adopting a conservative language and attitude.

26 To Simone Weil from Auguste Detœuf

Printed with the preceding letter in *Nouveaux Cahiers*, 15 December 1937.

[1937]

Ma chère amie,

The conversation you report is most interesting; I agree, though without generalizing to the extent that you do, that it reflects a very widespread state of mind. But it does not inspire the same reflections in me as in you. You reason with your soul, which identifies itself through kindness and love of justice with the soul of the workers; but the problem here is to understand two employers, who may once have been workers but who have certainly been employers for a long time.

Do you mind if we leave aside whatever may be rather grotesque and also rather odious in the fact of being portly and well-nourished. Your two industrialists share that misfortune not only with me but also with some of the workers' representatives and even with some of the workers themselves, who do not simply on that account consider that all is for the best in the best of all possible worlds. If I insist upon this point, which is certainly a minor one for you, it is because, throughout your objective account of the conversation and your pitilessly logical comments, this single touch of picturesque description does really appeal to the imagination; and this, as I see it, disturbs the serenity which is desirable.

So let us forget, if you will, the physical aspect of the two employers. What is the upshot of their conversation? Unquestionably, that they are exasperated, that they feel they have nothing more to lose, that they are disposed to shut down their factories to resist a law on the engagement of staff by which they would lose certain prerogatives which they consider indispensable for carrying on their business, and that a general strike of employers would be in their eyes a patriotic uprising.

You tell them that they have much more to lose than they believe, that they are flirting with a method of action which they condemn in their employees, and that their factories would be kept open in spite of them; and your conclusion is that the tendency towards sabotage by employers is growing.

And there is some truth in all this; but in my opinion it is a grain of truth from which, in the short run, nothing practical and nothing good can be developed.

Put yourself for a moment in the place of those two employers. These men believed themselves to be all-powerful in their firms; they have risked all their money in them; they have probably toiled long and hard, with a great deal of serious worry; they have been battling for years against the whole world: their competitors, their suppliers, their customers, their employees. They have become conditioned to see the world as full of enemies and to be able to count on no one apart from a few exceptional employees, whose devotion they take for granted most of the time. It seems to them they have never made demands on anybody and never asked anything except to be left in peace to tackle their own problems. To tackle them, it is true, by sometimes cheating and sometimes ruining somebody. But without remorse, without the faintest compunction, because they are only doing what everybody does; they are playing the game as it is played. No one has ever told them anything about social solidarity; no one they meet ever practises it. They are convinced of having done their duty by trying to make money; and they welcome the further idea that by looking after themselves, which is their chief motive, they are also enriching the community and doing a service to the nation. They are all the more convinced of this when they see others alongside them making more money than they by simply acting as brokers, middlemen, and speculators, and sometimes robbing the till, with impunity.

Add to all this that the events of recent years have convinced them that under this régime nothing but threats and violence are effective; that if you shout loud enough and treat the State with sufficient contumely and threaten to disregard the laws, you can be sure (if there are enough of you) not only of going unpunished but also of gaining your point. And you expect that they, alone, should go on trying not to embarrass the government – a government supported by a party which aims at totally dispossessing them!

I don't mean by this that their reasons are sound or their feelings right; I only ask you to recognize that unless they were more than human they could hardly think and feel otherwise.

When they talk about 'the end' and say they have 'nothing more to lose' they are, in a way, exaggerating; it is an attempt to get from their colleagues the support they have always lacked and also to convince one another that they possess more energy and solidarity than is in fact the case. But they truly believe what they say. And here you must really use your own imagination to try to grasp that these men have not so much imagination as you credit them with. For them, to have nothing more to lose means to have to give up their business, their *raison d'être*, their social surroundings, everything that makes up their existence. Never having known hunger, they cannot imagine hunger; never having known exile, they cannot imagine exile. But they do know examples of bankruptcy, ruin, social failure, inability to give one's children the advantages ordained for them from all eternity. And the destruction of the familiar conditions of their existence is, for them, the destruction of their existence. Suppose you were told: You will always have enough to eat and you will be kept warm and cared for, but you will be an imbecile and people will regard you as a piece of human wreckage; wouldn't you say: 'I should have nothing more to

From Auguste Detœuf 1937

lose'? What your mental activity and your social, moral and aesthetic interests are for you is all associated for them with their factory, a factory which has always functioned in a certain way and which they cannot imagine functioning differently. I purposely leave aside whatever fine and noble and disinterested traits they may possess. Yet there is something of all that, too; but to discern it you need to have regarded them with sympathy for a long time.

So if you will grant me that your two employers can hardly think otherwise than as they do, let us pass to a second point. Are they useless and will they be dispensed with, as you suggest? Neither, in my opinion. Though it is comparatively easy to replace the manager of a big firm by an official, the small employer can only be replaced by another employer. Under officialdom his business would soon come to a halt. His activity and resourcefulness, his daily adaptation to ever-changing circumstances, which call for the continual taking of decisions and risks and new responsibilities – all this is entirely alien to the role of a paid official, and especially the paid official of a State. Of all the difficulties the Russian economy has encountered, those which arise from the suppression of the little industries, the small employers, the independent craftsmen, are the most serious; they have not been overcome, and they will not be. Whatever new Economy is envisaged, the small and middling employer will remain. You think he fails to understand the situation; and indeed he will not understand it overnight, but he can learn to understand it. In the last eighteen months he has already learnt a lot more than people think.

So don't make the same mistake as he. You have need of him, although he wants to do some things that you find absurd. If you want him not to do them, you must try to calm him. A certain control over the engagement and dismissal of staff is necessary: it must be established, but it must be limited to the *strictly necessary minimum*; and moreover, is it really against the small employers that control in the interest of the mass of workers should be enforced? I don't think so. If the engagement of staff is properly managed in the big industries don't you think the natural working of supply and demand will lead to proper methods in the small ones? If you try to control too many businesses you create too many officials and a system of control that cannot be enforced and a continual state of friction. The education of the small and middling employer ought not to be done by direct but by indirect methods. He is accustomed to adapting himself to the trend of things; he is protesting today because he is confronted not by things but by the power of men – men whom he has not chosen and whom he considers tyrannical.

Don't try to impose your will on him by regulations which he doesn't understand – you won't succeed. On the other hand, you won't be able to replace him, and not only because the State would fail lamentably if it tried to replace him, but also because it will never dare to try. The workers are a concentrated mass, it is true; but they only represent a quarter of the country's population, and they cannot impose their will on it. Because they have been immoderate, through lack of experience, in their wage claims a great part of the country disowns them, at heart if not in words. In France of all countries the running of small businesses by the State will never be contemplated. And on the other hand, since you can't run them under your own direct control you can be sure that your innumerable regulations, diverse and inevitably inhuman, will very soon be evaded and ridiculed and become obsolete.

Your two employers are exasperated; though not, you may be sure, to the point of forgetting their personal interests, which, to a great extent, coincide with the general interest. A concerted strike against the threat of a too strict law on the engagement of staff is a possibility I do not exclude; because it is a question of measures which would directly affect every employer in what he considers his vital activity. But that would be no more than a demonstration. The real cause for anxiety lies elsewhere; it is the question of the spirit in which the legislation will be applied – a legislation which will perhaps be bureaucratic, and perhaps meddlesome, and perhaps economically unsound, or even anti-social; and a legislation which will not be understood by some of those to whom it is applied. We must have a law which is understood, that is to say, a law which does not totally transform the existing régime; a law which prevents abuses, but without claiming to control the employer in the current exercise of his authority. And this is possible. But one must first wish it – and not let oneself be carried away so that one creates disorder on the pretext of establishing some order; and exasperates a section of the people, and perhaps the most economically active section, on the pretext of establishing social peace; and promulgates laws, through a weak government like our present

From Auguste Detœuf 1937

one, which that government will from the very outset be incapable of enforcing.

One must put up with a few corpulent gentlemen who don't always think very clearly in order not to have – instead of a few unemployed who are more or less taken care of – a whole people dying of hunger and exposed to every hazard.

A. Detœuf

PART II
1937-1942

In August 1936, almost immediately the Spanish civil war broke out, Simone Weil had gone to Spain and joined the Anarchist militia. But fortunately she was invalided back to France before the end of the year, having been badly burned in an accident with cooking-oil. This accident almost certainly saved her life, which she could hardly have failed to lose either through enemy action or through protesting against atrocities on her own side (see 'Journal d'Espagne' in *Écrits historiques et politiques* and letter no. 35 in this volume). In the spring of 1937 she had several months' holiday in Italy; but her never very robust health was beginning to deteriorate and although she took up an appointment at the *lycée* of St. Quentin in October 1937, she was obliged to resign in January 1938.

From this time onward the headaches which had afflicted her almost continually for the past eight years became more severe and she spent most of the time in Paris with her parents. She did no teaching, but wrote a lot, including some poetry – from which she had abstained for many years. She was with her parents at a mountain resort above Nice when the war broke out, and they returned immediately to Paris, where they remained until just before the entry of the Germans in 1940. They then went to Marseille, whence they sailed for America on 14 May 1942. In the interval she had met Father Perrin, who unsuccessfully urged her to be baptized, and Gustave Thibon, who arranged for her to get a labourer's job in the grape-harvest.

27 To Jean Posternak

> Simone Weil had met Professor Posternak, who was then a medical student, when she was staying near Montana.

Milan [Spring, 1937]

Cher ami,

Here I am in Milan, and yet – strange to say – I have still not forgotten the people who languish in the nordic mists (in which connexion you should look up the Goethe poems at la Moubra and read one of the Roman elegies which begins (allowing for grammatical slips): 'O! wie war ich in Rom so froh!'[1] and goes on to describe a 'Mond heller wie nordischer Tag'.[2])

Particularly, I have not forgotten that you will have seen your musician friend on Sunday and if you did your duty will have asked him several bizarre questions. You promised to write to me about this. It will be safest to write to poste restante, Florence. At the same time tell me everything that occurs to you about Italy, including Milan because I shall certainly stop here on my way back; and including Venetia, too, because I don't know if I shall resist the temptation of a Milan-Venice round trip when I am here again.

On arriving at Pallanza I walked about eight miles along the lake (towards Switzerland) and as it seemed rather long to walk back I got a lift on a cart loaded with sacks of flour. Conversation with the driver, an engaging youth, was strictly limited by my ignorance of the language, but he made it clear to me that his views are not those of the friend to whom you've given me an introduction. Such was my first contact with the Italian people . . . . When I got to Stresa (at 8.30 p.m.) by the boat from Pallanza, a Pallanza school-teacher – taking pity on me as a solitary traveller – invited me to spend the night at her house in a village of 200 inhabitants on the mountain above Stresa. There, I was subjected to some ardent fascist propaganda; and I was able to see how people live, and eat, and think, in a village which is poor, but a bit above the peasant level. That was my second contact and, without prejudice, much less sympathetic. Lake Maggiore is very beautiful, but it is only now that I feel I am in Italy.

[1] In Rome, how happy I was! [2] Moon as bright as northern day.

To Jean Posternak 1937

I arrived in Milan at the same time as the Re Imperator,[1] who had come to close the Exhibition and Fair. The town packed full. Milan is a populous city of the kind I like and I foresee that in a few days I shall think I was born here. The people are really sympathetic. I am writing this at a delightful little café in Piazza Beccaria; just now the waiter was peeping over my shoulder at what I was writing, and when I looked up his smile was charming. Tonight they are doing Verdi's *Aida* at the Scala, and I am going to try to get standing room (no seats left). My very dear friend Stendhal will intercede for me, I think.

I forgot to ask you if there exists to your knowledge a really satisfactory book, in Italian or any other language, on Italian art (and music)?

I hope Plato has arrived and that you are reading the *Phaedrus* between two hearings of the Fourth Brandenburg andante, and that you are plunged in ecstasy.

Don't forget, if you are sending me any useful tips, to deal not only with works of art but also with interesting quarters of towns, and restaurants, and any spectacles of low life or high life, so long as they are characteristic.... As you know, everything interests me.

At Pallanza, Stresa, etc., you see phrases of Mussolini written up everywhere, all of them more or less directly referring to Abyssinia. But not at Milan.

I can breathe better here. If only Florence is uncontaminated....

χαῖρε

S. Weil

P.S. χαῖρε is the Greek word for good-bye, and it means: Be joyful.

P.P.S. When the spring reaches Montana I recommend for spring reading the first lines of Lucretius' *De Rerum Natura*:

> Aeneadum genetrix, hominum divumque voluptas,
> alma Venus, subter coeli labentia signa
> quae mare navigerum, quae terras frugiferentis
> concelebras, per te quoniam genus omne animantum
> concipitur, visitque exortum lumina solis:
> te, dea, te fugiunt venti, te nubila coeli
> adventumque tuum; tibi suavis daedala tellus
> summittit flores, tibi rident aequora ponti,
> placatumque nitet diffuso lumine caelum.

That is enough, I think, to make you want to continue.

[1] King Emperor, as the fascists styled the King of Italy.

28 To the same

Florence [Spring, 1937]

Cher ami,

Your prayers cannot be very efficacious, because I am writing to the sound of rain. You must commit a great many sins; take care. You may reply that I am in the same case; but I didn't pray. Whatever weather comes, I give it a friendly welcome. This vernal and Florentine rain is charming, and anyway one has no need of sunshine in the Medici chapel and I see no reason against spending days in it. I have already spent hours. This art is too moving, like the Third Symphony. How mournful the Dawn is! She is awakening to a bitter life, to a day of too much hardship; the awakening of Electra. One could engrave for her motto the beautiful lines:

> Seule, je n'ai plus la force de tirer
> le poids du chagrin qui m'entraîne à terre.[1]

The Night too is the sleep of a slave, who is not relaxed but who sleeps in order to suffer less. In this connexion, the lines

> Caro m'è 'l sonno, e più l'esser di sasso
> mentre che 'l danno e la vergogna dura, etc,[2]

are really Michelangelo's; at least, they are to be found in a good edition of his *Rime*. (Where there is also a sonnet on the night with this tercet:

> O ombra del morir, per cui si ferma
> ogni miseria a l'alma, al cor nemica,
> ultimo degli afflitti e buon remedio . . .)[3]

One understands better the lines 'Caro, etc.' and the feeling conveyed by the statues if one remembers that it was upon them that Michelangelo was working when he dropped everything to go to the defence of Florence (like Archimedes to that of Syracuse) and fortify San Miniato against Alessandro de' Medici; and that he was defeated, and saw Florence subjected for ten years to this Alessandro, who spent his time in buying or raping women, until the day of his assassination. (This is the subject of Musset's *Lorenzaccio*.)

[1] Alone, I have no longer the strength to lift the weight of grief that drags me down to earth.
[2] To sleep is welcome, and still more welcome to be made of stone, so long as the harm and the shame endure.
[3] O shade of death, which sets a term to every misery that oppresses the soul and heart, last of afflictions and best remedy. . . .

To Jean Posternak 1937

In this connexion, I have thought a lot about the question you raised (whether dictatorships stifle civilization or encourage it). Florence was almost a democracy in the proper sense of the word up to 1378, the date of the wool-workers' revolt. Dante, Giotto, and Petrarch belong to this period. After the suppression of the revolt the succeeding governments were more authoritarian, but always with party struggles and freedom of opinion. Machiavelli considers that freedom of opinion came to an end in 1466. Brunelleschi, Ghiberti, Donatello, Verrocchio, and many others, and a great number of monuments, came before that date. Vinci was fourteen at the time, Michelangelo was born six years later, and Machiavelli in 1469. From 1469 to 1492 Lorenzo the Magnificent exercised an authority tempered by the appearances of republican equality. After his death party strife broke out again and it was not until 1527 that Florence definitely lost its status as a city. In the next period there were only (so far as I remember) Benvenuto Cellini and Giambologna. Galileo too, but later still.

One can sum it up by concluding that periods of creative vitality and intellectual ferment are also periods of great freedom and even of civil discord; and that after such periods only a strong authority can promote further development, by creating stability and by compelling thought to concentrate itself and find devious expression; and this is also favourable to art, which lives by transposing.

While here I have re-read with passionate interest Machiavelli's *Istorie Fiorentine*. It has passages finer than Tacitus, if that is possible. It brings everything here to life.

At Milan, after an hour or two of contemplation I perceived the secret of the composition of the Last Supper. (At the time there seemed to me to be no valid reason for not spending one's whole life in that convent refectory.) There is a point on the hair on the right side of Christ's head towards which all the perspective lines of the roof converge and also, approximately, the lines formed by the apostles' hands on each side of him. But this convergence (which is discreetly emphasized by the arc above the window, of whose circle the same point is the centre) exists only in the two-dimensional space of the picture and not in the three-dimensional space which it evokes. Thus there is a double composition, one in two-dimensional and one in three-dimensional space; and the eye is led back from everywhere towards the face of Christ, by a secret, unperceived influence which helps to make his serenity appear supernatural. In addition, several of the lines formed by the pose or gesture of the apostles (especially the two angelic apostles, John and Philip) are approximately parallel to the arms of Christ.

I have read somewhere that Rembrandt, already at the height of his genius, came to Milan to study the Last Supper and went away with his conception of painting deeply revived.

Vinci surely possessed a secret, which he died (prematurely, though at sixty-seven) without having revealed. (As though Goethe had died before writing the second Faust.) And surely this secret was a Pythagorean conception of life. A complete edition of him, with all the hitherto unpublished things, is appearing in Rome now.

At Milan I had the happy surprise of finding in the Castello an extraordinary ceiling with foliage by him, of whose existence I was unaware.

I liked Milan very much. I had the luck to be staying between the delicious piazzas, Beccaria and Fontana. (Do you know the little marionnette theatre, with its delightful music, in Piazza Beccaria?) And Milan has some industrial suburban landscapes which are very moving; at least, to me they are. I spent hours among them. I possess the gift (which I purchased dearly) of reading the eyes of a shift of workers beginning or ending their day's work; and I had an opportunity to make use of this gift.

It was the day after the official announcement of an all-round wage increase of from 10% to 12%. (The day's papers were full of grateful acknowledgements.) Alas! What I read in their eyes was what I used to read in my work-mates' eyes, and what was visible in my own, at the most painful moments.... Whatever gain may have been realized this time, the sense of servitude in labour has not been dispelled but only muffled.

The same evening, in the same district, I went to a cinema just opposite a big textile factory (seats 1 lira, romantic-serial film). Palpitating audience; applause when the traitor was unmasked. During the news-reel (which ignored the country where I was last year)[1] three or four people tried to start applause for a certain sequence of pictures. The response of the rest of the audience was complete silence.

I record; I draw no conclusions. And anyway there are also the

[1] Spain, where the civil war was still in progress.

country districts. But I must add that a priest, of the typically Italian variety, whom I met in a train and who honoured me with his confidence, explained to me that the state of opinion has changed a lot in the last ten months – which I have found confirmed in other ways.

At Bologna I fell to the temptation of trains labelled for Ferrara and Ravenna. Two really beautiful towns. Do you remember the Diamanti palace? At Ravenna – it was market day – humanity was beautiful too, especially the young peasants. When Providence places beautiful people among beautiful things, it is a superabundance of grace. Every day, in this country, one notes in certain men of the people a nobility and a simplicity of manner and attitude which compel admiration.

Do you by chance know where Horace's Anio and Tibur were? I have been wondering ever since I was at Ravenna, because the charming orchards before you get there reminded me of the delicious lines:

> Me non tam patiens Lacedaemon,
> Non tam Larissae percussit campus opimae,
> Quam domus Albuneae resonantis
> Ac praeceps Anio et Tiburni lucus et uda
> Mobilibus pomaria rivis . . . .[1]

As for Florence, it is my own city. Surely I must have lived a previous life among its olives. As soon as I saw the lovely bridges across the Arno I wondered how I had stayed away so long. And Florence wondered too, no doubt, because towns love to be loved. I think I definitely won't go to Venice this time. Florence and Venice at one time is a lot; and I have no heart left for loving Venice, because Florence has taken it.

There are still many lovely things here which I haven't seen; because it is not my habit to visit towns, I let them seep into me by osmosis. But I have gone – on foot, as one should – along the Viale dei Colli, which was intoxicating from the scent of its flowers and its multitude of olive trees. San Miniato is very beautiful at sunset. At the Pitti I looked long at Giorgione's music party (which some idiots have recently attributed to Titian). I have developed a particular tenderness for Benvenuto Cellini's Perseus in the charming Loggia dei Lanci, and especially for the little figures at the bottom (the naked virgin, the genie who flies without wings). . . . Etc., etc.

Here are the outstanding features of the *Maggio musicale* (thanks to

[1] Horace, *Odes* I.7.

which, incidentally, one gets the impression that the population of Florence includes singularly few Italians); I send them so that you can give me expert advice, as quick as possible, because it may modify my plans:

Verdi's *Otello*, conducted by Sabata

Tristan and Iseult; conductor, Elmendorff; singers, Karin Branzell, Anny Konetzi, Hans Grahl, Jos. von Manowarda; orchestra of the Teatro di Stato di Monaco di Baviera (?)

Stravinsky's *Oedipus Rex* and Malpieri's *La Passione*, conducted by Molinari

Marriage of Figaro: conductor, Bruno Walter; singers, Favero, Novotna, Tassinari, Stabile, Pasero

Monteverdi's *Incoronazione di Poppaea*, conducted by Marinuzzi (Boboli gardens)

Write to me at poste restante, Rome, as I am going there for Whitsun (for the religious music) and staying a few days. On the way back I shall follow the steps of St. Francis, having traced them in the *Fioretti* for this special purpose, and then I shall reimmerse myself in Florence.

I owe you apologies for the books being delayed. No doubt it's my fault. That sort of stupidity is pretty frequent with me, alas. To win forgiveness I enclose two Michelangelo sonnets to Tommaso Cavalieri; I copied them for my pleasure, to understand them better (they are quite difficult). They are an excellent illustration of the *Phaedrus*. Ever since I've been in Florence I have been looking to see if I can recognize Tommaso Cavalieri, but I haven't seen him yet. Perhaps it's as well, because if I did meet him I should only be able to be dragged away from Florence by force.

I also send Dante's lines on Saint Francis. I think you will be ravished. I think that in the whole of poetry there is little to equal the powerful beauty of the lines on poverty:

> .... dove Maria rimase giuso
> Ella con Cristo salse en sulla croce.[1]

I looked in the *Fioretti* for the episode of the halt by the beautiful spring, and found it even better than I remembered, especially the words of Saint Francis:

---

[1] ... where Mary stayed below,
She went up on to the cross with Christ (*Paradiso*, XI.71-72).

E questo è quello che io riputo gran tesoro, ove non e cosa verun apparecchiata per l'industria humana; ma ciò che ci è si è apparecchiato dalla providenza divina, siccome si vede manifestamente nel pane accattato, nella mensa di pietra cosi bella e nella fonte cosi chiara: e però io voglio che noi preghiamo a Iddio che'l tesoro della santa povertà cosi nobile, il quale ha per servidore Iddio, ci faccia amare con tutto il cuore.[1]

That is how I understand the meaning of pure pleasures.

S.W.

Of Italian music I have so far heard Verdi's *Aida* (agreeable, but no more), Donizetti's *L'Elisir d'Amore* (delicious) and, here, Rossini's *Il Signor Bruschino* (very, very pretty).

How does the *Odyssey* impress you? There are two lines in it which to me are miraculously true, and which V. Bérard translates quite badly, repeated every time Ulysses escapes from an adventure after losing some of his men:

> They sailed on with afflicted hearts,
> Glad to have escaped death, having lost their dear companions.

29 To her mother

(A fragment)

Rome [Whitsun, 1937]

[. . . . . .] I have been in Rome for three and a half days, and it seems like a whole epoch. I felt at home here more quickly than in the other towns I've been to, and I had expected the contrary. Perhaps it is because the first thing I did here was to listen to some good music. I arrived about midday on Saturday and congratulated myself on having the rest of the day to look for a hotel. But after I'd got my breath, bought and studied a town-plan, and had lunch, it was already 2.30. In the train from Milan to Bologna I had met a priest (the very type of the shrewd, subtle Italian priest; he told me some interesting things

---

[1] And this is what I call a great treasure, where nothing has been provided by human labour but everything has been given by divine providence, as we may see clearly in the bread we have begged, and the fine table of stone, and the spring of clear water; and so I would have us pray God that he will cause us to love with all our hearts this treasure of holy poverty, who is so noble that God himself is her servant.

about the present 'Stimmung', and he spoke freely after I had told him, what I in fact believe, that in the end the Right will probably win in France) and this priest had told me that one can hear Gregorian plainsong at S. Anselmo. Finding by the map that the way to S. Anselmo (the Aventine) was by the Forum, the Colosseum, and the Palatine, I decided to go there on the chance, and to go on foot. On the way I saw advertisements of the Adriano (which has replaced the Augusteo as a concert hall) announcing religious music, on the same evening, by the choir of the Greek Catholic church of Zagreb. (Not to be missed if it comes to Paris!) The Palatine, with the new excavations, being on my way, I went there and walked among the ancient stones right to the far end. (Impression of overwhelming grandeur.) At the end, no way out – so I had to go all the way back to the Viale Imperiale and then retrace my steps the whole way along the street outside the enclosure. All this under a blazing sun, and blaspheming against the vaunted Organization. Reached S. Anselmo at 6 o'clock, just in time for a very impressive liturgical ceremony which lasted an hour. On the way I had inquired at several hotels which were all full. On leaving S. Anselmo (which is a pure jewel of a Benedictine monastery looking down on the Tiber) I went to the Adriano (part of the way by tram). There was just time to dine and go to the concert (seat 3 lire). Marvellous choral singing, rather of the Ukrainian type. Music by modern composers but, as was plain to hear, entirely based upon old liturgical themes. Coming out at midnight I still had to find somewhere to sleep . . . . I crossed the Tiber again and in the end luckily found a hotel, where I still am. I had left my rucksack at a restaurant near the station, which complicated things . . . .

The next day, Whit Sunday mass at St. Peter's, with the little choirboys from the Sistine. I don't know whose music it was, but doubtless Palestrina's. Divine. The music, the voices, the words of the liturgy, the architecture, the crowd, many of them kneeling, which included many men and women of the people, the latter with kerchiefs on their heads – there you have the comprehensive art which Wagner was seeking. I seem to remember you don't like St. Peter's? Certainly it was considerably spoiled by the idiot Pope who altered the original plan of Bramante and Michelangelo (a cross with four equal limbs); but even as it is I love it beyond measure, as well as the piazza in front of it. It really deserves to be the universal church of Christianity. I have seen nothing else in Italian architecture to approach that divine cupola of Michelangelo. Brunelleschi's cupolas at Florence (the Duomo and even San Lorenzo, which is much better) are not nearly so good. The Pope kneeling in prayer below the dome and just over the ashes of St. Peter is very beautiful. (Who the deuce is he by?) After the mass I went to the Catholic Press exhibition, where my ticket was stamped – it was interesting. Then back to S. Anselmo for Vespers. Then to St. Peter's again for more Vespers. Found a very sympathetic *trattoria* not far from St. Peter's, with delicious wines. After that I still had to go and retrieve my rucksack. At the end of a day like that, spent entirely in listening to religious music, one has a very good feeling. If Paradise is like St. Peter's with the Sistine choir it's worth going there.

On Monday I went again to hear mass at St. Peter's. After it I wandered long and fruitlessly in the streets around the Vatican looking for a missal. There was nothing anywhere except horrible little books with the most insipid Italian texts. That is something I would never have foreseen. Then again to S. Anselmo, where I was disappointed to find there were no Vespers. (Just below, I found a café where they have remarkable ices for 1 lira 60.) I then walked (via the Capitol, the Forum, and the 'Forum of Imperial Italy', which is quite impressive, but not when one has just seen the Colosseum) to beyond the Villa Borghese to an address given me by the young man at la Moubra, who has provided me with various useful tips about Italy. This was the address of an ardent young fascist student, the son of a high official of the régime; he was pleasant, cordial, and pretty naïve. Then back to the Ponte Umberto, near which I am staying, still on foot. Out again to finish the evening at a cinema; the film was over but after it there was a little comedy, of which I understood nothing, but it was very pleasant. After all that, this morning my foot hurt and I was limping . . . . (That burn doesn't seem to want to heal . . . .)[1]

Today I spent three hours in the Vatican museums. No one had told me that the *Pinacoteca* has a St. Jerome by Vinci, painted on wood. It is extraordinary; and I would give all the rest of the *Pinacoteca* twenty times over for it. This St. Jerome and the Giorgione 'Concert' at the Pitti, and the foreshortened Christ at the Brera will be the three really intense memories I shall keep of the museums of Italian paintings.

[1] Presumably a reference to her accident with hot oil in the Spanish civil war the previous year.

I saw the famous Raphael frescoes, which I naturally admired; but I would not want to contemplate them for hours. And I at last had the joy of seeing the Sistine. But, alas, more than a third of it is now hidden by scaffolding. On the other hand one sees much better than I expected. Remembering André, I half-lay back on one of the benches. But in my case it ended in a sharp altercation with the custodian! I shall complain to the administration and see what happens. As for the Greek statues, I only had time for a passing look. I shall have to go back.

That's all I have done today, except for a theatre in the evening. A well-acted piece, quite good (and interesting from the point of view of the spirit of the régime). I was only able to follow it dimly. After the theatre, I went to the Colosseum. (Where the devil has one read about the Colosseum by moonlight? It must be 'Childe Harold'?) There was a half moon and a clear sky. Unfortunately also a good many electric lights. All the same, the Colosseum at midnight is something impressive. I stayed there about three quarters of an hour, and when I remembered it might be as well to go home I was just able to catch a tram which must have been the last. (Though there is an all-night bus service, every half hour.) Which reminds me that it is perhaps also time to go to bed....

30 To Jean Posternak

Florence [Spring, 1937]

Cher ami,
         Your directions for the *Maggio musicale* were in line with my own inclination, so I complied with them. I had never heard *Figaro*, apart from excerpts, and as Bruno Walter's conducting was beyond all praise you can easily imagine the impression it made on me. And yet the impression paled beside the *Incoronazione di Poppaea*, played in the Boboli garden amphitheatre under the stars with the Pitti palace for background. I bitterly regretted your absence, because it was a marvel you would really have appreciated, a marvel to be remembered all one's life. But I like to believe you will hear it one day. The public was cool (pack of brutes!). Luckily, however, my enjoyment was enough to fill a whole amphitheatre. Music of such simplicity, serenity, and sweetness, of such dancing movement.... You remember my reaction when you put anything at all on the gramophone after Bach?

Well, there are melodies of Monteverdi which I would admire even after the famous andante.

This return to Florence has been a delight. If the first contact with Florence is delightful, how much more so to return to it as to a home after a short journey! And that is exactly the impression I had. Definitely, I shall not go to Venice this time. It is certain that I shall love it (if only from deference to you) if I ever see it; but it is equally certain that it will never be so close to my heart as Florence. The beauties of Florence are of a kind which d'Annunzio could never celebrate, or so I imagine. I say this in praise of Florence, because I am far from sharing your sympathy for the *Fuoco*, which you advised me in one of your letters to read. It is a way of understanding art and life which horrifies me, and I am convinced the man will soon be in profound and justified oblivion.

I shall have collected in a short time at Florence a certain number of pure joys. Fiesole (whence I descended just to listen to Mozart...), San Miniato (where I returned twice, Florence's most beautiful church in my opinion), the old sacristy of San Lorenzo, the bas-reliefs of the Campanile, the Giotto frescoes at Santa Croce, Giorgione's Concert, David, the Dawn and the Night... and mingled with them some verses of Dante, Petrarch, Michelangelo, and Lorenzo the Magnificent. (Do you know his poems? I didn't know till I came here that he wrote any; some of them are lovely:

> Quant' è bella giovinezza[1]
> Che si sfugge tuttavia....)

Rossini, Mozart, Monteverdi; Galileo – for I have just purchased his complete works and spent some luminous hours one afternoon perusing his extraordinary original insights about uniformly accelerated motion. That is as aesthetically pleasing as anything, especially when one reads it here. And Machiavelli, etc., etc. How I wish I knew and understood the underlying connexion between all these flowers of the Italian genius, instead of merely enjoying them on the surface.... I have also made a mental collection of a great many Florentine 'fiaschetterie' (charming word!) because I almost always eat in them (pasta al sugo, 70c. to 1 lira) and always at a different one. Near the Carmine (with the beautiful Masaccio frescoes) there is one which is always full

---

[1] How lovely is youth, although so fleeting....

of young workmen and little old pensioners who enjoy themselves by making up songs, both words and music! How I pity the unfortunates who have plenty of money and eat in restaurants at 8 or 10 lire.

And just conceive that in addition to this I also frequent the House of the Fascio, in a delightful old palace where I was taken by one of the founders of the Florence Fascio – a railwayman by profession and a former trade unionist (this was our common subject) with whom I got into conversation at a café terrace in Piazza Vittorio Emmanuele. In the Casa del Fascio there is an information bureau for foreigners, in charge of a young intellectual – sincere, intelligent and, of course, attractive (they are chosen for that). In his office I met a marquis of one of the oldest Florentine families – very rich, very fascist, very interesting. Among the things he told me (I did not hide my own opinions) some were sympathetic, others less so. It would take too long to relate. At the Dopolavoro office I was given a collection of stories written by workers. Lamentable, compared to those in the papers I read (do you remember?). The fatuousness of paternalism in all its horror. To me, this is significant.

At this point I must tell you about my meeting with your friend A. I would be very interested to know what he said about it, if he has written to you.... I think that if you could have been there behind a screen you'd have had a good laugh. For my part, I have wanted very much for a long time to have a frank conversation with exactly the sort of young man he is – that is to say, holding the opinions you know and at the same time possessing intelligence and personality, so that he is not a mere echo. He seemed to me to be like that; with one of those characters which always interest me, full of repressed ardour and unavowed ambitions. So I am grateful to you for the introduction; but I doubt if he has any such feeling. I fairly made him gasp. And yet I didn't do it on purpose.

He thinks that my legitimate and normal place in society is in the depths of a salt-mine. (He would send me there, I think, if he is consistent, as soon as his people govern France.) And I quite agree with him. If I had any choice in the matter I would prefer hardship and starvation in a salt-mine to living with the narrow and limited horizon of these young people. I should feel the mine less suffocating than that atmosphere – the nationalistic obsession, the adoration of power in its most brutal form, namely the collectivity (see Plato's 'great beast',

To Jean Posternak 1937

Republic, Book VI), the camouflaged deification of death. By contrast, what you wrote to me about Toscanini (you know what I mean) seemed like a great breath of fresh air. There are still men in the world who feel themselves compatriots of all men, in the noble tradition of Marcus Aurelius and Goethe.

Thank heaven, the people who are obsessed by all these myths are not the only people in this country; there are also men and women of the people, and young fellows in blue overalls, whose faces and manners have visibly been moulded only by daily contact with problems of real life. Although your friend shares with them that Italian nationality which he prizes so much, I believe I am much closer to them than he. I was thinking this particularly in the train from Rome to Terontola (junction for Assisi) in a compartment full of splendid types of young working men, back from Abyssinia, with whom I had no difficulty in fraternizing (I am not speaking of opinions but of human contact).

At Assisi I forgot all about Milan, Florence, Rome and the rest; I was so overcome by such graceful landscapes, so miraculously evangelical and Franciscan, and the touching little chapels, and all the blissful memories, and those noble examples of the human race, the Umbrian peasants – so well-favoured, so healthy, so vigorous and happy and gentle. I had never dreamed of such a marvellous country. A conundrum: everything in and around Assisi is Franciscan – everything, except what has been put up in honour of St. Francis (apart from the lovely Giotto frescoes); so that one might believe Providence had created those smiling fields and those humble and touching little chapels in preparation for his appearance. Did you notice that the chapel where he prayed, in Santa Maria degli Angeli (the abominable great church built around it), is a little marvel of architecture? – As superior to the works of the majority of famous architects as a popular song is to those of the majority of famous musicians.

I might almost have spent the rest of my life – if women were admitted – in that tiny little convent of the Carceri, about an hour above Assisi. There could be no serener, more paradisal view than Umbria seen from up there. St. Francis knew how to choose the most delicious places in which to live in poverty; he was not at all an ascetic. In that place, a completely believing young Franciscan who, if he died now, would surely go straight to heaven, showed the bed of a torrent which has been dry ever since St. Francis begged its waters to stop flowing because they interrupted his meditations. Since then (said the young Franciscan) this torrent has only flowed when some great misfortune was about to fall upon Italy; for example, in 1915, the year when Italy entered the war.

That very same day, Assisi was full of posters celebrating the anniversary, which has been made a national festival, of Italy's entering the war; they spoke of 'that day on which, for the first time after a long age of materialism, spirit triumphed over matter . . . that day, feast of veterans and future combatants . . . .'

I concluded that, in strict logic, that young Franciscan, and St. Francis, and the torrent, ought to be put in prison.

There it is! But they won't have St. Francis with them, any more than Toscanini.

In other ways, apart from this exaltation of war, there are many things in the system that would appeal to me. But – as I think I have explained to you – I believe the system has an essential need for this exaltation; which shocks me not so much for humanitarian reasons as because it rings false. The seduction of war is only too real, but it has nothing to do with all these hollow words; which, moreover, seem even more hollow in this country, among this people. The other evening, at Fiesole, as I was waiting to take the return bus, a workman of the town got into conversation with me. Seeing the books in my hand he said he would have liked to study but that he had a very humble job, he was a mason; and further, that Fiesole certainly had a lovely situation and life would be fine, only he earned really too little and his life was too hard – all this in the most unaffected way and with a gay smile. I asked him if he had any family and he replied that he was too fond of liberty to want to marry and that, being mad about music, he went for walks every Sunday with some companions and his guitar (so there's a man who cannot often think about the things that so preoccupy your friend). How can one help loving such a people?

I was glad to see that you are reading Plato in the proper state of mind, that is to say, in ecstasy. As for the other dialogues, what can I suggest? In French, only the *Gorgias* and the *Theaetetus* are more or less tolerably translated (and even so . . . !) For the *Republic*, the sublimest dialogue, I can only suggest this: In Paris, I will translate the finest passages for you and you can then look for a decent translation in some other language, using mine as a standard of reference. If you find nothing, learn Greek. . . . It is an easy language. You could also write to Mario Meunier, begging him, in the name of all the unfortunates in the same plight as you, to continue his work.

You seem to me to attach a lot of importance to the reasoning about immortality. I myself attach little. It is a factual question, which cannot be decided in advance by any reasoning. And what does it matter to us? The problem of a future after death can have no effect upon the data of any real problem in life. The problem is to raise oneself in this life to the level of eternal things (mens sentit experiturque se aeternam esse, said Spinoza), by struggling free from bondage to what is perpetually renewed and destroyed. And if everything disappears when we die, it is all the more important not to bungle this life which is given us, but to manage to have saved one's soul before it disappears. I am convinced that this is the real thought of Socrates and Plato (as also of the Gospel) and that all the rest is only symbols and metaphors. The real problem of the *Phaedo* is whether the soul is of the same nature as things that are born and die, or of a different nature. And on this point the arguments seem to me perfectly conclusive, the most conclusive of all being the evocation of the kind of man that Socrates was. For the *Iliad* I would advise you to wait for my comments on the translation you mention. There has never been anything to equal the *Iliad*; one must make sure of reading it properly. It fills me with pity that you should be unable to read such a beautiful thing in the original – so much so that I feel obliged to send you a few extracts.

[. . . .]

P.S. I have said nothing about Rome. I remember it above all as an orgy of Greek statues (that was the impression I got; they, or at least those of the purest style, are the only things more beautiful than Michelangelo. Since them, when has there been an expression – except by Bach – of that perfect and divine equilibrium between man and the universe?), and also the Whit Sunday mass in St. Peter's, with the choirs of men and children. Divine music under that divine cupola, among the kneeling crowd in which one saw many rugged faces of men and women of the people. And since there is nothing more beautiful than the texts of the Catholic liturgy, it is a real example of that all-inclusive art which Wagner aimed at. But even better, because the public also participates.

31 To the same

[Paris, 1937]

Cher ami,
     You must be thinking I have forgotten my promise about the *Republic*. But I have remembered it very often, only I have not been well since my return, and am therefore incapable of work. I don't know if it is the effect of not seeing any more olive trees, which is a privation I always feel very much. My feeling when I think of Italy can only be described by the word 'Heimweh'. I cannot read the name of Giotto, for example, or think of the name of a street in Florence, without a pang. And the impression of the *Incoronazione* is still with me, so that I feel that even in my dying moment I shall have a thought for the scene of the death of Seneca. I long to return there at the first opportunity. On the other hand, I feel that the sadness of the fall of Bilbao would be all the more bitter if I was in the country where that fall is a victory, at least for those who monopolize the right to speak.

I hope there are all sorts of valuable people at la Moubra, who can make a warm and lively atmosphere around you. What you say about the young German mathematician has a pleasant sound. I think you will end by becoming friends. One day he is sure to feel the influence of that singular phenomenon by which your room became the centre of social life at la Moubra; an influence which touched even the typical middling French class, which is usually so impermeable.... Ask him if he has heard of my brother, and also of 'Bourbaki' (collective name for a group of young mathematicians inspired by my brother, who are preparing a revolution in analysis). I hope you will induce him to make you do some mathematics. Remember the words Plato caused to be engraved on the door of his Academy (where Eudoxus taught ...): 'None enters here unless he is a geometer.'

You speak of Descartes without mentioning the *Rules for the Direction of the Mind*. Have you left it out? To me, it is the best of all – his first work, when he was still young and unknown, and without thought of publication; like an intellectual version of the *Confessions*.

I too, as soon as I got back, hastened to read de Broglie. I hardly dare to confess that it made a mixed impression on me. His intuition of genius, it seems to me, consists essentially in having perceived that the appearance of whole numbers in atomic phenomena, after Planck's

To Jean Posternak 1937

sensational discovery about the stable states of electrons, implies something analogous to wave interference. This intuition was confirmed by the amazing experiment of the diffraction of electrons by means of crystals or diffraction gratings. All that is physics, and of the most beautiful kind. But as for considering the wave concept as the *basic* concept of the structure of matter, surely that would be absurd? One can only conceive a wave by means of the notions of impact and pressure, as applied to fluids. Remember Huyghens' comparison with agate balls, at the beginning of his admirable thesis. (In this connexion, Fresnel's is also prodigiously interesting.) On the other hand, the image of waves and the image of corpuscles are incompatible; and what is there extraordinary about that? It shows the need to elaborate a third image to bring together the analogies represented by the other two. And if that should prove to be impossible, I see nothing to be shocked at in the fact that one has to refer to two incompatible images in order to give an account of a phenomenon – for images never do more than represent analogies in a manner 'acceptable to the heart', as Pascal would say.

In quantum mechanics, moreover, formulas are arrived at which include terms which fail to satisfy the commutative law of multiplication; and in the symbolism of wave mechanics this bizarre mathematical phenomenon appears to correspond to the duality of the 'wave' and the 'corpuscle' aspects of matter. In any case, it is admitted that this non-commutativity corresponds to the impossibility of measuring two magnitudes simultaneously and with accuracy (or according to the wave theory, to determine simultaneously both position and velocity). This impossibility is expressed by the 'uncertainty principle'. I fail to see anything in all this that could disprove determinism. Why, because we are unable to determine two magnitudes simultaneously by measurement, should it follow that these magnitudes are *in themselves* indeterminate? The question itself is meaningless. Is it sought to establish the impossibility of our acquiring the necessary data for a concrete conception of nature as determined? But that is something which simple common sense has always allowed us to recognize. It requires no knowledge of physics to understand that we never in any case possess all the data of the problems to which we try to reduce natural phenomena. To study any phenomenon, we eliminate by abstraction, on the one hand, all surrounding events and, on the other hand, all events on a smaller scale; and in this way we imagine a sort of doubly closed vessel or retort, in which we ourselves do not believe; for we know that it is implied in the essential principle of determinism that nothing in nature can be isolated from the rest. In particular we know very well that the mere fact of observing and measuring modifies the thing observed and measured. By convention, these modifications are regarded as 'negligible' (a word which has no place in basic theory), but it was obvious beforehand that the further we descended in the scale of magnitudes the closer we should approach to a limit at which they could no longer be 'neglected'. It is already a fine achievement to be able to measure mathematically the imperfection of our measures. One can imagine, on a scale much smaller still than the atomic, other corpuscles of which we shall doubtless never know *either* the position *or* the velocity; and within these corpuscles ... and so on. Determinism has never been more than a directing hypothesis for science, and that is what it will always be. De Broglie introduced probability into his description of phenomena, but that does not at all imply that we ought to substitute probability for necessity in our conception of phenomena; on the contrary, probability only enters our thought when we are faced by a problem whose solution we believe to be strictly determined by the data, but of some of whose data we are ignorant.

For a long time (because these matters have been talked about for years) I have tried and failed to see the revolutionary implications for our general conception of science which are supposed to inhere in de Broglie's 'uncertainty principle'. To see them in that light, one must have completely lost the idea of what science is.

What I find much more disturbing is the fact that 'Planck's constant' appears in all mathematical expressions, and yet nobody knows how to translate it into terms of physics. If anyone succeeds, it will be he and not de Broglie who will have achieved the synthesis between the two hypotheses of waves and corpuscles.

For many reasons, I believe as you do that science is entering a period of crisis graver than that of the fifth century, which is accompanied, as then, by a moral crisis and a subservience to purely political values, in other words, to power. The new phenomenon of the totalitarian State makes this crisis infinitely formidable, and may turn it into a death-agony.

To Jean Posternak 1937

That is why I see two categories of men – on the one hand those who think and love (how often, reading the political posters in Italy, did I not vividly recall the beautiful line spoken by Sophocles' Antigone: 'I was born to share, not hate, but love'), and on the other hand those whose minds and hearts are abased before power camouflaged as ideas.

If the crisis of science in our age is comparable to that of the fifth century, then there is an obvious duty: to make another effort of thought comparable to that of Eudoxus.

Apropos of the totalitarian State, if A. appeared to me obsessed by the nationalistic idea it was not because he talked a lot about Italy and the Duce, etc. I don't judge by such superficial signs. It was because I thought I detected the imprint of this obsession in his thoughts and feelings, so far as he revealed them to me, and in his whole behaviour and manner. Also perhaps because I could not perceive in him any other main preoccupation. If I was to some extent wrong, I am delighted for his sake. All I wish for him – because he does interest me – is that by virtue of friendship he may be infected with your enthusiasm for Plato.

Did you show him the *Nouveaux Cahiers*? I thought I had told you about Detœuf. He is a manager of big electrical engineering companies. An independent mind and a man of rare goodness. I like him very much. It was he who enabled me to become a factory worker, by getting me into one of his plants, from which I moved on to others. They were very unhappy places. His goodness did not reach as far as his workers.

As you observe, Giraudoux's *Electra* is not mine. (Who will bring mine to light?) I admire the same things in it that you do. The central idea (the banefulness of conscience) is powerful and fine, but its dramatic treatment is null, especially in the second act.

Why have I not the n existences I need, in order to devote one of them to the theatre! I am also haunted by an idea for a statue, because of having looked at so many in Italy. A statue of Justice: a naked woman, standing, her knees a little bent from fatigue (sometimes I see her kneeling, with chained feet, but it would not be so sculptural) her hands chained behind her back, leaning – with a serene face in spite of all – towards a balance (sculpted in high relief in front of her) with unequal arms, which hold two equal weights at unequal levels.

As you are cultivating acquaintance with my friend Montaigne (another compatriot of all men) you must also love the man who inspired his best pages and to whom I am even more tenderly attached: La Boétie, a young Stoic straight out of Plutarch.

The new *Iliad* from Budé's is much, much less good than the *Odyssey*, although much superior to previous translations. If you buy it, do at least buy text and translation together. Who knows? ... There is no attempt at rhythm, and although it is accurate it is not always scrupulously accurate enough to render the amazing force and simplicity of Homer's language. Is this the translation you mentioned to me? Or is there another one?

Contrary to what you supposed, France has never been so calm. Everyone has lost interest in politics, from sheer fatigue; for the past year the interest had been too intense. I see no harm in this lull, but may the gods not break it by raising the curtain on the great international drama. You, at any rate, are not eligible at present for cannon-fodder. So much the better.

χαῖρε
S. Weil

32 To the same

[1938]

Cher ami,

I did answer your letter, but having written the reply I omitted to send it. This sometimes happens with me. Then when I remembered the omission I was too lazy to re-write my letter. So I am now belatedly renewing our correspondence. First, to describe and dismiss my personal affairs: I took a new post in October, an hour and a half's journey from Paris, but had to give it up in January, being physically incapable of continuing (chronic and violent headaches, to which I have been liable for years, and extreme fatigue). This will explain to you why I have been for months and months in a certain state of physical depression which has made many things impossible for me, and particularly writing letters.

So your question about the poem I sent you, entitled *Prometheus*, has been left in the air. I thought that my sending it without any author's name would sufficiently indicate that it was my own. I am glad to hear you liked it. I sent another copy, at the same time, to Valéry; and he acknowledged it – which, apparently, is unusual for him – very pleasantly. I have slightly altered it since, and one day I will send you

To Jean Posternak 1938

a revised version. I am sending you two others today, and the beginning of a third which I am now working on. I hope they will please you enough to re-establish contact between us, if I may use an electrical metaphor, should the gap in our correspondence have been so long as to make it necessary – which, however, I do not think. For when, among other things, one has listened together – or what is called listening – to the andante of the Fourth Brandenburg Concerto, that makes a bond which is capable, I think, of resisting silence and the lapse of time.

Since returning from Italy – which, incidentally, reawakened the impulse to write poetry which I had repressed, for various reasons, since adolescence – I have developed two new loves. One is for Lawrence – not D. H., the novelist, who is completely uninteresting, but the one who, from 1916 to 1918, led to victory the Arab rising between Mecca and Damascus. If you want to learn to recognize the prodigious combination which makes an authentic hero – a perfectly lucid thinker, an artist, a scholar, and with all that a kind of saint as well – read his *Seven Pillars of Wisdom* (French translation published by Payot, I think). Never since the *Iliad*, so far as I know, has a war been described with such sincerity and such complete absence of rhetoric, either heroic or hair-raising. In short, I do not know any historical figure in any age who expresses to such a degree what I like to admire. Military heroism is sufficiently rare, lucidity of mind is rarer still; the combination of the two is almost unexampled. It is an almost superhuman degree of heroism.

The other love is Goya, whom I did not know – never having been to Madrid, alas – and whom I have got to know a little through a few canvases in a recent exhibition, some of them prodigious. He immediately joined the small group of painters who speak to my soul – Vinci, Giotto, Masaccio, Giorgione, Rembrandt. The works of the others evoke a higher or lower degree of pleasure and admiration, but up to now it is only with those few that I have the feeling of a sort of immediate spiritual contact, of the same kind that I feel with Bach, Monteverdi, Sophocles, Homer, etc. There has been a recent edition of Goya's *Disasters of War*; it arouses an equal degree of horror and admiration.

Must I speak of France? It is a pretty sad country just now. The spirit of June 1936 is dead, or rather putrefying. The persistent hold of the Communist Party over the workers is what is most distressing for anyone who has dedicated some of his love and hope to the working class. This hold was scarcely less strong when I was at Montana; but what is desolating is that it has persisted. The strikes in the industries working for national defence are a scandal. If their motive was pacifist, they would have the beauty which goes with any vigorous assertion of faith; but most of these metal-workers are very far from being pacifists. Almost all of them are in favour of armaments, and especially the communists; and yet they hold up production in order to increase wages which are already abnormally high in the working class, although the country will soon be bled white in paying for military expenses. Very probably this is a complicated political manoeuvre of the Communist Party, which wants to join the Government and push it into war.

For the rest, France is in process of being transformed into a second-class power. This was virtually accomplished as soon as Germany became united; but it is always a long time before a historical transformation is expressed in institutions, and this particular one has been obscured for the last twenty years, thanks to the formidable coalition which was victorious in 1918. I see no objection to France becoming a small nation in Europe. It seems to me that freedom, justice, art, thought, and similar kinds of greatness can be found in a small country as well as in a great one. But the change from a first-class power to a second-class power is hard for a people still intoxicated by Louis XIV and Napoleon – who always believed himself to be an object both of terror and of love to the whole universe. It is because nobody wants to admit this change that it involves such an incredible amount of lying, false information, demagogy, mixed boastfulness and panic (appalling mixture!) and demoralization – in other words, an unbreathable moral atmosphere.

At the moment, there are two possibilities. One is war with Germany for the sake of Czecho-Slovakia. Public opinion is scarcely interested in that remote country, but the Quai d'Orsay resolutely prefers war to a German hegemony in central Europe; and as for the Communist Party, any Franco-German war suits their book. Other politicians, except for the few who follow Flandin, are influenced by the Quai d'Orsay. What may perhaps prevent violent measures is the generally recognized weakness of the French army.

The other possibility is an anti-democratic *coup d'état*, supported by

To Jean Posternak 1938

Daladier and the army, accompanied by a very violent outbreak of anti-semitism (of which there are signs everywhere) and by brutal measures against the parties and organizations of the Left. Of the two possibilities I prefer this one, because it would be less murderous of French youth as a whole.

It is also possible that nothing will happen, in which case we shall go on expecting one or other of those possibilities. This prolonged suspense, relieved by increasingly little hope, even for those who are most blind to events, is making almost everyone more and more nervous. In Paris especially – the provinces are always less excitable – people are in the mood for every kind of panic.

I have long foreseen all this – since 1932, to be precise – so it is not the bewildering shock for me that it is for some people. Nevertheless, it is singularly joyless. For some years I have held the theory that joy is an indispensable ingredient in human life, for the health of the mind; so that a complete absence of joy would be equivalent to madness. If there is any truth in this, French sanity is becoming endangered – to say nothing of the rest of Europe.

I hope and believe it is different in Switzerland, in spite of the new and dangerous frontier with Germany since the *Anschluss*.

You wrote me that you would be leaving la Moubra in January, so I count on this letter finding you at home. And yet my very lively wishes for your complete and rapid cure are somewhat checked by the international situation. If there were a European catastrophe involving Switzerland I would not regret a prolongation of your illness which would protect your life.

Best wishes,
S. Weil

P.S. Send a line by return, will you? So that I know this letter has found you.

33 To Gaston Bergery

A Leftist member of the Chambre des Députés and editor of *La Flèche*, in which he campaigned against 'the Trusts' and the '200 families'.

[1938]

Dear Comrade Bergery,

I was glad to see that you squarely faced the question of Czecho-Slovakia in *La Flèche*. Forgive me for returning to it: the subject is so important and so agonizing that it is difficult not to think of it continually. I note first of all that one at least of the two conditions you lay down for defending Czecho-Slovakia can probably be ruled out – namely, the cohesion of the country to be defended. But whatever the immediate and practical importance of this point, it does not affect the wider problem raised by your article, for you relate the Czecho-Slovakian situation to the whole question of Germany's grip on central Europe and her hegemony in Europe. In my view this latter question ought to be directly examined in all its scope. For three-quarters of a century it has been crucial and never more so than today; it dominates our whole policy, both external and internal.

Your thought is that a German hegemony in Europe, with its corollary of French weakness, would tempt Germany to armed aggression against France. It is impossible effectively to dismiss this fear, and it is impossible to make light of it. And yet a firm French line, however ably sustained, could also end in war, and war could end in defeat and invasion with all their extreme consequences. So it may be said that either line could, if the worst comes to the worst, lead to the same final result (though the first, it seems to me, would involve a less grievous train of bloodshed and disaster for Europe and the world). The question is whether the worst is more likely to happen if the first line is followed or the second; and further, assuming that the best should happen, which of the two lines would lead to the better results.

Let us begin with the second point. What is the best conceivable result of a policy based on preserving the European balance of power? It is that France, in alliance with England, should arrest the German drive towards hegemony, without Germany's daring to resort to war. Since a dynamic drive is the essence of Germany's political system – a fact which must never be forgotten – France will only be able to contain the German will to expansion by remaining strong and vigilant, by turning all her attention outwards, by remaining continually ready for

To Gaston Bergery 1938

war and forever on the alert, as Péguy said. The liaison with England will have to be close and constant; which, incidentally, so long as the City remains what it is, will not make the struggle against the Trusts any easier. The war budget will have to be maintained and increased, or doubled. There is no need to emphasize the resulting misery, both material and moral – nervous tension, regimentation of minds, infringements of liberty, individual and collective anxiety. Yet this state of affairs would have to continue for as long as the German menace existed; and the question is whether this would be possible – morally, politically, or economically. From the economic and technical point of view alone, is it possible for France to support – or to support as long as Germany can – an armaments programme which will have to be continually renewed? Is it possible, even if she sacrifices all her remaining liberty and democracy in the effort? And if it is not possible, what sense is there in a policy which can do no more than postpone the alternative of war or abdication?

But even if it is possible, what hope does it offer? A change of régime in Germany? It is no doubt true that a serious defeat in prestige would bring down the régime. But it is equally true that Hitler is aware of this and that rather than accept such a defeat he would choose war in the most unfavourable conditions. The mere use of threats to slow down, turn aside, or even arrest his drive would not be enough to bring him down; indeed, the resulting state of alert on both sides of the Rhine would be more likely to create a French national-socialism among us.

We still hold in reserve, of course, the great and beautiful project of a multilateral negotiation, in the spirit of justice, to bring about the general pacification of Europe. This project was undoubtedly the one hope of salvation, but I fear it has been held in reserve so long that it is dead. Before Hitler came, it would have been ludicrously easy for France to adopt it; she did nothing of the sort; one pays for these things, and we are paying now. Again, in May or June, 1936, Blum could have taken advantage of a great mass-movement and of the wind of change that was blowing across France; the very wide power which events bestowed on him for several weeks would have enabled him to break conspicuously and solemnly with French foreign policy since 1918 and to make the 'spectacular' gesture which you have always demanded. He did no such thing, and that is why he fell. But now, although it is bitter and painful to have to say so, I believe it is too late.

For internal reasons, to begin with; because, after the great upsurge of 1936 and its running to waste, I think it will be some time before there is another great popular movement which could make possible a spectacular and solemn revision of French policy. But more especially because Hitler has said and repeated several times in the last year or two that he will either obtain his claims by force or else by unconditional agreement, without bargaining or compromise. In general, when he talks like this he acts accordingly; and in this case I believe he is in a position to do so – materially, politically, and morally. Materially, I think he has succeeded by now in altering the balance of power sufficiently in his favour to have good hopes of being able to get what he wants, at the opportune moment, without offering anything in exchange. Politically, he doubtless considers that from the point of view of internal policy, which is always paramount for dictators, his uncompromisingness is more dynamic, more imaginatively compelling, and more intoxicating for a people which has for years been exposed helpless to humiliation and to seeing its requests refused. Morally, no matter how just and generous the French proposals might be, Hitler's position would still be the stronger. For he can always say: So long as we were only able to appeal to justice, we were kept crushed under the burden of an oppressive treaty; now that we are strong enough to seize what we have a right to, we are offered the negotiations that were always previously refused; but we have no need of them now and we no longer ask for them. It seems clear to me that this attitude is necessarily prescribed for him by the logic of his movement.

French opposition to a German hegemony offers no future except the vicious circle which is implicit in the very notion of a European balance of power. If neither nation can tolerate the other's hegemony in Europe without sacrificing its own security, the only safe alternative is to exercise a certain hegemony itself – which obliges the other to try to wrest it away, and so on. The idea of security contains an internal contradiction; because, on the plane of force, which is where the problem of security arises, the only security is to be a little stronger than the people across the way, who thus lose their own security; therefore, to make the organization of peace dependent upon the establishment of general security, as France has done for so long, is to proclaim the impossibility of peace. Even if the vicious circle inherent in the doctrine of a European balance of power does not necessarily involve war, it does in any case involve the ever-increasing militarization of civil life. Will France be less enslaved to Germany by submitting to an indefinitely prolonged state of siege than by submitting to some form of political subordination?

Suppose, on the other hand, that France allows Germany to establish her hegemony in central Europe and later, doubtless, in the rest of Europe, what would be the best one could hope for? Nothing very attractive in this case either. All one could hope is that once France withdrew behind her frontiers, reduced her military system to a more modest and essentially defensive scale, ceased to obstruct Germany's diplomatic aims, and showed herself accommodating, to say the least, in the economic sphere, then Germany might not go to the trouble of invading her. This is certainly a possible hope. And it is also possible in this case that France might achieve within her own frontiers, if she would make the effort, a revival of culture and civilization and a social renewal – and without opposition from Germany. No doubt the German superiority of strength would impose certain discriminations in France, especially against the Communists and against the Jews. In my eyes, and probably in those of the majority of French people, this would hardly matter in itself. One can easily conceive that the essential might remain intact, and that those who still care about the public good in our country might be enabled, at last, to take a little effective action about housing and schools, and the problem of reconciling the demands of industrial production with the dignity of the workers, and to undertake a massive popularization of the marvels of art and science and thought, and other appropriate tasks of peace.

Comparing these two hypotheses which, I repeat, represent the best results to be hoped for from the two policies, it seems to me very clear that the second, although it implies a sad renunciation for a nation formerly of the first rank, is by a long way preferable. It offers a precarious future, but still a future; whereas the other offers none, it offers only an indefinite and doubtless aggravated continuation of an almost unendurable present.

One must also ask what probability there is of the best or the worst outcome for each of the two policies. Would Germany resist the temptation of absorbing a relatively weak France into her totalitarian system, either by military occupation or by some very rigorous kind of political and economic domination? Perhaps so, perhaps not. It will depend not only upon the relations of power but also upon the extent to which France has kept effectively alive some of her moral and spiritual resources; it will also depend upon how long the dynamic German drive is maintained. That sort of dynamism does not break down only as the result of defeat, it also wears itself out in the end by success. By wearing out in this way, even with France reduced for a time to a vassal state, the German political régime might evolve in a manner which would completely transform the problem of German hegemony in Europe. One must remember that political régimes are unstable; it is not wise to treat them as fixed data when framing a long-term foreign policy.

To give you my whole thought, it is this: A war in Europe would be certain disaster, in all circumstances, for everybody and from every point of view, whereas a German hegemony in Europe, however bitter the prospect, might in the end not be a disaster for Europe. If one bears in mind that national-socialism in its present extremely tense manifestation may be impermanent, then one can imagine in the next phase of history several possible consequences of such a hegemony, and not all of them disastrous.

And then, if France wants to check the continual growth of German power, is it actually possible for her to do so? Is it not in the nature of things that central Europe should fall under German domination? The maintenance of the status quo in Czecho-Slovakia is inconceivable; it can be defended neither in fact nor in law. And since the Sudeten territory includes both the natural defences of Czecho-Slovakia and also a great part of her industrial resources, I cannot imagine even any internal reform which could prevent this territory from remaining practically at Germany's mercy. Some such reform might just conceivably have been possible in 1930; but not now, in view of the bitterness of the Sudeten Germans and the military and economic power of Germany – with the complicity of Hungary and Poland she could completely encircle Czecho-Slovakia – and the undeniable political intelligence of Hitler. The only question, I think, is in what circumstances he will impose his will, and whether with or without brutality, and whether swiftly or gradually.

Even if France and England could oppose an effective barrier to Germany's drive into central Europe, would Hitler hesitate from going to war to break the barrier? The contrary seems to me probable. It may be that he would prefer not to go to war at all, even if he acquires

To Gaston Bergery 1938

sufficient resources to sustain a long war; but he certainly wants to possess those resources, so as to be able to speak to Europe in the tone he must use in order to continue to speak as master to the Germans. So far as conjecture is possible in such a matter, I believe that in order to acquire those resources he would risk a war if necessary, and if he had no other way of acquiring them. Is not the real aim of war nowadays the acquisition of the means for making war?

In such a war, France supported by England alone – for it is better to say nothing of Russia – would be very likely to lose, and she could only win by wearing herself out and inflicting more ruin on herself than a victorious enemy could do. And after the war where would Europe stand in comparison with the other continents?

Which alternative would be most likely to tempt Germany to war: a comparatively weak France, or a barrier erected by a still comparatively strong France against German ambitions? It is very difficult to say. Perhaps one can call the chances roughly equal, though if anything with a slight difference in favour of the policy of withdrawing behind our frontiers. And if it is true that this policy is also the one which, in the event of its relative success, offers the more favourable outlook, then I conclude it is the best policy; on the understanding, of course, that France should use the position she still occupies to make one more serious attempt, even though without much hope, to negotiate the great European settlement.

The most serious obstacle to the policy of withdrawal is that France is an empire. But that is a dishonouring embarrassment, for it does not mean maintaining her own independence but maintaining the dependence in which she holds millions of other people. If France wished to adopt the policy of withdrawal without seeing her colonial empire purely and simply snatched away from her, the policy would need to be accompanied by the rapid development of her colonies towards a large measure of autonomy, of various different kinds. In my eyes, this consideration alone, even if there were no other, would suffice to make the policy of withdrawal desirable; for I must confess that even if France were to lose some of her own independence this would be less shameful, to my way of thinking, than to continue to trample the Arabs and Indo-Chinese and others beneath her feet.

I believe, too, that the moral atmosphere would be cleared by the disappearance of all the lies, hypocrisy, and demagogy that go with the effort France has been making these last twenty years to play a role beyond her strength. To sum up – although this policy is a precarious and in some respects a painful one, it seems to me the only one that offers even a faint possibility of human progress or a fresh start. And if we ought to adopt it, I think it is urgent that we make up our minds to it as soon as possible.

That is why I deplore that there should not be a man like you behind it – someone who has the sympathy of all who love independence, intelligence, and honesty, who is not compromised by the blunders and crimes of the past, and who may one day therefore possess great authority with a large section of the people – rather than a Flandin in whom nobody can feel confidence in any way.

I have certainly taken up too much of your time; but having started on such a subject it seemed best to deal at once with all the aspects in which I see it. I hope you will soon give the readers of *La Flèche* your considered views in the matter. They certainly expect you to, because among all those who talk about it, whether as politicians or private individuals, you are the only one, when all is said and done, and although you are at present outside the government, who speaks like a statesman.

Very sincerely,
S. Weil

34 To an Oxford Poet

> Mr. Charles G. Bell, now of St. John's College, Annapolis, visited Solesmes for the Easter services in 1938, when he was an Oxford undergraduate. He remembers meeting there 'a thin, intense young woman' who read Marlowe and was deeply interested in the English metaphysical poets. It is thought that this may be the draft of a letter to him. (Written in English)

[1938]

Dear boy,

I have re-read *Lear* since I came home, and though I admire it more and more every time, I can't understand *your* reasons of admiring it. It is more like Sophocles than anything I know. Such should be – with all suitable transformations – the poetry of our age, which is an age of real, not metaphysical misery. Misery is always metaphysical; but it can be merely so, or it can be brought home to the soul through the pain and humiliation suffered by the body. That I call real misery.

To an Oxford Poet 1938

It was not till Christ had known the physical agony of crucifixion, the shame of blows and mockery, that he uttered his immortal cry, a question which shall remain unanswered through all times on this earth 'My God, why hast thou forsaken me?' When poetry struggles toward the expressing of pain and misery, it can be great poetry only if that cry sounds through every word. So it does in the *Iliad*, when Homer says:

> He who receives [from Zeus] the evil gifts is made a prey to shame;
> Dreadful hunger chases him forth across the holy earth;
> He wanders, honoured neither by gods nor men.
> (XXIV. 531-3)

So it does sometimes in Eschylus, nearly always in Sophocles. And so it does in *Lear*. Lear is a man forsaken by heaven and earth, helpless, and broken with misery and shame. His suffering has something great in it inasmuch as he is broken, not bended. Such is also the greatness of Sophocles' heroes. The very essence of the tragedy can be found in lines such as:

> ... Life and death! I am ashamed
> That thou hast power to shake my manhood thus;
> That these hot tears, which break from me perforce,
> Should make thee worth them ...
>
> . . . .
>
> O let me not be mad, not mad, sweet heaven!
> Keep me in temper: I would not be mad!
>
> . . . .
>
> ... O heavens,
> If you do love old men, if your sweet sway
> Allow obedience, if yourselves are old,
> Make it your cause ...
>
> . . . .
>
> You heavens, give me that patience, patience I need!
> You see me here, you gods, a poor old man,
> As full of grief as age; wretched in both:
> If it be you that stirs these daughters' hearts
> Against their father, fool me not so much
> To bear it tamely; touch me with noble anger,
> And let not women's weapons, water-drops,
> Stain my man's cheeks! ...
> ... You think I'll weep;
> No, I'll not weep:

> I have full cause of weeping; but this heart
> Shall break into a hundred thousand flaws
> Or ere I'll weep, O fool, I shall go mad!
> ... O Regan, Goneril!
> Your kind old father, whose frank heart gave you all –
> O, that way madness lies; let me shut that;
> No more of that.

And at last:

> Why should a dog, a horse, a rat have life,
> And thou no breath at all?

Helplessness – I do not mean weakness of character, but utter lack of material force – breathes forth in these lines all its bitterness. For it is bitter; nothing in the world is so bitter. Yet it is better for the soul than triumph and power, because there is truth in it; it is not, like these, poisoned with delusions and lies. For instance, the vilest prostitute in the streets, is better than a self-righteous woman born in a rich family. Still such misery is shameful; the soul yearns for a truth not mingled with misery, shame and bondage, and dares not think it can't be found in this world. I believe it can. And those who live in pain, as I think, all believe that it can, or at least that it could. For this reason, the nobleness of suffering is not to be spoken of lightly or too often; it can too easily become mere litterature in the mouth of people who have not suffered pain that can break the very soul. Do you realise there are millions and millions of people on earth who suffer nearly always, from birth to death? It is a pity they have not learned expression; they would say the truth about suffering. Yet they have sometimes expressed themselves – through anonymous melodies, songs, legends, religions – and then they have sometimes, as I think, surpassed the greatest geniuses.

Well, enough of that. You certainly have talent – which in itself is worthless. Who knows if maturity may not bring genius? That is 'on the knees of the gods'. Genius is distinct from talent, to my mind, by its deep regard and intelligence for the common life of common people – I mean people without talent. The most beautiful poetry is the poetry which can best express, in its truth, the life of people who can't write poetry. Outside of that, there is only clever poetry; and mankind can do very well without clever poetry. Cleverness makes the aristocracy of intelligence; the soul of genius is *caritas*, in the Christian signification of the word; the sense that every human being is all-important. That, at least, is my creed.

You will excuse me, I hope, if my English is not quite correct.

With friendly remembrance

Simone Weil

Have you still my address? 3, rue Auguste-Comte, Paris 6e.

35 To Georges Bernanos

[1938]

Monsieur,

However silly it may be to write to an author, since his profession must always involve him in a flood of correspondence, I cannot refrain from doing so after having read *Les Grands cimetières sous la lune*. Not that it is the first book of yours to touch me. The *Journal d'un curé de campagne* is in my opinion the best of them, at least of those I have read, and really a great book. But the fact that I have liked other books of yours gave me no reason for intruding upon you to say so. This last one, however, is a different matter. I have had an experience which corresponds to yours, although it was much shorter and was less profound; and although it was apparently – but only apparently – embraced in a different spirit.

I am not a Catholic, although – and this must no doubt appear presumptuous to any Catholic, coming from a non-Catholic – nothing that is Catholic, nothing that is Christian, has ever seemed alien to me. I have sometimes told myself that if only there were a notice on church doors forbidding entry to anyone with an income above a certain figure, and a low one, I would be converted at once. From my childhood onwards I sympathized with those organizations which spring from the lowest and least regarded social strata, until the time when I realized that such organizations are of a kind to discourage all sympathy. The last one in which I felt some confidence was the Spanish C.N.T.[1] I had travelled a little in Spain before the civil war; only a little, but enough to feel the affection which it is hard not to feel for the Spanish people. I had seen the anarchist movement as the natural expression of that people's greatness and of its flaws, of its worthiest aspirations and of its

[1] *Confederacion Nacional de Trabajadores*, the anarchist trade union organization.

unworthiest. The C.N.T. and F.A.I.[1] were an extraordinary mixture, to which anybody at all was admitted and in which, consequently, one found immorality, cynicism, fanaticism and cruelty, but also love and fraternal spirit and, above all, that concern for honour which is so beautiful in the humiliated. It seemed to me that the idealists preponderated over the elements of violence and disorder. In July, 1936, I was in Paris. I do not love war; but what has always seemed to me most horrible in war is the position of those in the rear. When I realized that, try as I would, I could not prevent myself from participating morally in that war – in other words, from hoping all day and every day for the victory of one side and the defeat of the other – I decided that, for me, Paris was the rear and I took the train to Barcelona, with the intention of enlisting. This was at the beginning of August 1936.

My stay in Spain was brought to a compulsory end by an accident. I was a few days in Barcelona, and then in the remote Aragonese countryside on the banks of the Ebro, about ten miles from Saragossa, at the very place where the river was recently crossed by Yaguë's troops; then I was at Sitges, in the palace converted into a hospital, and then again in Barcelona. A stay of about two months in all. I left Spain against my will and with the intention of returning; but later I decided voluntarily not to do so. I no longer felt any inner compulsion to participate in a war which, instead of being what it had appeared when it began – a war of famished peasants against landed proprietors and their clerical supporters – had become a war between Russia on the one hand and Germany and Italy on the other.

I recognize the smell of civil war, the smell of blood and terror, which exhales from your book; I have breathed it too. I must admit that I neither saw nor heard of anything which quite equalled the ignominy of certain facts you relate, such as the murders of elderly peasants or the *Ballillas*[2] chasing old people and beating them with truncheons. But for all that, I heard quite enough. I was very nearly present at the execution of a priest. In the minutes of suspense I was asking myself whether I should simply look on or whether I should try to intervene and get myself shot as well. I still don't know which I would have done if a lucky chance had not prevented the execution.

So many incidents come crowding ... but they would take too long

[1] *Federacion Anarquista Iberica*, the anarchist political party.
[2] An Italian fascist corps.

to tell; and to what purpose? Let one suffice. I was at Sitges when the militiamen returned, defeated, from the expedition to Majorca. They had been decimated. Out of forty young boys from Sitges nine were dead, as was learnt when the remaining thirty-one came back. The very next night there were nine revenge operations. In that little town, in which nothing at all had happened in July, they killed nine so-called fascists. Among the nine was a baker, aged about thirty, whose crime, so I was told, was that he had not joined the 'Somaten'[1] militia. His old father, whose only child and only support he was, went mad. One more incident: In a light engagement a small international party of militiamen from various countries captured a boy of fifteen who was a member of the Falange. As soon as he was captured, and still trembling from the sight of his comrades being killed alongside him, he said he had been enrolled compulsorily. He was searched and a medal of the Virgin and a Falange card were found on him. Then he was sent to Durruti, the leader of the column, who lectured him for an hour on the beauties of the anarchist ideal and gave him the choice between death and enrolling immediately in the ranks of his captors, against his comrades of yesterday. Durruti gave this child twenty-four hours to think it over, and when the time was up he said no and was shot. Yet Durruti was in some ways an admirable man. Although I only heard of it afterwards, the death of this little hero has never ceased to weigh on my conscience. Another incident: A village was finally captured by the red militia after having been taken and re-taken over and over again. In the cellars there were found a handful of haggard, terrified, famished creatures and among them three or four young men. The militiamen reasoned as follows: If these young men stayed behind and waited for the fascists the last time we retired from here, it means that they must be fascists too. They therefore shot them immediately, but gave some food to the others and thought themselves very humane. Finally, here is an incident from the rear: Two anarchists once told me how they and some comrades captured two priests. They killed one of them on the spot with a revolver, in front of the other, and then told the survivor that he could go. When he was twenty yards away they shot him down. The man who told me this story was much surprised when I didn't laugh.

At Barcelona an average of fifty people were killed every night in punitive raids. This is proportionately much less than in Majorca be-

---

[1] The meaning of this slogan is obscure. Possibly 'We are ready' (*Somos atentos*).

cause Barcelona is a town of nearly a million inhabitants; moreover, it had been the scene of a three-day battle of sanguinary street-fighting. But statistics are probably not to the point in such a matter. The point is the attitude towards murder. Never once, either among Spaniards or even among the French who were in Spain as combatants or as visitors – the latter being usually dim and harmless intellectuals – never once did I hear anyone express, even in private intimacy, any repulsion or disgust or even disapproval of useless bloodshed. You speak about fear. Yes, it is true that fear played some part in all this butchery; but where I was it did not appear to play the large part that you assign to it. Men who seemed to be brave – there was one at least whose courage I personally witnessed – would retail with cheery fraternal chuckles at convivial meal-times how many priests they had murdered, or how many 'fascists', the latter being a very elastic term. My own feeling was that when once a certain class of people has been placed by the temporal and spiritual authorities outside the ranks of those whose life has value, then nothing comes more naturally to men than murder. As soon as men know that they can kill without fear of punishment or blame, they kill; or at least they encourage killers with approving smiles. If anyone happens to feel a slight distaste to begin with, he keeps quiet and he soon begins to suppress it for fear of seeming unmanly. People get carried away by a sort of intoxication which is irresistible without a fortitude of soul which I am bound to consider exceptional since I have met with it nowhere. On the other hand I met peaceable Frenchmen, for whom I had never before felt contempt and who would never have dreamed of doing any killing themselves, but who savoured that blood-polluted atmosphere with visible pleasure. For them I shall never again be able to feel any esteem.

The very purpose of the whole struggle is soon lost in an atmosphere of this sort. For the purpose can only be defined in terms of the public good, of the welfare of men – and men have become valueless. In a country where the great majority of the poor are peasants the essential aim of every extreme-left party should be an improvement of the peasants' conditions; and perhaps the main issue of this war, at the beginning, was the redistribution of land. But those peasants of Aragon, so poor and so splendid in the pride they have cherished through all their humiliations – one cannot say that they were even an object of curiosity to the militiamen. Although there was no insolence, no injury,

To Georges Bernanos 1938

no brutality – at least I saw none and I know that theft and rape were capital crimes in the anarchist militias – nevertheless, between the armed forces and the civilian population there was an abyss, exactly like the abyss between the rich and the poor. One felt it in the attitude of the two groups, the one always rather humble, submissive and timid, the other confident, off-hand and condescending.

One sets out as a volunteer, with the idea of sacrifice, and finds oneself in a war which resembles a war of mercenaries, only with much more cruelty and with less human respect for the enemy.

I could say much more on the same lines, but I must limit myself. Having been in Spain, I now continually listen to and read all sorts of observations about Spain, but I could not point to a single person, except you alone, who has been exposed to the atmosphere of the civil war and has resisted it. What do I care that you are a royalist, a disciple of Drumont? You are incomparably nearer to me than my comrades of the Aragon militias – and yet I loved them.

What you say about nationalism, war, and French foreign policy after the war is equally sympathetic to me. I was ten years old at the time of Versailles, and up to then I had been patriotically thrilled as children are in war-time. But the will to humiliate the defeated enemy which revealed itself so loathsomely everywhere at that time (and in the following years) was enough to cure me once for all of that naïve sort of patriotism. I suffer more from the humiliations inflicted by my country than from those inflicted on her.

I am afraid I have bothered you with a very long letter. I will only add an expression of my keen admiration.

S. Weil

Mlle Simone Weil, 3 rue Auguste-Comte, Paris (VIe)

P.S. I wrote my address automatically. I expect, for one thing, that you have better to do than to answer letters. And in any case I am going to Italy for a month or two and if a letter from you should be forwarded it might be held up somewhere.

36 To Jean Giraudoux

(A draft of a letter.) Giraudoux was Minister of Propaganda in 1939-40.

[1939 or 1940]

Monsieur et cher archicube,[1]
 Your function is an excuse for the liberty I take in writing to you. You speak to the public, so the public should be able to speak to you. My admiration and sympathy for your writing and especially your plays have several times given me the wish, so natural to readers, of approaching you on the strength of the traditional camaraderie of the rue d'Ulm[2] and of a few common friends. But one should resist that sort of wish, because the sympathy between authors and readers is necessarily unilateral; and as for expressions of admiration, nothing is more boring to listen to. But today it is different. You have addressed the women of France, and I am one of them; so I have a share, one twenty-millionth I suppose, of the right to address you. And although it is my admiration for you which makes me write, it is not admiration that I am going to express.

I did not hear your speech; I read it in *Le Temps*. There is a passage in it which caused me acute pain. I have always been proud of you as one of those whose names can be mentioned when one is looking for reasons why present-day France can be loved; and that is why I would wish you always to speak the truth, even on the wireless. Without doubt, you believe you speak it; but I wish with all my heart that I could persuade you to ask yourself if you are doing so when you assert that France's colonial dominions are attached to her by any links except subordination and exploitation.

I would give my life and more if possible to believe that this is true; for it is dreadful to feel guilty through involuntary complicity. But it is not true. To any informed person who has studied the question its untruth is absolutely clear. How many men we are now compelling to die for our country after depriving them of their own! Did not France acquire Annam by conquest? Was it not a peaceful, united, organized country, with a historic culture, and enriched by Chinese, Hindu, and Buddhist influences? In particular, they have a common idea, for which they use the word karma, which is exactly identical with the Greek

[1] i.e. former student or 'old boy' of the École Normale Supérieure.
[2] Address of the École Normale Supérieure.

idea, unfortunately forgotten by us, of nemesis as the automatic punishment for excess. We have killed their culture; we forbid them access to the manuscripts of their language; we have imposed upon a small section of them our own culture, which has no roots among them and can do them no good. Although there is chronic famine in the north of their country, the plentiful rice of the south is exported abroad. There is an annual tax which is the same for the poor as for the rich. Parents are reduced to selling their children, as they used to do in the Roman provinces. Families sell the shrines of their ancestors, their most valued possession, and not even so as to get food, but simply to pay the tax. I shall never forget hearing an agricultural expert of the Colonial Ministry frigidly explain that people are right to hit the coolies on the plantations because they are so weak from overwork and privation that any other form of punishment would be more cruel. Have you not heard of the machine-gunning of some unarmed peasants who had come to say they could not pay their tax? Has anyone dared to deny the atrocities after the Yen-Bay troubles? Villages were destroyed from the air; the Foreign Legion was unleashed in Tonkin to kill indiscriminately; young people employed in the prisons heard the screams of the tortured all day long. And, alas, one could add much more of the same kind. And in Africa, are you not aware of the mass-expropriation of Arabs and blacks after the first war? And how can it be said that we brought culture to the Arabs, when it was they who preserved the traditions of Greece for us through the Middle Ages? Yet I have read, in Paris, newspapers published by Arabs in French, because neither they nor their public could read Arabic. Did you not read in the newspapers about a year ago that there was a strike in a Tunisian mine because the Moslem workers were expected to work as hard as usual during Ramadan, that is to say, while they were fasting? How could the Moslems put up with such a thing, and others like it, unless they were being held down by force?

I realize that this letter exposes me, under the decree of 24 May 1938, to from one to five years in prison. I do not feel in danger; but suppose I were, what do I care? Perpetual prison could not hurt me more than the fact of being unable, because of the colonies, to think that France's cause is just.

37 To A.W.

(An extract)

[Between January and April 1940]

[...] I have succeeded in getting the book on Babylonian and Egyptian mathematics. [....] I would like to write to the author about a question which he leaves unanswered: How were the Egyptians able, with a geometry which he says was very crude and empirical, to find a remarkably close approximation to π – namely, area of circle $=(\frac{8}{9}d)^2$. This seems to me fairly easy to imagine, if one assumes very rough-and-ready methods. Having divided the circumscribed square into 81 little squares one might consider that the circle's area could be found by subtracting from each corner three of these squares plus approximately the sum of three half-squares.

There is one really amusing Babylonian problem; they give the dimensions of a canal to be dug, and the daily output of a worker in volume of earth displaced, and the *combined total of working-days and workers*. What has to be discovered is the number of working-days and the number of workers. I wonder what our pupils' parents would say if a problem so formulated was set in an exam today? It would be amusing to make the experiment. Strange folk, those Babylonians! Personally I don't much like their spirit of abstraction. The Sumerians must have been much nicer people. In the first place, it was they who invented all the Mesopotamian myths, and myths are a lot more interesting than algebra. But as for you, you must be a direct descendant of the Babylonians. I myself quite agree with the Pythagorean saying that God is ever a geometer – but not that he does algebra. Anyway, and however that may be, I was glad to find in the last letter I've had from you that you deny belonging to the abstract school.

I remember you said at Chançay or Dieulefit[1] that these studies of Egypt and Babylon throw doubt on the creative role hitherto attributed to the Greeks in mathematics. But I think that up to now (and leaving aside the possibility of further discoveries) they have rather confirmed it. The Babylonians appear to have been devoted to abstract exercises concerning numbers, and the Egyptians appear to have proceeded purely empirically. The application of a rational method to concrete problems and to the study of nature seems to have been peculiar to the

---

[1] Places where a group of mathematicians held conferences.

To A. W. 1940

Greeks. (Though it is true that one would need to know the Babylonian astronomy before one could decide.) What is singular is that the Greeks must have known Babylonian algebra and yet there is no trace of it among them before Diophantus (who belongs, unless I am mistaken, to the fourth century A.D.). The algebraic geometry of the Pythagoreans is something quite different. The explanation is probably connected with religion; it would seem that the secret religion of the Pythagoreans must have agreed with geometry and not with algebra. If the Roman Empire had not destroyed all the esoteric cults, perhaps we should understand something about these enigmas. [. . . .]

38 To the same

(An extract)

[Between January and April 1940]

[. . .] I am not sure if the discovery of incommensurables is a sufficient explanation of the obstinate refusal of algebra by the Greeks. They must have known Babylonian algebra from the earliest times. According to the tradition, Pythagoras made a journey to Babylon in order to study there. Obviously, they transposed this algebra into geometry long before Apollonius. The transpositions of this kind which are found in Apollonius are concerned, no doubt, with bi-quadratic equations; all those of the 2nd degree can be solved when once the properties of the triangle inscribed in the semi-circle are known, a discovery which is attributed to Pythagoras. (In this way one finds two quantities of which one knows either the sum and the product or the difference and the product.) But what is singular is that this transposition of algebra into geometry seems to be, not a side issue, but the very mainspring of geometrical invention throughout the history of Greek geometry.

The legend concerning Thales' discovery of the similarity of triangles (at the time when a man's shadow is equal to the man, the pyramid's shadow is equal to the pyramid) relates that discovery to the problem of a proportion with one unknown term.

Nothing is known about the next discovery, made by Pythagoras, of the properties of the right-angled triangle. But here is my hypothesis, which certainly accords with the spirit of Pythagorean research. It is that this discovery came out of the problem of finding the geometrical mean between two known quantities. Two similar triangles having two non-homologous sides equal represent a proportion between three quantities.

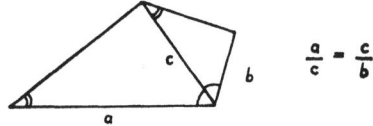

$$\frac{a}{c} = \frac{c}{b}$$

If the two extremes are constructed on the same straight line the figure becomes a right-angled triangle (because the angle between a and b becomes 180°, whose half is a right angle). The essential property of the right-angled triangle is that it is formed by the juxtaposition of two triangles similar to it and to one another. I think it was this property that Pythagoras discovered first. The right-angled triangle also provides the solution of the reciprocal problem: to find the extremes, when the geometrical mean and the sum or the difference of the extremes are known.

As for conics and their properties, the discoverer in this case is said to have been Menaechmus, a pupil of Plato and one of the two geometers who solved the problem, set by Apollo, of doubling the cube. (The other was Archytas, who solved it by the torus.) Menaechmus solved the problem by conics (two parabolas or a parabola and a hyperbola). So it seems to me that there is no doubt that he invented them for this purpose. And the problem of doubling the cube comes down to that of finding *two* geometrical means between two known quantities.

It is easy to imagine the process of discovery, because the cone consists of a circle with a variable diameter and the parabola gives the series of all the geometrical means between a fixed and a variable term.

So there is a continuous series of problems: proportion between four terms of which one is unknown – geometrical progression of three terms of which the middle term is unknown – geometrical progression of four terms of which the two middle terms are unknown.

Just as the properties of the right-angled triangle made it possible to solve problems of the 2nd degree, so the properties of the conics made it possible for those of the 3rd and 4th degree.

Note that, whereas we solve equations on the assumption that expressions like $\sqrt{\ }$, $\sqrt[3]{\ }$, etc., have meaning, the Greeks gave each of them a meaning before they tackled problems of the corresponding degree.

To A. W. 1940

Note, too, that the assimilation of the unknown to a variable goes back at least as far as Menaechmus, if not further. One can hardly suppose that the Babylonians, with their numerical equations, possessed this idea. The Greeks of the 5th century possessed the idea of function and also that of representing functions by lines. One gets the impression, from the story of Menaechmus, that curves were for them a means of studying functions, much rather than an object of study in themselves.

In all this we see a progressive development whose continuity is at no point interrupted by any drama due to the incommensurables. Most certainly, there *was* a drama of the incommensurables and its repercussions were immense. The popularization of that discovery brought the concept of truth into a discredit which still endures today; it brought, or at least assisted in bringing, to birth the idea that it is equally possible to prove two contradictory theses; this point of view was diffused among the masses by the sophists, along with a learning of inferior quality, directed solely towards the acquisition of power; as a result of this there arose, from the end of the 5th century, both demagogy and the imperialism that always goes with it, which brought the Hellenic civilization to ruin; it was this process (reinforced, of course, by other factors such as the Persian wars) which enabled the Roman arms finally to kill Greece, with no possibility of resurrection. My conclusion is that the gods did right when they destroyed in a shipwreck the Pythagorean who was guilty of divulging the discovery of incommensurables.

But among geometers and philosophers I do not believe there was any drama. What ruined Pythagoreanism (in so far as it was ruined) was something quite different – namely, the wholesale massacre of Pythagoreans in Magna Graecia. Moreover, the pentagram, which represents a relation between incommensurables (cutting a segment in extreme and mean ratio), was one of the Pythagoreans' symbols. But Archytas (one of the survivors) was a great geometer and was the master of Eudoxus, inventor of the theory of the real numbers and of the concept of limit and the concept of integration as expounded in Euclid. There is no reason to think that the Pythagoreans, when they spoke of number, were referring only to integers. Quite the contrary, when they said that justice, etc., etc., are numbers it seems to me they made it clear that they were using the word to describe every kind of proportion. They were certainly capable of conceiving the real numbers.

In my opinion, the essential point of the discovery of incommensurables is outside geometry. It consists in this, that certain problems concerning numbers are sometimes susceptible of solution and sometimes insoluble; such as the problem of a geometrical mean between two given numbers. This by itself is enough to prove that number in the strict sense of the word cannot be the key to everything. Now, when was this perceived? I don't know if there is any information on this point. In any case it could have been perceived before the beginning of geometry. It was sufficient to make a special study of problems of proportion. And in that case the geometrical procedure for finding geometrical means (height of right-angled triangle) would be seen *immediately*, as soon as it was discovered, as not being subject to any similar limitation. One might almost suggest that the Greeks studied the triangle in order to find proportions which could be expressed otherwise than by integers and that consequently they conceived the straight line as a *function* from the beginning, just as they did later with the parabola. Objections can be raised against this thesis, but they fail, in my opinion, if one remembers the custom of secrecy among Greek thinkers and their practice of only diffusing a doctrine in a garbled form. If it was Eudoxus who completed and perfected the theory of the real numbers, that need in no way preclude earlier geometers from having glimpsed the idea and constantly attempted to grasp it.

It may be asked why the Greeks were so attached to the study of proportion. This was certainly a matter of religious preoccupation and therefore (since they were Greeks) partly of aesthetics. The link between mathematical preoccupation on the one hand and philosophico-religious preoccupation on the other is historically confirmed for the age of Pythagoras; but it certainly goes back much further. Thus Plato, who was an extreme traditionalist, speaks often of 'the ancients, who were much closer than we are to the light . . .' (evidently alluding to an antiquity much more remote than Pythagoras); on the other hand, he placed over the door of the Academy 'None enters here unless he is a geometer' and he said 'God is ever a geometer'. These two attitudes would be in contradiction – which cannot be – unless the preoccupations from which Greek geometry emerged (if not the geometry itself) were of very ancient date; one may suppose that they were derived either from the pre-Hellenic inhabitants of Greece, or from Egypt, or

To A. W. 1940

from both. Moreover, Orphism (which has this double origin) inspired both Pythagoreanism and Platonism (which are practically equivalent) to such an extent that one may wonder whether Pythagoras and Plato did much more than write commentaries on it. Thales was almost certainly initiated into some Greek and Egyptian mysteries and was consequently steeped in a philosophic and religious atmosphere similar to that of Pythagoreanism.

I think therefore that from a fairly remote antiquity the idea of proportion had been the theme of a meditation which was one of the chief methods, and perhaps the chief method, of purifying the soul. There can be no doubt that this idea was at the centre of Greek aesthetics and geometry and philosophy.

What constitutes the originality of the Greeks in mathematics is not, I believe, their refusal to admit approximations. There are no approximations in the Babylonian problems; and for a very simple reason: they are constructed from their solutions. Thus there are dozens (or hundreds, I can't remember) of problems of the 4th degree with two unknowns, all having the same solution. This shows that the Babylonians were only interested in method and not in solving actual problems. In the same way, in the canal problem which I quoted to you, the sum of workers and working-days is obviously never the datum. They amused themselves by supposing the datum to be unknown and the unknown to be known. It is a game which evidently does the greatest honour to their feeling for 'disinterested research'. (Did they have scholarships and prizes to stimulate them?) But it is only a game.

This game must have seemed profane, or even impious, to the Greeks. Otherwise, why should they not have translated the treatises on algebra, which must have existed in Babylonian, at the same time that they transposed them into geometry? The work of Diophantus could have been written many centuries earlier than it was; but the Greeks attached no value to a method of reasoning for its own sake; they valued it in so far as it enabled concrete problems to be studied efficiently. And this was not because they were avid for technical applications but because their sole aim was to conceive more and more clearly an identity of structure between the human mind and the universe. Purity of soul was their one concern; to 'imitate God' was the secret of it; the imitation of God was assisted by the study of mathematics, in so far as one conceived the universe to be subject to mathematical laws, which made the geometer an imitator of the supreme lawgiver. Clearly, the mathematical games of the Babylonians, in which the solutions were given before the data, were useless for this purpose. The data they needed were ones which are really provided by the world, or by action upon the world; so it was necessary to find ratios which did not necessitate preparing the problems artificially in order to make them 'come out right', as is the case with integers.

It is for the Greeks that mathematics was really an art. It had the same purpose as their art, to reveal palpably a kinship between the human mind and the universe, so that the world is seen as 'the city of all rational beings'. And it did really possess a concrete subject-matter which existed, like that of every other art without exception, in the physical sense of the word; this subject-matter was space; that is, the actual datum of space to which all human actions are subjected as a material condition. Their geometry was a science of nature; and their physics (I am thinking of the Pythagoreans' music and above all of Archimedes' mechanics and his study of floating bodies) was a geometry in which the hypotheses were introduced as postulates.

I fear that our tendency today is rather towards the Babylonian conception: towards mathematics as a game, more than as an art. I wonder how many mathematicians today regard mathematics as a method for purifying the soul and 'imitating God'? Then again, it seems to me to lack a concrete subject-matter. There is a great deal of axiomatic work, which makes an apparent resemblance to Greek methods; but is not the choice of the axioms to a great extent arbitrary? You speak of 'concrete material'; but does the material essentially consist of anything except the sum-total of mathematical work achieved up to now? In that case, present-day mathematics would be a screen between man and the universe (and therefore between man and God, conceived in the Greek manner) instead of a contact between them. But perhaps I calumniate it.

Apropos of the Greeks, have you heard anything about a certain Autran who has just published a book on Homer? He puts forward a sensational theory, which is that the Lycians and Phoenicians of the second millennium B.C. were Dravidians. His arguments, which are philological, do not appear to be negligible – so far as one can judge without knowing the Dravidian languages or the inscriptions he quotes. But the theory is very attractive – too attractive, even – in this sense,

To A. W. 1940

that it offers an extremely simple explanation of the analogies between Greek thought and Indian thought. The differences might perhaps be sufficiently accounted for by climate. In any case, how can one help feeling nostalgia for an age in which one and the same thought could be found everywhere, in all peoples, in all countries; when ideas circulated throughout a prodigious area, which at the same time enjoyed all the riches of diversity? Today, as under the Roman Empire, uniformity is clamped down everywhere, blotting out all traditional variety, and at the same time ideas have almost ceased to circulate. Well, there we are! In 1,000 years' time perhaps things will be a little better.

39 To the same

An extract from a draft of a letter

[Between January and April 1940]

The discovery of incommensurables comprises two separate discoveries: (1) That there are certain operations in integers (e.g. $\sqrt{2}$) which do not lead to any rational number and (2) that, on the other hand, these numerically indefinable results correspond to segments. The thing is generally presented the other way round; it is supposed that the first discovery was that the diagonal of the square is $\sqrt{2}$ and that this led to the search for the value of $\sqrt{2}$, or at any rate that it was through seeking a common measure for segments that it was discovered that in certain cases there is no such measure. But it is an arbitrary and altogether implausible assumption that the geometrical aspect of this idea was studied before the arithmetical. The study of numbers began long before the study of lines. The Babylonians must necessarily have perceived that their algebraic methods only produced solutions in cases where the data were suitably selected – so they selected the data to conform to the solution. What did they think about the other cases? We cannot know whether they believed they were held up by excessively complicated calculations or by an impossibility.

But as regards the Pythagoreans or pre-Pythagoreans the matter is much clearer. Since they studied numerical proportions and every kind of numerical mean, they must have sought for the geometrical mean between a number and its double, as they did for the harmonic and the arithmetical mean. (Perhaps they envisaged this problem in the form of doubling the square; the problem of Delos suggests this, by analogy.) It must have seemed to them difficult to find a rational number for the geometrical mean between a number and its double. But they called arithmetic 'the science of even and odd', which suggests that they must have asked themselves whether a number formed in a given manner is even or odd.

Consequently one may suppose that they asked this question about the geometrical mean between a number and its double, when this mean is a whole number. They could easily prove that it is an even number and also an odd number; for this it is sufficient to know that only the square of an even number can be even, which is obvious almost at sight, especially if one represents a square number with dots. Therefore this mean (as a whole number) never exists. It can easily be deduced from this that it never exists as a fraction either.

Aristotle says that the incommensurability of the diagonal is demonstrated per absurdum: if it were commensurable, the even would be equal to the odd. That is the oldest text on the subject.

That the root $\sqrt{n.2n}$ does not exist may have been a cause of distress. But there was nothing to prevent Pythagoras from knowing this *before* he evolved his doctrine. Let us suppose he did; in that case he would have been overwhelmed with joy, not despair, at the discovery about the diagonal of the square. Because, to begin with, a numerical relation which cannot be numerically expressed exists nevertheless, defined by completely determined quantities. And then, to comprehend that relation, as such, requires a purer activity of the mind, more independent of the senses, than any relation between numbers.

So great a shock of joy might well have inspired the formula 'everything is number', i.e.: in everything without exception there are relations *analogous* to numerical relations. In any other sense the formula would be stupid, because everything is not number.

I think that is what happened. Because the discovery of incommensurables had tremendous repercussions; one senses this from the number and the kind of allusions made to it. It is continually being cited as a choice example. But if it had been a stir of distress one would feel this in the allusions; what one in fact feels is the contrary. Thus when Socrates, in the *Meno*, wants to prove that all souls come from the 'intelligible heaven'[1] and know by 'recollection' he questions a slave

[1] Presumably a translation of νοητὸς τόπος. Cf. *Republic*, 517b.

To A. W. 1940

about the duplication of the square. So this problem is linked with a knowledge which bears eminent witness to the soul's divine origin. The *Epinomis* (apocrypha of Plato) says: 'What is called by the altogether ridiculous name of geometry is in fact the assimilation (ὁμοίωσις) to one another of numbers (ἀριθμῶν) not naturally similar, an assimilation made manifest by the necessity (πρὸς μοῖραν) of plane objects; whoever is able to understand it sees clearly that this marvel is not of human but of divine origin.'

In my opinion, this text defines geometry as the science of the real numbers. I cannot see any other interpretation.

Plato also puts the incommensurables at the beginning of the *Theaetetus*, the dialogue concerning **knowledge**.

Thales may have acquired an intuitive knowledge of his theorem by representing numerical proportions by means of a plane diagram.

If, as I suppose, Pythagoras constructed a right-angled triangle from two similar triangles in order to form geometrical means, and if he thus obtained, what he knew he could not obtain arithmetically, the geometrical mean between a number and its double – then the note of exultation which is audible in every reference to geometry, and especially to incommensurables, is quite understandable. To find numerical relations which enable one to know in advance the character (even, odd, square, etc.) of numbers which one has not found, and to find non-numerical relations which are as exact as the relations between numbers – these are two intoxicating achievements.

All this implies of course that the idea of proportion as expounded in the fifth book of Euclid existed long before Eudoxus. This is what I meant to suggest by pointing out that Eudoxus was of Pythagorean origin. Without some such theory, Plato's philosophy is unintelligible. He was a contemporary of Eudoxus; but there is no tradition and no 'internal evidence'° (it seems to me) to suggest that he received at any time in his life a revelation from one of his contemporaries. Would he have put into Socrates' mouth an allusion to the diagonal of the square if this had been a subject of scandal in Socrates' day?

However, I am quite willing to believe that the giving of formal proofs only began after the discovery of incommensurables.

There may very well have been crisis and scandal among minds of inferior scientific and philosophic formation. It is indeed more than

---
° In English in the original. See p. ix.

likely. Who knows if the demonstration of the even being equal to the odd may not have been the model for the demonstrations proving a thesis and its contrary (the basis of sophistry) which pullulated in the fifth century and demoralized Athens?

– We are far from agreeing about Nietzsche. Not that I feel any inclination to take him lightly; all I feel is an invincible and almost physical repulsion. Even when he is expressing what I myself think, I find him literally intolerable. I would rather take it on trust that he is a great man than go and see for myself; why go near something that gives me a pain? But I don't see how a lover of wisdom who ends up as he did can be regarded as successful. Admitting that physical factors counted for something in his case, a little humility is seemly in the afflicted – not an unbounded arrogance. If affliction evokes arrogance as a sort of compensation, the case deserves pity but not esteem and still less admiration.

Above all, how can one admit that he was capable of understanding anything about Greece? (To begin with, imagine looking to Wagner to revive it! . . .) His view of the Dionysian man was evidently a self-portrait, but if his view were correct Greece would have foundered as he did.

He was completely mistaken about Dionysus – to say nothing of opposing him to Apollo, which is pure fantasy, because the Greeks confused them in the myths and seem sometimes to have regarded them as identical. Why didn't he take into account Herodotus – who did know what he was talking about – and who said that Dionysus is Osiris? It follows from this that he is the God whom man must imitate in order to save his soul; who was united with man by suffering and death; and with whom man can and ought to be reunited in perfection and bliss. Exactly like Christ.

Neither *hubris*, nor cosmic frenzy, nor Wagner have anything to do with it.

I cannot accept any catastrophic interpretation of Greece and its history, nor that it should be said that they clung 'desperately' to proportion and felt intensely the disproportion between man and God (they were not Hebrews!). True, their conception of existence was a sad one, as it is for all whose eyes are open; but their sadness had a motive; it had meaning *in relation to* the happiness for which man is made and of which he is deprived by the harsh constraints of this world.

To A. W. 1940

They had no taste for affliction, disaster, disequilibrium. Whereas there are so many modern people (and notably Nietzsche, I believe) in whom sadness is connected with a loss of the very instinct for happiness; they feel a need to annihilate themselves. In my opinion, there is no anguish in the Greeks. That is what makes them dear to me. In struggling against anguish one never produces serenity; the struggle against anguish only produces new forms of anguish. But the Greeks possessed grace from the beginning.

In order to discuss the question of mysticism in Greece one must agree upon this distinction. There are people who simply experience states of ecstasy; there are other people who devote themselves almost exclusively to the study of these states, who describe and classify them and, so far as it is possible, induce them. It is the latter who are generally called mystics; and that is why St. Francis is not, I believe, regarded as such. Mysticism in the second sense came into Hellenic civilization with the gnostics and neo-Platonists – perhaps not uninfluenced, as you suggest, by the 'gymno-sophists'. It is possible that in the earlier period the Greeks voluntarily abstained from such studies, believing that there are some things which ought not to be formulated and extending this obligation of secrecy, in certain matters, even to the soul's dialogue with itself. In parenthesis, if they did so believe I think they were quite right; I admire St. Teresa but I think she would be even more admirable if she had never written. But that they knew states of ecstasy and set a high value on them there can be no doubt. The writings of Plato are a sufficient witness. (The role he attributes to love is in itself sufficiently characteristic.) And when, in eulogizing the μανία which emanates from the gods, he says that Dionysus inspires the μανία of the mysteries, it seems to me the passage can only be interpreted as referring to states of ecstasy. Because it cannot refer to states of collective semi-delirium. Where rites combined with teaching are accompanied by states of ecstasy it seems to me that mystical practices are implied.

In this connexion, the fact that Aeschylus was initiated at Eleusis is no reason for distinguishing between him and the rest of Greek thought, because practically everybody was. Diogenes the Cynic is an exception; but that was part of his Cynicism and is an indication that everybody else was initiated. I am speaking of those who matter.

There is a very singular passage in the *Philebus*: 'It is a gift from the gods to men, so it seems to me, thrown down from among them thanks to some Prometheus at the same time as some extremely bright fire; and the ancients (παλαιοί), being better than us and dwelling closer to the gods, have handed on this oracle: that all the things which are said to be everlasting are made out of the one and the many and have the limited and the unlimited inherent in them.'[1] (He goes on to explain that in every field of research it is necessary to grasp the single idea which governs it and then to pass on to the 'many'; that is to say, to posit a certain number of ideas which permit us to qualify and set in order all the things which the single governing idea embraces; and only after finishing this task to pass on to the infinite variety of the things in question. For example: (1) Sound – (2) High pitch, low pitch, interval, etc. – (3) Sounds. He says that modern men do not know how to use this method.) This passage sounds Pythagorean; but the Pythagoreans were too recent to be the παλαιοί referred to. So the reference must be to the pre-Hellenic inhabitants of Greece, or of some foreign country, probably Egypt. But the tone of the passage (gods, Prometheus, oracle, etc.) suggests a religious descent. Presumably it was from Orphism and consequently, perhaps, from the doctrine of the mysteries. Here, in any case, we have proof (which nobody, so far as I know, has pointed out) that what is to our eyes the most original part of the Pythagorean and Platonic doctrines is of very ancient origin. This conception of number as forming a sort of mean between unity (which is the property of thought) and the limitless (ἄπειρος) quantity which is presented in the object is singularly luminous. The prescribed direction (one→many→infinite) entirely precludes what we call induction and generalization. It is remarkable that this method was scrupulously followed by Greek science.

In the same way, with regard to things seen, proportion enables thought to grasp all at once a complex variety in which, without the aid of proportion, it would lose itself. The human soul is exiled in time and space, which rob it of its unity; all the methods of purification are simply techniques for freeing it from the effects of time, so that it may come to feel almost at home in its place of exile. The mere fact of being able to grasp, all at once, a multiplicity of points of view concerning one and the same object makes the soul happy; but regularity and diversity must be so combined that thought is continually on the point

[1] Plato, *Philebus*, 16c.

To A. W. 1940

of losing itself in diversity and continually being rescued by regularity. However, thought is not satisfied with objects fabricated to produce this effect; it aspires to conceive the world itself as analogous to a work of art, to architecture, or dance, or music. For this purpose it is necessary to find in the world regularity within diversity; in other words, to find proportions. It is impossible to admire a work of art without thinking oneself, in a way, its creator and without, in a sense, becoming so; and in the same way, to admire the universe as if it were a work of art is to become, in a manner, its creator. And this leads to a purging of the passions and desires related to the situation of one little human body within the world; they become meaningless when thought takes the world itself for its object. But proportion is indispensable for this result, because without it there can be no equilibrium between thought and the diverse, complex, and changing material of the world. On the other hand, proportion has no value in itself, but only in so far as it is applied, both in the arts and in the natural sciences. Applied in this way, it detaches the mind from desire and leads it towards contemplation, which excludes desire. (All of this, of course, is unsupported, or only remotely supported, by texts.)

In the eyes of the Greeks, the very principle of the soul's salvation was measure, balance, proportion, harmony; because desire is always unmeasured and boundless. Therefore, to conceive the universe as an equilibrium and a harmony is to make it like a mirror of salvation. In relations between men, also, the good consists in abolishing the uncontrolled and unlimited; that is what justice is (so it can only be defined by equality). And it is the same for a man's relations with himself. There is a text in the *Gorgias* on 'geometric equality' as the supreme law of the universe and at the same time the condition for the soul's salvation. These ideas, it seems to me, compose the very atmosphere of the tragedies of Aeschylus.

If, by the sense of disproportion between thought and the world, you meant the sense of being an exile in the world, then I agree; the Greeks experienced intensely the feeling that the soul is in exile. It was from them that this feeling passed into Christianity. Such a feeling does not involve anguish, however, but only bitterness. Moreover, if the Stoics – as I am convinced – invented nothing, but only reproduced in their language the thought of Orphism, Pythagoras, Socrates, Plato, etc., one can then say that this place of the soul's exile is precisely its fatherland, if only it knew how to recognize it. Who knows if the story in the *Odyssey* of Ulysses waking up in Ithaca and not recognizing it is not a symbol with this meaning? The *Odyssey* is obviously packed with philosophical symbols (Sirens, etc.). More than any other people, the Greeks possessed the feeling of necessity. It is a bitter feeling, but it precludes anguish.

Besides, I will never admit that anyone in the 19th century understood anything at all about Greece. Which disposes of a lot of questions.

Your theory that an artist's doctrine has no effect on his art appears to me untenable. I agree that there are problems of the eye and the hand which demand his exclusive attention. But I think his conception of the world and of human life decides what those problems of the eye and hand shall be. This only applies, it is true, to artists of the very first order. But to me the others are not of much interest. I don't believe it can be maintained that the art of Giotto, to mention only him, was unconnected with the Franciscan spirit. And in science, too, I don't think it can be considered irrelevant that Galileo was a Platonist. In general, I don't believe that a man of the very highest order accepts a view of human life, or of the good, etc., which is imposed on him by chance, from outside. (Though he may accept a label for it in this way.) I believe on the contrary that every activity of such a man is closely related to all his other activities. The mystery of very great art is precisely this, that an artist's doctrine passes into the work of his hands; and it matters little whether he can also express it in words.

(*An alternative draft of the preceding paragraph*)
I am quite willing to believe that for many sculptors and painters it is a matter of indifference whether they hold one conception of the world or another. They, I think, are the ones who don't interest me. But it seems to me difficult to maintain that in the case of Giotto there was no connexion between his art and his admiration for St. Francis – or in the case of Leonardo, the Platonic theories – or in the case of the cathedrals, Catholicism (including the heresies). Not that I believe that artists turn aside from the problems occupying their eyes and hands to plunge into abstract speculation (though that, too, may sometimes happen) but I think that the problems which occupy their eyes and hands depend upon the way they conceive human life and the world. This applies only to those of the very highest class. In general, I think

that in men of the very highest class any activity of any kind is closely linked with all their other activities. It is true, of course, that the labels they sometimes accept, which depend upon the age they live in and the sphere in which they move, may be a matter of indifference; but a label is not a doctrine. Clearly, it is the mystery of very great art that the artist's doctrine is expressed through the work of his hands. And I would say the same of science. But very great men are few (moreover, one may disagree about classifying them); and for all the others what you say is perfectly true. And incidentally, don't fail to note that the majority of doctrines are similar in essentials; where there are thought to be differences they often do not exist.

[....] the idea of art as something that induces madness or that it is the proper sphere of the mad is one of the worst blasphemies one can utter. [....]

40 To Edoardo Volterra

> Professor Volterra was in France as an exile from fascist Italy. Simone Weil looked after his correspondence while he was away from Paris on a journey.

[1940]

Dear Edoardo,

I have got the papers on Ptolemy. Those are the ones you wanted me to send, I think? But on looking through them I have found a few incorrect turns of phrase. Here are some examples – 'l'histoire d'Alexandre II montre sa soumission', incorrect. It should be 'montre quelle fut sa soumission', or better, 'fait voir combien il se montra soumis'. – 'il se trompe sur des évènements qui ont eu lieu sous les règnes d'Alexandre I et Ptolémée'. This makes no sense; the meaning, I imagine, is 'il confond avec des évènements...' – 'par cela il détruisait l'argument...'; it should be 'ainsi' or 'par là'; 'par cela' is never French. – 'Il raconte l'étonnement qui l'avait frappé...'. One uses 'raconter' for an event, not an emotion (one uses 'exprimer' for an emotion), and it ought to be 'qui l'a frappé' – 'on leur donnait les moyens pour conquérir...'. Very incorrect. It should be either: 'le moyen de...' (if the means is regarded as sufficient by itself) or else: 'un moyen pour', or again 'la possibilité de...' – I suppose there's nothing to be done about these points? I thought I would mention them on the chance, and meanwhile I'll wait for your instructions before posting the copies. Anyway, the mistakes are few in number and not serious; I could correct them by hand on each copy, if you like?

The part about the agrarian law and Cicero's attitude is very interesting. The Gracchi certainly cannot have foreseen that their ideas would give rise to a project for the general expropriation of everything and everybody.

I do not find the argument on the validity of testaments in Egypt convincing. The king's rights over the country were not those of proprietorship but of absolute sovereignty, deriving from his divinity. If he had been its proprietor he could have sold the country, as a whole or in lots, which, I imagine, is not conceivable for Egypt? I doubt whether the quality of divinity can be passed on by testament. It would be of singular interest to study the various forms of sovereign-worship in antiquity (Persia, Egypt, Rome). Excuse these passing reflections.

The fact that there were no individual proprietors in Egypt proves, unless I am mistaken, that the king's right was not a proprietary right, since it was inalienable. Is it not of the essence of the proprietary right, in the strict sense of the word, that it is alienable unless limited by the order of a superior power?

One statement which struck me in this paper was the following: 'Upon the juridical capacity of the Roman people, which was the source of all law, there was no restriction.' Does this mean that the collectivity, the people as a whole, was the sole source of law and that individuals possessed only such rights as the collectivity loaned to them? This is of urgent interest to me because a French jurist has recently published something about two opposed conceptions of law, one of which recognizes while the other denies the rights of individuals as such. And it so happens: (1) that I have just written something about the analogy between ancient Rome and certain modern phenomena; but as I didn't know whether this analogy held good also for the conception of law, I left that aspect aside; and (2) since law everywhere in the West, except England, I think, is based upon Roman law, the opposition established by the above-mentioned jurist ought to be invalid. It would be a great help to me if you would think this over and give me your considered opinion.

[....]

I hope you are enjoying your books and the country. I urgently recommend you to re-read Marcus Aurelius. Ἀνθρώπῳ οὐδενὶ συμβαίνειν τι δύναται ὃ οὐκ ἔστιν ἀνθρωπικὸν σύμπτωμα – Πᾶν μοι καρπὸς ὃ φέρουσιν αἱ σαὶ ὧραι, ὦ φύσις . . . . ὦ πόλι φίλη Διός.[1] And Epictetus. Δοῦλος Ἐπίκτητος γενόμην, καὶ σώματι πηρὸς – καὶ πενίην Ἴρος, καὶ φίλος ἀθανάτοις.[2] And Aeschylus and Sophocles. Is it not an extraordinary privilege today to understand the one language in which men have known how to express with nobility the relations between man and destiny? And ought we not to show ourselves worthy by making practical use of it? Forgive me for reminding you of this: all of us are continually in need of being reminded of such things. Write to let me know if I can do anything for you. I am at your disposal, as you know. Best wishes to you both.

Simone Weil

41 To Déodat Roché

This letter appeared in the *Cahiers d'Études Cathares*, No. 2, April-June 1949.

23 January 1940 [sic, for 1941]

I have read at Ballard's your article for the Oc number,[3] 'The Cathars and Spiritual Love'. Thanks to Ballard I had previously read your paper on Catharism. These two pieces have made a strong impression on me.

I have long been greatly attracted to the Cathars, although knowing little about them. One of the chief reasons for this attraction is their opinion about the Old Testament, which you express so well in your article when you say so truly that the worship of power caused the Hebrews to lose the idea of good and evil. I have always been kept away from Christianity by its ranking these stories, so full of pitiless cruelty, as sacred texts; and the more so because for twenty centuries these stories have never ceased to influence all the currents of Christian thought – at least if one means by Christianity the churches so denominated today. St. Francis of Assisi himself, who was as clear of this taint as it is possible to be, founded an Order which quickly began to participate in murder and massacre almost immediately after it was formed. I have never been able to understand how it is possible for a reasonable mind to regard the Jehovah of the Bible and the Father who

[1] Meditations, Book IV, 23.
[2] Palatine Anthology, 7.676.
[3] A special number of the *Cahiers du Sud*, devoted to 'Le Génie d'oc'.

is invoked in the Gospel as one and the same being. The influence of the Old Testament and of the Roman Empire, whose tradition was continued by the Papacy, are to my mind the two essential sources of the corruption of Christianity.

Your studies have confirmed a thought of mine which I already had before reading them. It is that Catharism was the last living expression in Europe of pre-Roman antiquity. I believe that before the conquests of Rome the countries of the Mediterranean and the Near East formed a civilization, which was not homogeneous because it varied greatly from one country to another, but was continuous; and I believe that one and the same thought inhabited all its best minds and was expressed in various forms in the mysteries and the initiatory sects of Egypt, Thrace, Greece, and Persia, and that the works of Plato are the most perfect written expression which we possess of that thought. The scarcity of texts makes it, of course, impossible to prove this opinion. But one indication among others is the fact that Plato himself always presents his doctrine as issuing from an ancient tradition, but without ever stating its country of origin. The simplest explanation, in my opinion, is that the philosophical and religious traditions of the countries he knew were merged in one single stream of thought. It is from this thought that Christianity issued; but only the Gnostics, Manichaeans, and Cathars seem to have kept really faithful to it. They alone really escaped the coarseness of mind and baseness of heart which were disseminated over vast territories by the Roman domination and which still, today, compose the atmosphere of Europe.

There is something more in the Manichaeans than in antiquity, or at least than in antiquity as known to us; there are some magnificent conceptions, such as the descent of divinity among men and the rending of the spirit and its dispersal throughout matter. But what above all makes the fact of Catharism a sort of miracle is that it was a religion and not simply a philosophy. I mean that around Toulouse in the 12th century the highest thought dwelt within a whole human environment and not only in the minds of a certain number of individuals. That, it seems to me, is the sole difference between philosophy and religion, so long as religion is something not dogmatic.

No thought attains to its fullest existence unless it is incarnated in a human environment, and by environment I mean something open to the world around, something which is steeped in the surrounding society and is in contact with the whole of it, and not simply a closed circle of disciples around a master. For the lack of such an environment in which to breathe, a superior mind makes a philosophy for itself; but that is a second best and it produces thought of a lesser degree of reality. Probably there was an environment for the Pythagoreans, but this is a subject about which we have practically no knowledge. In Plato's time there was no longer anything of the sort; and one feels continually in his work his regret for the absence of such an environment, a nostalgic regret.

Excuse these rambling reflections; I only wanted you to see that my interest in the Cathars is not a matter of simple historical curiosity, or even of simple intellectual curiosity. It gave me joy to read in your article that Catharism may be regarded as a Christian Pythagoreanism or Platonism; for in my eyes there is nothing above Plato. Simple intellectual curiosity cannot give one contact with the thought of Pythagoras and Plato, because in regard to thought of that kind knowledge and adhesion are one single act of the mind. I believe it is the same as regards the Cathars.

Never has the revival of this kind of thought been so necessary as today. We are living at a time when most people feel, confusedly but keenly, that what was called enlightenment in the 18th century, including the sciences, provides an insufficient spiritual diet; but this feeling is now leading humanity into the darkest paths. There is an urgent need to refer back to those great epochs which favoured the kind of spiritual life of which all that is most precious in science and art is no more than a somewhat imperfect reflection.

That is why I so anxiously hope that your studies of Catharism will arouse the widespread public attention they deserve. But studies of such a theme, however good, cannot suffice. If only you could find a publisher, a collection of original texts, presented intelligibly to the public, would be infinitely desirable....

42 To Admiral Leahy

The draft of a letter to the United States Ambassador at Vichy, written in English.

10.3.41

Excellency,

I am emboldened to write to you by the thought that I am going to speak for many Frenchmen and Frenchwomen who in all parts of the country, in all classes of the population, are thinking many things which they cannot say. They feel deeply grateful for American generosity, but think that such generosity, to be wise, should be subject to some conditions. Two conditions, I think, are of great importance.

In the first place, of course, no help given to France should be in the least harmful or dangerous to the cause of England. Many men and women in France would gladly starve if they felt that through starvation they could be useful to England. Are not people killed in every war, men, women and children? In France, since we have ceased to fight, there is no killing any more, but, as we are still with our hearts on the side of one of the fighters, why should we not suffer and even die, if needful, for the cause which is still ours?

Up to this moment, however, there has not been any need for heroism; we have not yet felt hunger. It may come, of course, even to-morrow; but many people have complained before they were hungry. I am sure of that; for I am living with my father and mother in Marseille, which has been for some time, I believe, the town in the whole non-occupied zone where food is most scarce; my father and I have both lost our situations, so we take care to spend very little money; we had absolutely no food in store; we have never, up till now – and I mean literally never – stood in a 'queue'; yet till now we have eaten, not well, of course, but enough. So I think I can say that there is as yet no hunger in France. Of course, some people may go hungry for want of money; but if that is so, it is due to bad organisation of governmental help, not to scarcity of food. In 1934-35, when food was so plentiful, there was in France, I believe, more hunger than now. Indeed I know it, for during this time, as I wanted to see with my own eyes the life of the working men and women, I worked for a year as a factory girl and lived upon my salary; I have felt and seen hunger then, not now.

That, however, is not to the purpose. The second condition, I think, to which American generosity should be subject is a better treatment of aliens in France. You know, of course, all the facts about the bad treatment of aliens in this country, the concentration-camps, etc. – facts which I, as a Frenchwoman, can scarcely bear to think upon for very shame. In spite of all official promises, these shameful things are still going on. I even happen to know that in the 'camp du Vernet' there has lately been an aggravation.

For the sake of these unhappy people, for the sake, also, of the French men and women to whom honour is dearer than food, I think America should refuse to give any help till these cruel treatments have really ceased – ceased in fact, I mean, not merely upon paper; or, if some time must be allowed for a new and better organisation, it should be a short and quite definite length of time. That would be the only way to move the heavy state bureaucracy to action, since bureaucracy is often devoid of heart or mind, but has always a stomach. The U.S.A. have it now in their power, as suppliers of food, to put a stop to any cruelty going on in France. I beseech you, let them use that power. I would most gladly starve for such an end.

Gratefully and sincerely yours
S. W.

43 To A.W.

Extracts from four letters written from Marseille in 1941-2.

i.

[. . .] Recently, in trying to repeat Archimedes' mechanical method for the quadrature of the parabola I hit upon a different method from his, but analogous to it, and such as he might well have also used; it consists in using for integration the volume of the pyramid instead of the centre of gravity of the triangle. What I mean will be clear if you recall the passage in Archimedes; but it doesn't matter. The point I am concerned about is the following. The centre of gravity of the triangle is simply the point of intersection of the medians. This point of intersection, like the volume of the pyramid, gives the ratio $1/3$. In the same way the point of intersection of the medians of the parallelogram gives the ratio $1/2$, like the area of the triangle. Therefore, the theorems concerning points of intersection of the medians of parallelograms and triangles ought to imply something corresponding to the integrations which provide, respectively, the formulas $1/2 x^2$ and $1/3 x^3$. But in what way? That is what I do not see. What do you think about it? I don't know if I have made myself clear.

Can you tell me if Neugebauer has published anything new on ancient mathematics or astronomy since the book I have seen (which, I think, was of 1934)? [. . . .]

ii.

[. . .] I have been in real need of a physicist lately, to ask him the following question. Planck justifies the introduction of quanta of energy by the assimilation of entropy to a probability (strictly, the logarithm of a probability); because, in order to calculate the probability of a macroscopic state of a system, it is necessary to postulate a finite number of corresponding microscopic states (discrete states). So the justification is that the calculus of probabilities is numerical. But why was it not possible to use a continuous calculus of probabilities, with generalized number instead of discrete numbers? (Considering that there are games of chance in which probability is continuous.) There would then have been no need of quanta. Why could not this have been tried? Planck says nothing about it. T. does not know of any physicist here who could enlighten me. What do you think about this? [. . . .]

iii.

Your reply about Planck did not satisfy me. In the first place, while it is true that Planck's reasons have no more than a historical interest, it is also true that the reasons for which the theory of quanta is accepted today have only a historical interest, because the present moment, too, will soon be no more than history.

Secondly, this is how I see the question. There are two macroscopic states, A and B; there is a ratio between their respective entropies and, combining the two notions, between their respective probabilities; between the number of microscopic states corresponding to each of them, on this interpretation of probability. According to classical mechanics this number is infinite; therefore it is necessary to find a well-determined ratio between two infinites. Such ratios do exist; for example, between two segments if each is regarded as a set of points. The pointer of a roulette wheel may stop at any point on the disc; the number of possibilities is infinite. The probability of its stopping at green or red, for example, is proportional to the lengths of the arcs so coloured. To apply the notion of continuous probability it would be necessary to find some way of representing the relations between microscopic states and macroscopic states; an image, an analogy, such that the infinite number of microscopic states corresponding to a macroscopic state have finite ratios measurable by irrational numbers. It appears to me to be experimentally impossible to establish sufficiently precise measurements to exclude this possibility. (This seems to me obvious because rational and irrational numbers can be infinitely close.)

I have read a collection of Planck's lectures, of which one is entitled 'Genesis of Quantum Theory'; I have also read the part concerning quanta in his four-volume textbook of Physics; in both places he explicitly says that probability demands discontinuity; he makes no reference to the slightest attempt to use probability without sacrificing continuity. If he had made such an attempt and failed, it seems to me he would have mentioned it.

If I have succeeded in making clear the question I have in mind, I wish you would put it to a physicist.

[. . . .]

As regards Stévin, I made a thorough study of his *Arithmetic* in 1934 or 1935, and I have somewhere a whole notebook full of résumés and extracts from that work; I have not read his works on mechanics, but I have seen Lagrange's account of some of his ideas.

iv.

[. . . .] Have you read St. John of the Cross? It is my chief occupation at the moment. I have also been given a Sanskrit text of the Gita, transliterated into the Roman alphabet. The thought is extraordinarily similar in both. Mystical thought is identical in all countries. I believe that Plato should also be included, and that he took mathematics as material for mystical contemplation. [. . . .]

44 To Joë Bousquet

> Joë Bousquet was permanently paralysed as the result of a wound in the first world war. Simone Weil had sent him her Plan for an Organization of Front-Line Nurses and he had replied with a letter of commendation, of which she hoped to make use. See pages 145-153.

[Marseille] 12 May 1942

Cher ami,

First of all, thank you for what you have just done for me. If your letter is effective, as I hope, you will have done it, not for me but for others through me, for your younger brothers who should be infinitely dear to you since the same fate has struck them. Perhaps some of them will owe to you, just before the moment of death, the solace of an exchange of sympathy.

You are specially privileged in that the present state of the world is a reality for you. Perhaps even more so than for those who at this moment are killing and dying, wounding and being wounded, because they are taken unawares, without knowing where they are or what is happening to them; and, like you in your time, they are unable to think thoughts appropriate to their situation. As for the others, the people here for example, what is happening is a confused nightmare for some of them, though very few, and for the majority it is a vague background like a theatrical drop-scene. In either case it is unreal.

But you, on the other hand, for twenty years you have been repeating in thought that destiny which seized and then released so many men, but which seized you permanently; and which now returns again to seize millions of men. You, I repeat, are now really equipped to think it. Or if you are still not quite ready – as I think you are not – you have at least only a thin shell to break before emerging from the darkness inside the egg into the light of truth. It is a very ancient image. The egg is this world we see. The bird in it is Love, the Love which is God himself and which lives in the depths of every man, though at first as an invisible seed. When the shell is broken and the being is released, it still has this same world before it. But it is no longer inside. Space is opened and torn apart. The spirit, leaving the miserable body in some corner, is transported to a point outside space, which is not a point of view, which has no perspective, but from which this world is seen as it is, unconfused by perspective. Compared to what it is inside the egg, space has become an infinity to the second or rather the third power. The moment stands still. The whole of space is filled, even though sounds can be heard, with a dense silence which is not an absence of sound but is a positive object of sensation; it is the secret word, the word of Love who holds us in his arms from the beginning.

You, when once you have emerged from the shell, will know the reality of war, which is the most precious reality to know because war is unreality itself. To know the reality of war is the Pythagorean harmony, the unity of opposites; it is the plenitude of knowledge of the real. That is why you are infinitely privileged, because you have war permanently lodged in your body, waiting for years in patient fidelity until you are ripe to know it. Those who fell beside you did not have time to collect their thought from its frivolous wandering and focus it upon their destiny. And those who came back unwounded have all killed their past by oblivion, even if they have seemed to remember it, because war is affliction and it is as easy to direct one's thought voluntarily towards affliction as it would be to persuade an untrained dog to walk into a fire and let itself be burnt. To think affliction, it is necessary to bear it in one's flesh, driven very far in like a nail, and for a long time, so that thought may have time to grow strong enough to regard it. To regard it from outside, having succeeded in leaving the body and even, in a sense, the soul as well. Body and soul remain not only pierced through but nailed down at a fixed point. Whether or not affliction imposes literal immobility, there is always enforced immobility in this sense that a part of the soul is always steeped, monotonously, incessantly, and inextricably, in pain. Thanks to this immobility the infinitesimal seed of divine love placed in the soul can slowly grow and bear fruit in patience – $\dot{\epsilon}\nu\ \dot{\upsilon}\pi o\mu\epsilon\nu\hat{\eta}$ is the divinely beautiful Gospel expression. Translators say *in patientia*, but $\dot{\upsilon}\pi o\mu\dot{\epsilon}\nu\epsilon\iota\nu$ is quite another thing. It means to remain where one is, motionless, in expectation, unshaken and unmoved by any external shock.

Fortunate are those in whom the affliction which enters their flesh is the same one that afflicts the world itself in their time. They have the opportunity and the function of knowing the truth of the world's affliction and contemplating its reality. And that is the redemptive function itself. Twenty centuries ago, in the Roman Empire, slavery was the affliction of the age, and crucifixion was its extreme expression.

But alas for those who have this function and do not fulfil it.

When you say that you do not feel the difference between good and evil, your words are not serious if taken literally because you are speaking of another man in you who is clearly the evil in you; you are well aware – or when there is any doubt a careful scrutiny can nearly always dispel it – which of your thoughts, words and deeds strengthen that other man in you at your expense and which ones strengthen you at his. What you mean is that you have not yet consented to recognize this difference as the distinction between good and evil.

It is not an easy consent to give, because it commits one irrevocably. There is a kind of virginity in the soul as regards good, which is lost for ever once the soul has given this consent – just as a woman's virginity is lost after she has yielded to a man. The woman may become unfaithful, adulterous, but she will never again be a virgin. So she is frightened when she is about to yield. Love triumphs over this fear.

For every human being there is a point in time, a limit, unknown to anyone and above all to himself, but absolutely fixed, beyond which the soul cannot keep this virginity. If, before this precise moment, fixed from all eternity, it has not consented to be possessed by the good, it will immediately afterwards be possessed in spite of itself by the bad.

A man may yield to the bad at any moment of his life, because he yields to it unconsciously and unaware that he is admitting an external authority into his soul; and before surrendering her virginity to it the soul drugs herself with an opiate. To be possessed by the bad, it is not necessary to have consented to it; but the good never possesses the soul until she has said yes. And such is the fear of consummating the union that no soul has the power to say yes to the good unless she is urgently constrained by the almost immediate approach of the time-limit which will decide her eternal fate. For one man this time-limit may occur at the age of five, for another at the age of sixty. In any case, neither before nor after it has been reached is it possible to locate it temporally; in the sphere of duration this instantaneous and eternal choice can only be seen refracted. For those who have yielded to the bad a long time before the limiting moment is reached, this moment is no longer real. The most a human being can do is to guard intact his faculty for saying yes to the good, until the time when the limiting moment has almost been reached.

It appears to me certain that for you the limiting moment has not yet arrived. I lack the power to read men's hearts, but it seems to me that there are signs that it is not far distant. Your faculty for consent is certainly intact.

I think that when you have consented to the good you will break the shell, after an interval perhaps, but doubtless a short one; and the moment you are outside it there will be pardon for that bullet which once pierced the centre of your body, and thus also for the whole universe which drove it there.

The intelligence has a part in preparing the nuptial consent to God. It consists in looking at the evil in oneself and hating it. Not trying to get rid of it, but simply descrying it and keeping one's eyes fixed upon it until one feels repulsion – even before one has said yes to its opposite.

I believe that the root of evil, in everybody perhaps, but certainly in those whom affliction has touched and above all if the affliction is biological, is day-dreaming. It is the sole consolation, the unique resource of the afflicted; the one solace to help them bear the fearful burden of time; and a very innocent one, besides being indispensable. So how could it be possible to renounce it? It has only one disadvantage, which is that it is unreal. To renounce it for the love of truth is really to abandon all one's possessions in a mad excess of love and to follow him who is the personification of Truth. And it is really to bear the cross; because time is the cross.

While the limiting moment is still remote, it is not necessary to do this; but it is necessary to recognize day-dreaming for what it is. And even while one is sustained by it one must never forget for a moment that in all its forms – those that seem most inoffensive by their childishness, those that seem most respectable by their seriousness and their connexion with art or love or friendship – in all its forms without exception, it is falsehood. It excludes love. Love is real.

I would never dare to speak to you like this if all these thoughts were the product of my own mind. But although I am unwilling to place any reliance on such impressions, I do really have the feeling, in spite of myself, that God is addressing all this to you, for love of you, through me. In the same way, it does not matter if the consecrated host is made of the poorest quality flour, not even if it is three parts rotten.

You say that I pay for my moral qualities by distrust of myself. But my attitude towards myself, which is not distrust but a mixture of contempt and hatred and repulsion, is to be explained on a lower level –

on the level of biological mechanisms. For twelve years I have suffered from pain around the central point of the nervous system, the meeting-place of soul and body; this pain persists during sleep and has never stopped for a second. For a period of ten years it was so great, and was accompanied by such exhaustion, that the effort of attention and intellectual work was usually almost as despairing as that of a condemned man the day before his execution; and often much more so, for my efforts seemed completely sterile and without even any temporary result. I was sustained by the faith, which I acquired at the age of fourteen, that no true effort of attention is ever wasted, even though it may never have any visible result, either direct or indirect. Nevertheless, a time came when I thought my soul menaced, through exhaustion and an aggravation of the pain, by such a hideous and total breakdown that I spent several weeks of anguished uncertainty whether death was not my imperative duty – although it seemed to me appalling that my life should end in horror. As I told you, I was only able to calm myself by deciding to live conditionally, for a trial period.

A little earlier, when I had already been for years in this physical state, I worked for nearly a year in engineering factories in the Paris region. The combination of personal experience and sympathy for the wretched mass of people around me, in which I formed, even in my own eyes, an undistinguishable item, implanted so deep in my heart the affliction of social degradation that I have felt a slave ever since, in the Roman sense of the word.

During all this time, the word God had no place at all in my thoughts. It never had, until the day – about three and a half years ago – when I could no longer keep it out. At a moment of intense physical pain, while I was making the effort to love, although believing I had no right to give any name to the love, I felt, while completely unprepared for it (I had never read the mystics), a presence more personal, more certain, and more real than that of a human being; it was inaccessible both to sense and to imagination, and it resembled the love that irradiates the tenderest smile of somebody one loves. Since that moment, the name of God and the name of Christ have been more and more irresistibly mingled with my thoughts.

Until then my only faith had been the Stoic *amor fati* as Marcus Aurelius understood it, and I had always faithfully practised it – to love the universe as one's city, one's native country, the beloved fatherland of every soul; to cherish it for its beauty, in the total integrity of the order and necessity which are its substance, and all the events that occur in it.

The result was that the irreducible quantity of hatred and repulsion which goes with suffering and affliction recoiled entirely upon myself. And the quantity is very great, because the suffering in question is located at the very root of my every single thought, without exception.

This is so much the case that I absolutely cannot imagine the possibility that any human being could feel friendship for me. If I believe in yours it is only because I have confidence in you and you have assured me of it, so that my reason tells me to believe it. But this does not make it seem any the less impossible to my imagination.

Because of this propensity of my imagination I am all the more tenderly grateful to those who accomplish this impossibility. Because friendship is an incomparable, immeasurable boon to me, and a source of life – not metaphorically but literally. Since it is not only my body but my soul itself that is poisoned all through by suffering, it is impossible for my thought to dwell there and it is obliged to travel elsewhere. It can only dwell for brief moments in God; it dwells often among things; but it would be against nature for human thought never to dwell in anything human. Thus it is literally true that friendship gives to my thought all the life it has, apart from what comes to it from God or from the beauty of the world.

So you can see what you have done for me by giving me yours.

I say these things to you because you can understand them; for your last book contains a sentence, in which I recognize myself, about the mistake your friends make in thinking that you exist. That shows a type of sensibility which is only intelligible to those who experience existence directly and continuously as an evil. For them it is certainly very easy to do as Christ asks and deny themselves. Perhaps it is too easy. Perhaps it is without merit. And yet I believe that to have it made so easy is an immense privilege.

I am convinced that affliction on the one hand, and on the other hand joy, when it is a complete and pure commitment to perfect beauty, are the only two keys which give entry to the realm of purity, where one can breathe: the home of the real.

But each of them must be unmixed: the joy without a shadow of incompleteness, the affliction completely unconsoled.

You understand me, of course. That divine love which one touches in the depth of affliction, like Christ's resurrection through crucifixion, that love which is the central core and intangible essence of joy, is not a consolation. It leaves pain completely intact.

I am going to say something which is painful to think, more painful to say, and almost unbearably painful to say to those one loves. For anyone in affliction, evil can perhaps be defined as being everything that gives any consolation.

A pure joy, which in some cases may replace pain or in others may be superimposed on it, is not a consolation. On the other hand, there is often a consolation in morbidly aggravating one's pain. I don't know if I am expressing this properly; it is all quite clear to me.

The refuge of laziness and inertia, a temptation to which I succumb very often, almost every day, or I might say every hour, is a particularly despicable form of consolation. It compels me to despise myself.

I perceive that I have not answered your letter, and yet I have a lot to say about it. I must do it another time. Today I'll confine myself to thanking you for it.

Yours most truly,°

S. Weil

I enclose the English poem, *Love*,[1] which I recited to you. It has played a big role in my life, because I was repeating it to myself at the moment when Christ came to take possession of me for the first time. I thought I was only reciting a beautiful poem but, unknown to me, it was a prayer.

° In English in the original. See p. ix.
[1] George Herbert's poem, 'Love bade me welcome; yet my soul drew back. . . .'

PART III

1942-1943

On arriving in New York from Marseille in June 1942, Simone Weil immediately began to appeal for employment with the Free French in London, where she hoped to be given some arduous and dangerous mission to the Continent. She finally got to England at the end of November 1942, only to be bitterly disappointed. Her letters of 1943 reveal her misery at being given purely intellectual work. What these letters do not reveal, however, though I have referred to it in a note between letters 55 and 56, is that she virtually starved herself to death in England. She died, at the age of thirty-four, at a sanatorium near Ashford in Kent, on 24 August 1943, from an affection of the lungs complicated by voluntary malnutrition.

Suicide is doubtfully compatible with Simone Weil's philosophy, though it is true that she admired the Catharist *Perfecti*, who sometimes died from self-inflicted starvation. In her case, however, I think one can distinguish between deliberately suicidal behaviour and behaviour which she felt obliged to adopt for other reasons while accepting that it might or would prove fatal. She considered that as a Frenchwoman in England she had no right to eat more than the official rations of the civilian population in France, and having fallen ill she felt uneasy about eating any food at all while she was unable to contribute to the British war effort. This may be an unbalanced way of reasoning, but it is only suicidal in the sense that it is suicidal to refuse to get into a life-boat in order to leave more room for others.

45 To Maurice Schumann

New York, 30 July 1942

Cher ami,

      I very often listened to your praises in France. You are very popular there. Every time I heard you spoken of in this way I was delighted, and I remembered Henri IV and the lecture-room where we listened to Chartier.[1]

I embarked for New York from Marseille, where I had been for a year and a half, on 14 May. Although urged by my parents, who wanted to escape from anti-semitism without being separated from me, I would never have left if I had known how difficult it is to get from New York to London.

I had considerable responsibility for distributing one of the most important clandestine publications in the free zone, *Les Cahiers du Témoignage Chrétien*. I had the consolation, amid all the surrounding sadness, of sharing in the country's suffering; and I knew enough about my own particular type of imagination to be aware that France's misfortune would hurt me much more from a distance than when I was there. And so it does; and the passing of time only makes the pain more and more unbearable. Moreover, I have the feeling that by leaving France I committed an act of desertion. This thought is intolerable.

To leave was like tearing up my roots, and I forced myself to it solely in the hope that it would enable me to take a bigger and more effective part in the efforts and dangers and sufferings of this great struggle.

I had and still have two ideas, one or the other of which I would like to realize.

One of them is set forth in the enclosed paper. I believe it might save the lives of many soldiers, considering the number of deaths in battle due to lack of *immediate* care (cases of 'shock'°, 'exposure'°, loss of blood).

In the spring of '40 I tried to get it adopted in France, and was well on the way to success, but events moved too rapidly. I was in Paris, where I remained, in the belief that there would be fighting, until 13 June. On that day I left, having seen on the walls the placards proclaiming Paris an open city. Since the armistice my one desire has been

---

[1] Better known in England by his *nom de plume*, Alain.

to get to England. I made several attempts to do so, legally or illegally, but they all failed. A year and a half ago I let my parents begin negotiations, on my behalf as well as their own, to emigrate to America – in the belief that New York could be simply a stepping-stone to London. Everybody here tells me it was a mistake.

My second thought was that I could work more effectively in secret operations if I left France and returned with precise instructions and a mission – preferably dangerous.

I will not go into details about this because I have done so in another letter to you, which I have entrusted to a friend of my family's who is soon leaving for England.

It seems to me that the first condition for carrying out either of these ideas is to move from New York to London.

I imagine you are in a position to help me, and I urgently beg for your support. I really believe I can be useful; and I appeal to you as a comrade to get me out of the too painful moral situation in which I find myself.

A lot of people don't understand why it is a painful moral situation; but you certainly do. We used to have a great deal in common once, when we were students together. It gave me real joy when I learnt, in France, that you have an important position in London.

I confidently rely on you.

With all good wishes,
Simone Weil

(*Enclosure*)

PLAN FOR AN ORGANIZATION OF FRONT-LINE NURSES

The following project was favourably reported on in France, by the Army Commission of the Senate at the War Ministry, in May 1940. Owing to the rapid evolution of events, no attempt at putting it into practice was possible.

Attached hereto is a letter about the project from Joë Bousquet, a disabled veteran of the first world war. Wounded in the spine in 1918, he has been immobilized in bed ever since then by the resultant paraplegia. The experience of war has remained much closer to him than to those who resumed a normal life after 1918; on the other hand, his judgement is that of a mature man. Therefore his opinion is valuable.

The project is concerned with the formation of a special body of front-line nurses. It would be a very mobile organization and should in principle be always at the points of greatest danger, to give 'first aid'° during battles. It could start as an experiment with a small nucleus of ten, or even less; and it could come into operation at the shortest possible notice, because hardly any preparation is required. An elementary knowledge of nursing would suffice, because nothing can be done under fire except dressings, tourniquets, and perhaps injections.

The indispensable moral qualities for the work are not of a kind which can be taught, and it would be no problem to eliminate any women who volunteered without possessing them. The horrors of war are so distinct today in everyone's imagination that one can regard any woman who is capable of volunteering for such work as being very probably capable of performing it.

This project may appear impracticable at first sight, because of its novelty. But a little reflection will show that it is not only practicable but very easy to carry out. The consequences of its failure would be almost negligible, whereas its success would be of really considerable value.

It is easy to try out because it could be started with a very small number of volunteers; and just because the initial number would be so small, no organization would be required. If the first experiment succeeded, the original nucleus would be gradually enlarged and the organization would be developed *pari passu* with its requirements. In any case, the nature of its work would prevent the organization from ever becoming very large; nor is it necessary that it should be.

Nothing could prevent the experiment from succeeding, except the incapacity of the women engaged in it to fulfil their task.

There are only two risks. First, that the women's courage might fail under fire; and second, that their presence among the soldiers might have undesirable moral effects.

Neither could arise if the women who volunteer are of a quality which corresponds to their resolution. Soldiers would never show disrespect to a woman who was brave under fire. The sole necessary precaution would be to ensure that the women were only with the soldiers during battles and not during rest periods.

Clearly, these women would need to have a good deal of courage.

They would need to offer their lives as a sacrifice. They should be ready to be always at the most dangerous places and to face as much if not more danger than the soldiers who are facing the most; and this without being sustained by the offensive spirit but, on the contrary, devoting themselves to the wounded and dying.

But if the experiment succeeded, its advantages would be proportional to the difficulty.

This difficulty is more apparent than real, in view of the small number of volunteers and particularly of the first nucleus which, once again, could be fewer than ten. It is probable, and almost certain, that one could easily find ten women of sufficient courage.

For those who were added later to the original nucleus there would be the strong spur of emulation.

If, at the first experiment, the women should fail under fire, or behave unsuitably in their relations with the soldiers, it would be simple to disband the organization, return the women to the rear, and drop the whole scheme.

The experiment having been conducted on a minute scale and without publicity, the consequences would be nil, except for any resulting losses of life.

But these losses would be infinitesimal, in number, on the scale of the war. One can say negligible; because the death of two or three human beings is, in fact, hardly considered as a loss at all in an operation of war.

In a general way, there is no reason to regard the life of a woman, especially if she has passed her first youth without marrying or having children, as more valuable than a man's life; and all the less so if she has accepted the risk of death. It would be simple to make mothers, wives, and girls below a certain age ineligible.

The question of physical stamina is less important than it appears at first sight, even if the group had to work in very severe climates, because the nature of the work would make it easy to ensure long and frequent periods of rest. The women would not be called upon for long-sustained endurance like soldiers. It would be easy to proportion their efforts to their capacities.

At first, the fact that modern war is motorized may appear an obstacle; but on reflection it appears that this probably rather facilitates the scheme.

When infantry is moved up to the line in lorries there seems very little objection to arranging that in one of every so many lorries there shall be a place reserved for a woman. It would mean one rifle less, but the presence of this woman would have a material and moral effect which would certainly make that disadvantage negligible.

It may be thought that even if the experiment succeeded with a small nucleus it would be impossible to recruit larger numbers because of the difficulty of the work.

But even if the membership of the group never exceeded a few dozen, though this is unlikely, its value would still be very considerable.

Equally, if after a certain time the losses were considered too heavy to justify continuing the experiment, its achievements up to that time would remain and would far outweigh the losses.

Thus the objections which immediately arise on first consideration of this project are reduced to very little, one could almost say to nothing, on closer examination. Its advantages, on the other hand, become more obvious and appear all the greater the more clearly one considers them. The first and most obvious is the actual work which these women would regularly have to do. Being present at the most dangerous places and accompanying the soldiers under fire, which ordinary stretcher-bearers, first aid men, and nurses do not do, they would often be able to save lives by giving summary but immediate aid.

The moral support they would bring to all those they assisted would also be inestimable. They would comfort men's last moments by receiving messages for their families; they would mitigate by their presence and their words the agony of waiting, sometimes so long and so painfully, for the arrival of stretcher-bearers.

If that were all, it would be already a sufficient reason for organizing such a group of women. The considerable advantage it represents is offset by almost no disadvantages. But there are other considerations involved with this project which may perhaps be of capital importance in the general conduct of the war.

In order to estimate them, one must remember the essential role played in the present war by moral factors. They count for very much more than in past wars; and it is one of the main reasons for Hitler's successes that he was the first to see this.

Hitler has never lost sight of the essential need to strike everybody's imagination; his own people's, his enemies', and the innumerable spectators'. His own people's, in order to drive them incessantly forward; the enemy's, in order to provoke the maximum of psychological disarray; the spectators', in order to astonish and impress.

For this purpose, one of his most effective instruments has been such special bodies as the S.S., and the groups of parachutists who were the first to land in Crete, and others as well.

These groups consist of men selected for special tasks, who are prepared not only for risking their lives but for death. That is the essential point. They have a different inspiration from the rest of the army, an inspiration resembling a faith or a religious spirit.

Not that Hitlerism deserves to be called a religion. But it is quite undoubtedly a religion-substitute, and that is one of the principal causes of its power.

These men are unmoved by suffering and death, either for themselves or for all the rest of humanity. Their heroism originates from an extreme brutality. The groups they compose correspond perfectly to the spirit of the régime and the designs of their leader.

We cannot copy these methods of Hitler's. First, because we fight in a different spirit and with different motives; and also because, when it is a question of striking the imagination, copies never succeed. Only the new is striking.

But if we neither can nor ought to copy these methods, we do need to have their equivalents. This need is perhaps a vital one.

If the Russians have so far stood up to the Germans better than other people, one of the reasons may be that they dispose of psychological methods equivalent to Hitler's.

We ought not to copy the Russians either. We ought to create something new. This gift of creation is in itself a sign of moral vitality which will encourage the hopes of those who count upon us, while discouraging the enemy's hopes.

The value of special formations in which every member is ready to die can hardly be disputed. Not only can they be entrusted with tasks for which other troops are less suitable, but their mere existence is a powerful stimulant and source of inspiration for an army. For this, all that is necessary is that the spirit of sacrifice be expressed in acts and not words.

In our age, propaganda is an essential factor for success. It was the making of Hitler; nor has it been neglected by his enemies.

But although we give a lot of thought to propaganda for the rear, we think less about it for the front. Yet it is just as important there; only it requires different methods. At the rear, propaganda is carried on by words. At the front, verbal propaganda must be replaced by the propaganda of action.

The existence of special formations inspired by the spirit of total sacrifice is a continual propaganda of action. Such formations are necessarily the product of a religious inspiration; not in the sense of adherence to any definite church, but in a much less easily definable sense, for which nevertheless only the word religious is appropriate. There are circumstances in which this inspiration is an even more important factor for victory than the purely military ones. This can be verified by studying how Joan of Arc or Cromwell won their victories. It may well be that our own circumstances are of this kind. Our enemies are driven on by an idolatry, a substitute for religious faith. It may be that our victory depends upon the presence among us of a corresponding inspiration, but authentic and pure. And not only the presence of such an inspiration, but its expression in appropriate symbols. An inspiration is only active when it is expressed, and not in words but in deeds.

The S.S. are a perfect expression of the Hitlerian inspiration. If one may believe neutral reports, they exhibit at the front the heroism of brutality, and carry it to the extreme possible limits of courage. To demonstrate to the world that we are worth more than our enemies, we cannot claim to have more courage, because it would be quantitatively impossible. But we can and ought to demonstrate that our courage is qualitatively different, is courage of a more difficult and rarer kind. Theirs is a debased and brutal courage; it springs from the will to power and destruction. Just as our aims are different from theirs, so our courage too springs from a wholly different inspiration.

There could be no better symbol of our inspiration than the corps of women suggested here. The mere persistence of a few humane services in the very centre of the battle, the climax of inhumanity, would be a signal defiance of the inhumanity which the enemy has chosen for himself and which he compels us also to practise. The challenge would be all the more conspicuous because the services would be performed by women and with a maternal solicitude. These women would in fact be only a handful and the number of soldiers they could help would be proportionately small; but the effect of a moral symbol is independent of statistics.

A courage not inflamed by the impulse to kill, but capable of supporting, at the point of greatest danger, the prolonged spectacle of wounds and agony, is certainly of a rarer quality than that of the young S.S. fanatics.

A small group of women exerting day after day a courage of this kind would be a spectacle so new, so significant, and charged with such obvious meaning, that it would strike the imagination more than any of Hitler's conceptions have done. What is now necessary is to strike harder than he. This corps of women would undoubtedly offer one way of doing so.

Although composed of unarmed women, it would certainly impress the enemy soldiers, in the sense that their presence and their behaviour would be a new and unexpected revelation of the depth of the moral resources and resolution on our side.

The existence of this corps would equally impress the general public, both in the countries involved in the war and in the neutrals. Its symbolic force would be appreciated everywhere. The contrast between this force and the S.S. would make a more telling argument than any propaganda slogan. It would illustrate with supreme clarity the two roads between which humanity today is forced to choose.

And the impression upon our own soldiers would certainly be greater still.

The enemy's soldiers have an advantage over ours, from the purely military point of view, in having been separated from their families for ten years while they were being drilled for war. The war atmosphere seems natural to them, because they have scarcely known any other. Having breathed only the air of violence, destruction, and conquest, they have no conception of the value of home life. So, whatever its hardships, this war is not an upheaval for them, but simply the continuation and fruition of what went before.

But French and English and American youths have felt and still feel uprooted by it. Their previous experience was of quiet family life, and all they want is to return to it after a victory whose purpose is to safeguard it.

An aggressor country always enjoys a considerable initial advantage in morale, provided the aggression was prepared and premeditated.

The German aggression has uprooted our young men from their natural life and set them in an atmosphere which is alien to them, but natural to their enemies. In order to defend their homes they have to begin by leaving them, and indeed almost forgetting them, because they must live in surroundings where there is nothing to recall them. Thus the atmosphere of the war prevents them from remembering the war's purpose. On the side of the aggressor the exact opposite happens. So it is not surprising that the aggressor holds the initiative.

And that is why the impetus of aggression is never opposed with equal impetus unless the defenders are fighting on their own ground, near their homes, and almost desperate with the fear of losing them.

To transform our soldiers into brutal young fanatics like Hitler's youth is neither possible nor desirable. But their fire can be kindled to the full by keeping as clearly alive as possible the thought of the homes they are defending.

How could this be done better than by sending with them into the firing-line and wherever there is the most brutal carnage something which evokes the homes they have been obliged to leave, and which evokes them not sentimentally but inspiringly? In this way they would be spared a single moment of the depressing sense of a complete break between themselves and all that they love.

This corps of women could be precisely such a concrete and inspiring evocation of far distant homes.

The ancient Germans, those semi-nomadic tribes whom the Romans could never subjugate, were aware of the inspirational value of a feminine presence in the thick of battle. They used to place in the vanguard of their lines a young girl surrounded by the élite of their youthful warriors.

And the Russians today, it is said, find it an advantage to let women serve in the firing-line.

Besides caring for the wounded, the members of this feminine corps would be able to perform all sorts of other services. At critical moments, when there is too much to be done, it would be natural for officers and N.C.O.'s to make use of them for any task except the handling of weapons: for liaison, rallying-points, transmission of orders. At such times, assuming that they retained their sang-froid, their sex would be a positive asset for these tasks.

Clearly, they would need to have been carefully selected. The presence of women can be an embarrassment if they do not possess a certain amount of that cool and virile resolution which prevents them from setting any store by themselves in any circumstances whatever. This cool resolution is a quality not often found allied in the same person with the tenderness required for comforting pain and agony. But although the combination is rare, it can be found.

No woman would think of volunteering for the service outlined here unless she possessed both the tenderness and the cool resolution, or unless she was unbalanced. But those in the second category could easily be weeded out before the moment of coming under fire.

It would suffice, to begin with, to find about ten women genuinely fitted for such a task. These women certainly exist. It would be easy to find them.

It seems to me impossible to conceive any other way in which these few women could be so effectively used as in the work I have suggested. And in a struggle so severe and so vital we ought so far as possible to use every human being with the maximum of effectiveness.

Addendum. – Herewith an extract from the *Bulletin of the American College of Surgeons*, of April 1942 (p. 104):

'The early application of simple prophylactic or therapeutic measures can frequently prevent shock or overcome mild shock, whereas employment of all presently available methods may prove futile if shock has persisted and become increasingly severe upon the field.'

According to the American Red Cross, by far the greatest proportion of deaths in battle are the result of 'shock'°, 'exposure'°, and loss of blood, *which can only be prevented by immediate treatment.*

The American Red Cross has developed a system of plasma injections which can be operated *on the battle-field* in cases of shock, burns, and haemorrhage (ibid., p. 137).

46 To the same

New York, 30 July 1942

Cher ami,

This letter, which will be brought to you by Captain M.-F. goes into more detail than my first one, which no doubt you have received.

I am told that your particular job concerns liaison with the illegal work in France. There is no question that the liaison is insufficient. A.Ph. has said so plainly, and he is quite right.

It is probably important, both from the strictly military point of view and from the even more essential one of propaganda by deeds, that a bombardment should sometimes coincide with an act of sabotage.

And more generally, whatever strategic plans are being evolved at a high level, it is essential to establish and maintain a connexion between them and the illegal work in France.

From the point of view of morale it is absolutely essential. At the moment, the sense of lack of co-ordination is having a deplorable moral effect. And there will come a moment when the morale of the French people will be an essential factor for victory.

For all these reasons, agents must be sent over from time to time. (It is being done, of course; but I believe it would be well to send more.) Other kinds of liaison, however effective, can never entirely replace this kind.

A woman is as suitable for this type of mission as a man, even more so provided she has a sufficient amount of resolution, sang-froid, and spirit of sacrifice.

I really believe I could be useful in this way. I would accept any degree of risk (including certain death if the objective was sufficiently important). I will leave it at that. You know me well enough, I think, to know that what I say is the result of long and mature reflection, and that I have weighed everything and reached a cool resolve which, I like to think, I shall not go back on and which will express itself in act when the opportunity is allowed me.

I have had several chances to test my sang-froid in face of an imminent threat of death and have been satisfied that I possess it. You know me well enough to know also that I would not say this unless it were true.

I would willingly undertake a mission of sabotage. And as for the transmission of general instructions, I would be all the more suitable for that because I only left France on May 14 of this year and was in contact with the clandestine movements. In particular I know well, because I have collaborated with him, the organizer of the paper, *Les Cahiers du Témoignage Chrétien*, who is himself in continual contact with the leaders of other clandestine groups (in the unoccupied zone).

To Maurice Schumann 1942

Moreover, the police did not trace this activity of mine.

I beg you, get me over to London. Don't leave me to die of chagrin here. I appeal to you as a comrade.

Best wishes,
Simone Weil

47 To the same

New York [1942]

Cher ami,

Your letter brought me great encouragement at a time when the distress of being so far away from the scene of struggle and suffering, with the additional burden of moral isolation, was becoming very hard to bear.

It is a joy to discover that our views are very close. They were so when we were both young and they are perhaps more so now, after a parallel evolution.

Not that I am in a position to put 'tala' after my name. I have no right to, because I have not been baptized.

And yet it seems to me that if I did so sign myself I should not be lying. (Certainly not if one takes the word in its etymological sense.[1])

I adhere totally to the mysteries of the Christian faith, with the only kind of adherence which seems to me appropriate for mysteries. This adherence is love, not affirmation. Certainly I belong to Christ – or so I hope and believe.

But I am kept outside the Church by philosophical difficulties which I fear are irreducible. They do not concern the mysteries themselves but the accretions of definition with which the Church has seen fit to clothe them in the course of centuries; and above all the use in this connexion of the words *anathema sit*.

Nevertheless, although I am outside the Church or, more precisely, on the threshold, I cannot resist the feeling that I am really within it. Nothing is closer to me than those who are within it.

It is not an easy spiritual situation to define or make comprehensible. It would need pages and pages – or a book. . . . But I must confine myself now to these few words.

I am glad to know the *Témoignage Chrétien* people are your friends.

[1] The word is used at the *École Normale* to describe Catholic students. Professor André Weil tells me that one (possibly serious) etymological explanation is: Ceux qui vonT À LA messe (those who go to mass).

I felt a deep and lively friendship for their circles. I think they are much the best thing in France at this moment. May no harm come to them.

A thousand thanks for having spoken to A.Ph. about me. I am glad he is well-disposed towards me. I very much hope I shall see him if he comes here.

When it comes to saying what I think I could do, I am embarrassed. I am not a specialist, and I have no particular technical qualifications; all I have is the general culture which we both share, except that I have also (if it could be made use of) a certain personally acquired experience of working-class life. I worked at machines in several factories in the Paris region, including Renault, in 1934-5; I took a year's leave for that purpose. I still possess my certificates. And last summer I did agricultural labour, including six weeks as a harvester in a vineyard in the Gard.

Any really useful work, not requiring technical expertise but involving a high degree of hardship and danger, would suit me perfectly.

Hardship and danger are essential because of my particular mentality. Luckily it is not universal, because it would make all organized activities impossible, but as far as I am concerned I cannot change it; I know this by experience.

The suffering all over the world obsesses and overwhelms me to the point of annihilating my faculties and the only way I can revive them and release myself from the obsession is by getting for myself a large share of danger and hardship. That is a necessary condition before I can exert my capacity for work.

I beseech you to get for me, if you can, the amount of hardship and danger which can save me from being wasted by sterile chagrin. In my present situation I cannot live. It very nearly makes me despair.

I cannot believe it is impossible to give me what I need. It is unlikely there is so much demand for painful and dangerous jobs that not one is available. And even if that is so, it would be easy to make one. For there is plenty to be done; you know it as well as I do.

I have much to say about this; but by word of mouth, not by letter.

It seems to me, then, that the best thing would be to assign me to some provisional work, which you could easily choose for me yourself, you know me well enough for that, so as to get me to London quickly, as quickly as possible; and then I could be transferred to whatever seemed the most suitable operation, after full discussion. I would accept any provisional work anywhere – propaganda or press, for example, or anything else. But if it was a job not involving a high degree of hardship and danger I could only accept it provisionally; otherwise I should be consumed by the same chagrin in London as in New York, and it would paralyse me. It is unfortunate to have that sort of character; but that is really how I am, and I can do nothing about it; it is something too essential in me to be modified. The more so because it is not, I am certain, a question of character only, but of vocation.

In this respect, the project I sent you would have satisfied my needs perfectly, and I am very distressed that A.Ph. thinks it impracticable. I confess, however, that I have not yet lost all hope of its realization some day; I am, and have long been, so convinced that it is a thing that ought to be done.

In any case, there is other more urgent work at the present time, and I am hungry to take part in it without delay.

Only arrange for me to come. I know it is difficult just now. But I also know that people do manage it, including women. I very much hope you'll be able to help. If A.Ph. could take me in his luggage, as secretary or something, when he returns from here....

Anyway, I thank you very, very much.

Kindest wishes,
Simone Weil

I will very gladly do you an article, of course. You'll receive it soon.

48 To Jean Wahl

[New York, 1942]

Cher ami,

I have wanted to write to you for a long time. We only just missed one another at Marseille (a letter from you, posted at Aix, has followed me here). We shall not be here at the same time either. Are we destined to see one another again some day in Paris? Or never? Everything is so uncertain that one is forced to live from day to day, or else in eternity – or in both ways at once, which is the best.

You speak mysteriously in a way which seems to imply that certain people are spreading strange rumours about me? Is it being said, by any chance, that my sympathies tend towards Vichy? If so, you can deny it. In June 1940 I fervently hoped that Paris would be defended and I only left after I had seen with dismay the placards declaring it an open city. I stopped at Nevers in the hope there would be a front on the Loire. And I was dismayed again by the news of the armistice, after which I immediately resolved to try to get to England. I tried every possibility that offered, including dangerous ones. When I left France it was solely with the idea of getting to England. Meanwhile, before leaving France I took part in the distribution of illegal literature. As soon as I arrived here I wore everybody out with my supplications to be sent to England. And at last I am going there, thanks to André Philip, who has found a job for me with him (incidentally, he is a very, very excellent person, quite first class). Ever since the day when I decided, after a very painful inner struggle, that in spite of my pacifist inclinations it had become an overriding obligation in my eyes to work for Hitler's destruction, with or without any chance of success, ever since that day my resolve has not altered; and that day was the one on which Hitler entered Prague – in May 1939, if I remember right. My decision was tardy, perhaps; I left it too late, perhaps, before adopting that position. Indeed, I think so and I bitterly reproach myself for it. But anyhow, since I adopted the position I have not budged. So I beg you to deny categorically any rumours to the contrary.

What may have given rise to such rumours is the fact that I don't much like to hear perfectly comfortable people here using words like coward and traitor about people in France who are managing as best they can in a terrible situation. There is only a small number of Frenchmen to whom such words are almost certainly applicable; they ought not to be used about any others. There was a collective act of cowardice and treason, namely the armistice; and the whole nation bears responsibility for it, including Paul Reynaud, who ought never to have resigned. I myself was immediately appalled by the armistice, but in spite of that I think that all the French, including myself, are as much to blame for it as Pétain. From what I saw at the time, the nation as a whole welcomed the armistice with relief and so the nation bears an overall and indivisible responsibility for it. On the other hand, I think that, since then, Pétain has done just about as much as the general situation and his own physical and mental state allowed of to limit the damage. The word traitor should only be used about those of whom one feels certain that they desire Germany's victory and are doing what they can to that

To Jean Wahl 1942

end. As for the others, some of those who are prepared to work with Vichy or even with the Germans may have honourable motives which are justified by particular situations. And others may be constrained by pressures which they could only resist if they were heroes. Most of the people here, however, who set themselves up as judges have never had an opportunity to find out if they themselves are heroes. I detest facile, unjust, and false attitudes, and especially when the pressure of public opinion seems to make them almost obligatory.

I would very much have liked to see you, chiefly in order to know whether your personal experiences have modified your 'Weltanschauung', and how. After all that has happened I should think the word 'Dasein' must have a different resonance for you. There is nothing like misfortune for giving the sense of existence. Except when it gives the sense of unreality. It may give the one or the other; or even both of them. In any case, it seems to me that such experiences must give another meaning to all the words of the philosophic vocabulary.

I cannot detach myself sufficiently from what is going on to make the effort of drafting, composing, etc.; and yet a part of my mind is continuously occupied with matters absolutely remote from current events (though current problems are indirectly related to them). My solution is to fill notebook after notebook with thoughts hastily set down, in no order or sequence.

I believe that one identical thought is to be found – expressed very precisely and with only very slight differences of modality – in the ancient mythologies; in the philosophies of Pherekydes, Thales, Anaximander, Heraclitus, Pythagoras, Plato, and the Greek Stoics; in Greek poetry of the great age; in universal folklore; in the Upanishads and the Bhagavad-Gita; in the Chinese Taoist writings and in certain currents of Buddhism; in what remains of the sacred writings of Egypt; in the dogmas of the Christian faith and in the writings of the greatest Christian mystics, especially St. John of the Cross; and in certain heresies, especially the Cathar and Manichaean tradition. I believe that this thought is the truth, and that it requires today a modern and Western form of expression. That is to say, it requires to be expressed through the only approximately good thing we can call our own, namely science. This is all the less difficult because it is itself the origin of science. There are a few texts which indicate with certainty that Greek geometry arose out of religious thought; and this thought appears to resemble Christianity almost to the point of identity.

As regards the Jews, I think that Moses knew this wisdom and refused it because, like Maurras, he conceived religion as a simple instrument of national greatness; but when the Jewish nation had been destroyed by Nebuchadnezzar the Jews, completely disoriented and scattered among many nations, received this wisdom in the form of foreign influences and introduced it, so far as was possible, into their religion. Thus it inspired, in the Old Testament, the book of Job (which I believe to be a mutilated and adapted translation of a sacred book concerning an incarnated God who suffered, was put to death, and resurrected), most of the Psalms, the Song of Songs, the sapiential books (which derive perhaps from the same current which produced the works called hermetic, and perhaps also the writings attributed to Dionysius the Areopagite), and what is called the 'second Isaiah', and some of the minor prophets, and the books of Daniel and Tobias. Almost all the rest of the Old Testament is a tissue of horrors.

I think that the first eleven chapters of Genesis (up to Abraham) can only be a translation, mutilated and re-cast, of an Egyptian sacred book; that Abel, Enoch, and Noah are gods, and that Noah is identical with Osiris, Dionysus, and Prometheus. I think that Shem, Ham and Japhet correspond, if not to three races, at least to three human families, three forms of civilization; and that Ham alone witnessed the nakedness and intoxication of Noah, that is to say, received the revelation of mystical thought. The people of Ham, according to Genesis, are the Sumerians, Ethiopians, Egyptians, Phoenicians, and Aegeo-Cretans (Philistines); and no doubt the Iberians should be added. The people of Japhet and Shem everywhere conquered and destroyed the people of Ham; but they never had any spiritual life unless they consented to adopt the religious and philosophical thought of the conquered. Almost all the Hellenes consented, and so also did the Celts and the Babylonians and some of the Hebrews after the 6th century. Those who, from pride and will to power, refused to be instructed – such as the Spartans, the Romans, the Hebrews before Nebuchadnezzar, and probably the Assyrians – remained brutes, with no spiritual and hardly any intellectual life. The 'Hamitic' stream of thought is traceable everywhere as a thread of light all through pre-history and history. It even penetrated into Germanic mythology (in the story of

Baldi and the story of Odin hanged on the Tree of the World). But it is everywhere threatened with destruction by pride and the will to domination, the spirit of Japhet and Shem. It had been almost destroyed throughout the whole of the Roman Empire at the time of the birth of Christ, who was a perfect and consequently a divine expression of it, to judge by the writings which he inspired. Today, Hitler and many others are trying to abolish it throughout the whole world.

I will not hide from you that the 'existentialist' line of thought appears to me, so far as I know it, to be on the wrong side; on the side which is alien in thought to the revelation received and transmitted by Noah (to use that name for him) – on the side of force.

However that may be, such of my preoccupations as are not immediately related to current events are turned more or less in the direction I have outlined. Which does not prevent me from thinking at the same time continually about the present situation.

Well, I think I've given you more than a few 'hints'°. And now, in turn, I would much like to hear before my departure, which is imminent, something of what *you* are thinking.

... I hope you are not finding life in exile too painful.

With best wishes
Simone Weil

49 To her parents

[London] 16 December [1942]

Darlings,°

I am writing from Mme R.'s; her welcome couldn't have been kinder. I have only been at liberty in London for forty-eight hours. I sent you a cable yesterday. On arrival I was put into a clearing centre where one was strictly forbidden to telephone, write, or wire. This happens to everybody, and one is usually kept there from six to ten days. But I was unlucky (Antigone as usual!) and spent eighteen and a half days there. However, one was very well treated and it was very comfortable.

As to my first contacts with the French here, everyone has been very, very nice to me. Schumann as nice as possible. C. welcomed me as though we were old friends. My own little plans don't seem to be prospering. And that no doubt will give you pleasure. I don't yet know at all what my job will be, nor whether I shall be a civilian or in uniform. I am billeted provisionally with the French women volunteers.

I've had a letter from André, but nothing from you. I suppose a letter of yours was lost.

[....]

Needless to say how anxious I am for your news. Of course I worry about you and think about you a lot. But I am infinitely and completely glad to have crossed the sea again. Only, so far, I still continue to regret, for myself (for you it's altogether different), the decision I took last May. André asked me about this in his letter: you can tell him the answer. He may think my feeling strange, but that is how it is.

[....]

The journey was pleasant. A lot of rolling, but nobody in the ship was seasick. A few very cold days, but the ship was heated. No incidents. Agreeable moral atmosphere.

Needless to say, I'm already in love with London. I was before I arrived. Equally needless to say that I love England. I have not been disappointed in any way, quite the contrary. (The few shortcomings I've noticed so far were ones which I had already foreseen.)

Mme R. sends greetings, and so do the children. W. is very grown-up and has become very nice.

(Passage censored)

But don't go there on a cold or wet day. Telephone first.

Travel prospects for you don't look very brilliant so far; but I'll do my best, it goes without saying.

Your most loving,°

Simone

50 To the same

31-12-42

Darlings,

I wanted to wait for news from you, and also to let the holiday rush die down, before writing. I have heard nothing (since your letter of 13 November). Upon arrival, I arranged for two cables to be sent to you, as it was impossible for me to do it. Then I sent you two myself, the second one asking you for news by cable. But nothing has come.

To have no news of you hurts me only; so it does not matter. But I hardly dare think of the possibility that you may have no news of me.

I suppose you are still applying to the North Africa Delegation. If I

To her parents 1942

could influence you I would advise staying in New York until the world calms down. In a time like ours it is absurd for families to make plans for keeping together. Better be resigned to separation as a temporary necessity.

For my part, if I could know that you have news of me and that you are not unhappy, separation would cause me no pain. It is true that I don't know this. I don't even know if you are alive. So of course I am anxious. But I should be much more so if you started travelling again. The fun we had in planning out journeys was perhaps not sensible. America is, after all, the safest place at the moment; and if you didn't care about safety you should never have left Marseille.

As for me, I am perfectly all right as regards external things – apart from the question of lodgings, which is difficult and I am still in a temporary billet. Otherwise all goes well. Everybody is as nice as possible to me. I am given purely intellectual and entirely personal work to do, which I can do as and how I like. In brief, I ought to be very happy, were it not that, as you know, I have my own very particular notions of happiness. As you do not share them, you will feel no regret that they are unfulfilled. In fact – as you are well aware – I am not happy. But now at last life is no longer morally impossible for me, as it was when I was with you.

I like this town better and better, and the country, and the people in it. But it is one of the unhappy things about life in exile that it is almost impossible to tell the people around us that we like them, because it may seem like flattery. An English lady, a friend of Mme R.'s, to whom I said that I loved England, replied: 'I love France, but I don't believe any French people love England.'° Whether she was convinced of my sincerity in the end, I don't know.

In one sense, both things and people here seem to me exactly as I think I expected them to be, and in another sense perhaps better. Lawrence somewhere describes England by the terms 'humour and kindness'°; and one does meet with these traits continually in little incidents of daily life and in the most widely different circles. Especially *kindness*° – to a much greater degree than I would have dared hope. People here do not scream at one another as they do on the Continent; nor do they where you are now, but that is because their nerves are relaxed whereas here people's nerves are strained but they control them from self-respect and from a true generosity towards others. It may be that the war has a good deal to do with all this. People here have suffered just enough for it to be a tonic which stimulates dormant virtues. They have not been stunned as in France. Nevertheless, all things considered, it seems to me certain that at this moment of history they are worth more than us. (Which would not be difficult, it is true.)

I wrote as soon as I could to tell you that I had been kept in seclusion and unable to communicate for nineteen days. It is the general rule, but it's generally not so long. (Tell this to M. since he wants to know the way things are done.) I was unlucky. For the rest, one is perfectly well treated, both materially and morally. But in spite of this, everyone emerges from the process completely flat. It's an odd phenomenon. I was no exception. But after a few days of freedom the effect wears off completely.

[. . . .]

Mme R. couldn't be kinder to me. F. is more and more sympathetic. A curious thing, our minds seem to have moved on similar lines.

[. . . .]

I see the Lehigh river flooded. I hope Sylvie's[1] cradle wasn't washed away.

Love from my very soul,°

S.W.

51 To the same

8.1.43

Darlings,

I received your cable today. Until it came, I had had no news of you at all, except for your letter of 13 November. But what worried me much more than not hearing from you was the thought that perhaps you had heard nothing from me. But I feel reassured about that since you have had my first letter. No doubt you'll soon get the second. I hope you also had my cables. I sent two. In any case, so long as the correspondence gets through in one direction that's the chief thing. But if your letters continue to fail to reach me you must send a cable now and then – though not so often that it becomes ruinous.

I hope it is true that you are 'happy and perfectly well'°; but I hardly dare believe it.

From what people tell me here, there is scarcely any chance that you

[1] Simone Weil's niece, born just before her departure from America.

To her parents 1943

could come. There are only two categories of French doctors here: those who were established and practising here before the war – Anglo-French in effect – and army doctors who only treat the armed forces. It leaves a gap, because there are absolutely no arrangements for the civilian personnel (to which I belong). If anything were done to fill this gap, if one or more clinics were organized for French civilians, then you could easily come. But I can't undertake to try to push the idea. You know how I lack eloquence and persuasiveness; and I think I ought to use what little I have in connexion with matters of more general interest and of less personal concern to myself.

[. . . .]

I unfortunately missed M.-F. He is only in London occasionally and I wasn't able to meet him.

Although French circles here are naturally more united than in New York, the opportunities of seeing people are not so numerous – and the less so because, as you can imagine, I have not developed social habits. Perhaps it is wrong of me, but I can't help it. I work a lot; by which I mean that I spend a lot of time at it, but as I have been given purely intellectual work I cannot judge its quality and effects. Also, people continue to be much nicer to me than I would be inclined to think reasonable. But since everything that concerns the work and one's impressions about it is rather difficult to deal with by letter, and since my life at the moment amounts to nothing else, I can't tell you much about myself.

Not that I really work as much as I ought and would like to, because I lose an enormous amount of time whenever I go out in London. But nevertheless I am absolutely at home here now and I feel a tender love for this bomb-damaged town.

Before I became submerged in work I went to two concerts at the *National Gallery*.° But I think I told you about them. Another thing I'd like to be able to describe to you, as a drop of the purest essence of the English spirit at its most delightful, is a Food Ministry exhibition called *Potato Fair*.° Its purpose is to encourage people to eat potatoes in place of imported foodstuffs and it is designed like a show for children. The theme of the exhibition is presented in 'nursery rhymes'°; there are distorting mirrors to show what you become if you don't eat potatoes, and so on. What strikes me most about these people, in their present situation, is a good humour which is neither spontaneous nor yet artificial, but which arises from a spirit of tender and brotherly comradeship in an ordeal shared by everybody. I am convinced that, because of this, people are in reality happier here than they were a few years ago, in spite of the family separations, the overwork, and all the rest.

I have still not found a place to live. Write to me at Mme R.'s. This having no address makes me postpone from day to day the moment of getting in touch with people. I saw G., who will give you news of me. Physically, I am well; I am almost free from headaches; I live comfortably and take perfectly good care of myself. Moreover, there is no question of changing my job; I am regularly established in my present one. So, whatever you do, have no anxiety about me. I give you my word you would be wrong to have any. I will write to A. one of these days, and also to B., for whom I don't know if it will be possible to arrange anything.

Fondest love,°
S.

P.S. You should read Bernanos' *Lettre aux Anglais*; it is splendid. I saw M. and Mme B. who were as nice as possible and told me to remember them to André and you.

52 To the same

22 January 1943

Darlings,

I have had one letter, and then nothing more. The posts must be very irregular. G. will give you news of me. He'll tell you he found me comfortably installed in the depths of an office, in good health and complete tranquillity .... (I regret more and more the decision I took last May). Since I have been here the bombings have been nothing; less than they were in Paris. Materially, I manage very well. I've found a room, all by myself and without any outside help, although rooms are almost unprocurable. (My address: c/o Mrs. Francis, 31 Portland Road, Holland Park, London W.11; write to me there.) It's a good room and half the average price. The landlady is charming. I eat well, sleep well, and so on, and everyone is nice. Whether I am really working, in the true sense of the word, I don't know; but I do nothing else but try. If you were here you wouldn't see much of me.

To her parents 1943

And as to that, I have a suggestion: I am told that the Belgians, unlike us, have hospitals and clinics for civilians in England. Couldn't you get taken on by them? You might inquire at the Belgian Consulate.

It's true there's always the uncertainty about North Africa....

Tell A. to let me know exactly what he has in mind, if he wants something in the present set-up. C., whom I don't know, is in charge of Education. I must add that I haven't the slightest desire to pull strings for anybody – except myself, and certainly not with a view to advancement.... When I wanted to come here in the summer of '40, it was the losing side; today one is a little too conscious that it is the winning side (I mean among the French); and as I did not succeed in joining them at the right moment I am far from comfortable in this atmosphere, so far as my personal feelings are concerned.

[....]

For myself, I feel an ever more deadly chagrin at having been tempted, almost a year ago, to try something new.

Tell B. that I don't write because the things I have to tell him are difficult to put in writing. Tell him also that I mean to speak fully about him one day to A.Ph., but not until I have done some work for the latter which he finds satisfactory (if I can manage it). Let me know if by any chance B. has managed some other way. If so, it would be better. What need has he to be anything in the official circles of today? My own idea, for myself, as you know, was something quite different....

G. is to transmit to the Free French Delegation at New York an order from here for typing and sending: (1) the 'magnum opus' of 1934, (2) the article on factory life which I wrote for *Économie et Humanisme* (they have it, I think?), (3) the other article, of tala[1] tendency, which I wrote for the same review (entitled *Conditions d'un travail non servile*). They will be furious...! If you suggest doing the job yourself, see that you get paid! And if they do it in their office, keep an eye on them and try to see that it is done quickly and well....

There are a few new corrections to the poems:
(1) New ending for 'Les astres'[2] (definitely definitive this time, I think!).

> A votre aspect toute douleur importe peu.
> Nous nous taisons, nous chancelons sur nos chemins.

---
[1] See note on p. 155.   [2] Unpublished poem by Simone Weil.

Ils sont là dans le cœur soudain, les feux divins.
[*At the sight of you every sorrow becomes trivial.
We are speechless, we waver on our paths.
They are there suddenly in the heart, the fires divine.*]

(2) *Prométhée*,[1] verse 5 line 1: 'Plus lumineux fut le présent des nombres' [*More luminous was the gift of numbers*]; verse 6 line 1: 'L'aube est par lui une joie immortelle' [*Thanks to him, the dawn is an immortal joy*].

(3) *Jour*,[1] verse 3, lines 3–5: 'Toute cette splendeur posée – Comme une caresse en tous lieux – Nous reviendra tendre et limpide' [*All that splendour, like an omnipresent caress, tender and limpid will return to us*].

(4) *Violetta's Song*,[2] verse 2 ff: 'Le sommeil encor jamais n'avait comblé – Tant que cette nuit mon cœur qui le buvait – Mais il est venu, le jour doux à mes yeux – Plus que le sommeil ‖ Voici que l'appel du jour tant attendu – Touche la cité parmi la pierre et l'eau – Un frémissement dans l'air encor muet – A surgi partout ‖ Ton bonheur est là, viens et vois, ma cité – Épouse des mers, vois bien loin, vois tout près – Tant de flots gonflés de murmures heureux – Bénir ton éveil ‖ Sur la mer s'étend lentement la clarté – La fête bientôt', etc. (the rest unchanged). [*Never before had sleep so refreshed my heart as this night. But the day has come, more grateful to my eyes than sleep. See, the long awaited holiday wakens the stones and waters of the city. A tremor runs everywhere through the yet unbroken silence. Awake, O my city, your joy is here. Look, bride of the sea, look far, look near. Everywhere the murmuring waves are blessing you. Gently over the sea the light is spreading. Soon the festival . . .*]

It would be nice to produce, without hurry, a few copies of the collection of poems (including *Violetta*, preceded by Jaffier's last four lines).

Apart from that, no time to do anything to the play.

I would rather like these verses to appear all together, at the same time, in chronological order, somewhere . . . .

What is happening to K.'s review?

I am amused at your saying people have dropped you now that I am no longer there! When I was there it was like living in a desert and no one made any sign of life.

---
[1] Unpublished poem by Simone Weil.
[2] From Simone Weil's unfinished drama *Venise sauvée*.

To her parents 1943

I am going to have some money sent to you from the excess of my salary. Because, needless to say, I spend little .... If you don't need it, try to give it where it will be useful. But no doubt you'll have a use for it ....

I do so want you to be well, and not bored, and enjoying life in New York, and finding good books to read, and having good weather, and everything like that! If only I could believe that you're not unhappy, either of you ....

Fondest love°.

S.W.

53 To Maurice Schumann

The following undated letter is placed here by conjecture. It was clearly written some little time after Simone Weil's arrival in London on 14 December 1942, and before she entered the Middlesex Hospital in April 1943. Internal evidence suggests that it may have been written at about the same time as the preceding letter to her parents of 22 January.

London

I am horrified to see how many pages I have written without noticing. It is all merely personal. Of no interest. Don't read it until you really have some time to waste.

Cher ami,

As there are few opportunities for talking at leisure, perhaps it is better to write.

Anyway, nothing I can say could express my gratitude for your comprehension.

Only it is absurd that this comprehension should be expressed in praises which are utterly misplaced when applied to me, and which make me very uncomfortable.

The fact that it is possible to speak about thought in terms like superiority and inferiority is a proof of the unhealthy atmosphere in which we live. It would be a morbidly vain cook whose reaction to a meal was to compare it with his own productions.

A meal is not for comparison, it is for eating. In the same way words, whether written or spoken, are absorbed in so far as they are nourishing, that is to say in so far as they contain truth. That is their only use.

Nowadays this is quite forgotten.

We are born and grow up in falsehood. Truth only comes to us from outside, and it always comes from God. It makes no difference whether it comes direct or through human words. Every truth which penetrates into you and is welcomed by you was destined personally for you by God. If it happens to come through words, the flesh-and-blood creature who spoke them has no more importance or value than the paper on which the Gospel is printed – or than the she-ass through whom, in the Bible story, God chose to warn one of the prophets.

I was born with mediocre intellectual faculties. Be assured that I only say this because it is the fact. The state into which I fell when I was twenty ought soon to have extinguished them (and I did live and work for a long time with the daily impression that they were literally on the point of complete extinction). And they were in fact seriously impaired in a number of ways (as you may have had occasions to notice). But there are treasures of divine mercy for those who long for truth. In no circumstances, whatever may happen, are they left completely in darkness.

In return for this mercy there is the obligation to trample down everything in oneself that could obstruct the passage through one of the truth.

It is this obligation which compels me to write things which I know that I, personally, have no right to express.

I have no right to speak of love, because I know that love does not dwell in me. Where love dwells it flows like a continual fountain of supernatural energy. There are some words in Isaiah which are terrible for me: They that love God 'shall run and not be weary; and they shall walk, and not faint.' This makes it physically impossible for me to forget, even for a moment, that I am not of their number.

But that does not prevent me from leaving my pen at the disposal of any truths which deign to make use of it; I am forbidden to withhold it. When I speak of what is true I simply mean, of course, what appears to me manifestly to be so.

In the same way, I know that I personally have no right to make the slightest reservation about the things which I cannot avoid condemning.

I have never had more than an infinitesimal influence on the life of France, because of my lack of ability, and that infinitesimal influence has in fact been entirely for the bad. Consequently, before those who

To Maurice Schumann 1943 (?)

have done some good – which is certainly very much the case with you – I personally ought only to admire and be silent.

But that, too, cannot restrain me, because I owe the truth to those I love.

If by chance some truth has passed through me to reach you, that would at least give some meaning to my stay in this country.

– Although the thoughts which my pen transcribes are far above me, I adhere to them as what I believe to be the truth; and I think that I have been commanded by God to prove experimentally that they are not incompatible with an extreme form of action in war.

I believe I am not mistaken because, ever since 1914, war has always been in my thoughts and because I have always confusedly felt something of this kind, and it has grown increasingly clearer and more imperative.

Moreover, it does not seem to me to matter that the sense of a particular command from God is always inevitably clouded by uncertainty.

I believe that if anyone has this feeling mistakenly and yet, because of it, puts all his strength and faith and humility into an attempt to obey, then – so long as the thing is not evil in itself (which this wish of mine almost certainly is not) – by divine mercy it becomes a commandment of God although it was not before.

I am quite certain that if anyone believes, even mistakenly, that he has received a command from God and fails to perform it through lack of energy or faith or power of persuasion, he is guilty of disobedience.

That is my situation at the present moment.

It is a situation in my eyes infinitely worse than hell – assuming all that theology says about hell to be true. The damned are not in a state of disobedience; they are in the place where God's will has put them; their lot is in accord with perfect justice and truth. That is why I cannot be afraid of hell. But I am in terror of disobedience.

It is easy to understand why, in a situation which is to me infinitely worse than hell, I lose all dignity and discretion in my ceaseless, desperate appeals for release.

You are thinking perhaps – or even if not, a part of you may be thinking – that since I am not in the Church the words I am using cannot have their full meaning for me.

On this matter I think I owe you a confidence.

In my eyes, a Christian sacrament is a contact with God through a sensible symbol, employed by the Church and whose meaning derives from a teaching of Christ's.

Some would add that it must also have been officially promulgated by the Church. But I think this last condition is not absolutely necessary, and that there are exceptions for those who have legitimate reasons for remaining outside the Church. It goes without saying that I believe I am one of these; otherwise I would join the Church today. By legitimate reasons I mean legitimate in relation to myself and my particular vocation. I would never blame those who are in the Church; I would be more inclined to envy them.

Christ said: 'As Moses lifted up the serpent in the wilderness, even so must the Son of man be lifted up: that whosoever believeth in him should not perish....'

Whoever looked up at the brazen serpent lifted on a pole was preserved from the poison of snakes.

I think it is a sacrament simply to look at the host and the chalice during the elevation with this thought in mind.

For analogous reasons, I think the same about reciting the Lord's Prayer in Christ's own words (I am convinced the Greek text goes back to Christ; it is too beautiful), provided one's desire is to be nothing but an instrument for the repetition of Christ's own prayer.

Further, what certain texts affirm about the possibility of verifying some of the effects of the sacraments appears to me to coincide with my observations on myself.

Therefore, rightly or wrongly, I do not consider myself outside the Church as a source of sacramental life, but only outside it as a social reality.

It may be that I am wrong – but if so I must be the prey of an unheard-of devil, a devil who tempts you to feed on the spectacle of the mass – Maybe. But I am obliged to trust what appears to me to be true. What else could I trust?

– As to my capacity for action in war, I am extremely lacking in every sort of capacity, in every way, unfortunately.

Nevertheless, I am convinced that if I fell into the hands of the Germans I would have a better chance than others who are physically, intellectually, and morally far superior to me of dying without giving anything away.

This conviction rests upon a remark you made to me the other day,

To Maurice Schumann 1943 (?)

that human beings shrink from losing their dignity. The more a man possesses of strength, vigour, honour, and all other resources, and therefore the more he is worth, the more he feels this repugnance.

Consequently, a man in this situation will either succeed in maintaining, or almost maintaining, his dignity to the very end or else, if he reaches the limit of his endurance and collapses, he will abandon everything, including the obligation of secrecy.

Knowing this, the enemy operates methodically to destroy self-respect.

For my part, as soon as I had brought myself to the decision to participate, if I had the chance, in any serious work of sabotage (for various reasons, I did not make the same decision as regards propaganda), in other words, immediately after the armistice, I recognized that I would be obliged in certain circumstances to use my own will to break down my self-respect in face of the enemy.

This might be a painful operation, but not difficult once it became necessary.

All this was very evident to me because in the past I had called upon my reserves of self-control, to the extreme limit of nervous tension, for years, until in the end they partially failed – as you have had occasion to observe.

It seemed to me that in certain circumstances I might indeed be stimulated beyond my normal strength, by the presence of the enemy and the spur of honour; but that nevertheless if I had the keeping of secrets involving the safety of human lives I would have no right to count upon it.

I therefore decided that in those circumstances I would begin by forgetting all about my dignity and concentrate all my strength and attention solely upon the necessity of guarding my secrets.

I made up my mind that if ever I was involved in an operation I would always carry in my head an innocuous list of false avowals, carefully prepared in advance, so that they could be extorted from me during the process of breaking down my self-respect.

This method ought to be successful if one collapses before reaching the point where one has lost all self-control, because during the process of collapse one would be sufficiently lucid to bring out the false information.

It is unlikely that the enemy would detect this ruse.

On the other hand, the object being to die before giving anything away, it is necessary to reach as quickly as possible a state in which one is in fact incapable of doing so.

With me, precisely because of my physical weakness, this state would arrive fairly soon. A moderate amount of ill-treatment would put me definitely into the state where the mind is a blank.

Moreover, I am not altogether ignorant of the methods for stimulating ill-treatment. It ought to be possible if one starts, while one still possesses self-control, by coolly employing the rudest and most offensive provocation, for they are brutes who react to provocation; and then if one collapses almost immediately, for they are sadists who cannot resist trampling upon anything that shows signs of weakness.

As a whole, I believe these tactics are reasonable.

If I were obliged to put them into practice I should feel that they were as reliable as human prudence can make them and that if they fall short there is a strong hope that the divine mercy would assist.

For it is certain that there are treasures of divine mercy for those who abandon everything, including their honour, and pray only for the grace of not doing any harm.

Even when I was in the hands of the French police, from whom there was no danger of physical ill-treatment, I had to renew inwardly my resolve to abandon, if necessary, all concern for my dignity. Because if they had chosen to torment me verbally on a day when my pain was too bad I should have been unable to retain that concern and at the same time to concentrate upon not saying anything that could incriminate anybody.

As it happened, this problem did not arise; and I think that in fact it was I who made them a little uncomfortable by looking them steadily in the eye the whole morning and not answering their questions except with 'No' or 'I have nothing to add to my previous statements.'

But it was only by a lucky chance that I was in a state where I could do this.

In this way you can understand that the proposition I put to you – the proposition of the scapegoat – is an easy one for me. It implies nothing more than was incumbent on me in any case.

Owing to the physical deficiency of my nature, there is no possible half-way house for me between total sacrifice and cowardice. And I really cannot make the second choice. Or perhaps I would be only too glad to make it, but there is something stronger than me which forbids it.

And my intellectual situation is the same. I have no alternative between creative attention and mental nullity, because my capacity for every other kind of attention is paralysed.

Truly, I have had an undeserved blessing and I have turned it to wretchedly poor account.

– My need of your help compels me to speak about myself much more, I assure you, than I have ever done to anybody.

I don't want you to do me the injustice of imagining that I affect saintliness – you once seemed to say something to that effect. Above all I don't want at any price that you should think better of me than the truth allows.

I can tell you very plainly my position as regards saintliness.

To begin with, and incidentally, I do not like the way in which Christians today speak about saintliness. They speak about it in the way that a cultured banker or engineer or general might speak about poetic genius – a beautiful thing which they know they do not possess, which they love and admire, but which it would never occur to them for a moment to blame themselves for lacking.

In reality, it seems to me that saintliness is, if I dare say so, the minimum for a Christian. It is to the Christian what financial probity is to the merchant, or courage to the soldier, or objectivity to the scientist.

The virtue specific to the Christian is called sanctity. Or if not, what is its name?

But by a conspiracy as old as Christianity itself, and stronger with each century, this truth has been concealed, along with several others equally uncomfortable.

There exist in fact dishonest merchants, cowardly soldiers, etc., and also people who have chosen to love Christ but who are infinitely below the level of sanctity.

Of course I am one of them.

On the other hand, many of those instincts and reactions which seem to be essentially rooted in human nature, and ineradicable except by a supernatural conversion, are in fact only derived from the fund of vital energy possessed by every normal man.

If, as a result of circumstances, this fund is exhausted, then those instincts and reactions disappear with it. It takes time, and it involves a lot of very painful interior struggle. But once they have disappeared, that is the end. The process is irreversible, like growing older.

It is the existence of these irreversible processes that makes human life so tragic.

The end of this process is a state somewhat resembling, superficially, the detachment of the saints. It is upon this resemblance that the Gospel parables base their analogy between slaves and the disciples of Christ. But since the former state is the result of a purely mechanical process it has no value.

It is easy to discriminate between the two states. Sanctity is accompanied by a continual flow of supernatural energy which acts irresistibly upon all that surrounds it. The other state is accompanied by moral exhaustion and often – as in my case – by moral and physical exhaustion together.

The words of Isaiah which I quoted leave no possible doubt.

Some people, it is true, experience long and terrible afflictions without falling into this state. But, in the first place, men are endowed from the outset with very varying quantities of vitality (not to be confused with strength or health). And then, man has a very large freedom to postpone, in affliction, the moment of reaching the limit; he can do it by falsehood, by artificial compensations, and by resorting to all kinds of stimulants. And again, many people are in this state without its being perceived.

To come back to myself, having been automatically presented by circumstances with this *ersatz* of sanctity, I feel a perfectly clear obligation to make it the rule of my life, although it is valueless, solely for love of the genuine article. Not in the hope of acquiring it, but simply to pay it homage.

I have a strong feeling that if I failed flagrantly in this obligation I should quickly fall into extreme wickedness and baseness.

If I stay rigorously faithful to it, I am still far below those who, possessing their life intact and rich with zest and normal aspirations to happiness, give away even a fraction of it for the sake of justice and truth.

But that doesn't worry me, or, more accurately, I am glad of it.

All I wish for myself is to be one of those who are ordained to see themselves as unworthy slaves, having done no more than they were commanded.

To Maurice Schumann 1943 (?)

What fills me with anguish is the fear that, on the contrary, I am one of the disobedient.

– To return to the practical means for avoiding this, I can scarcely see myself explaining to the B.C.R.A.[1] people my tactics for dealing with torture.

(I hope I didn't upset you by explaining it in such detail. But after all, you have no right to feel more squeamish about me than about any little German peasant – who may be worth so much more than me and be so much more innocent.)

To you, at any rate, I hope I have given a clear account of myself, and that you will consider it offers all possible guarantees in default of actual achievements.

Apart from the tactics I have outlined and a readiness to offer my life unconditionally for any service, I have no special abilities except a certain intuition, with regard to agents provocateurs, for discerning who can be trusted. At least I think so, on the strength of several experiences in the past.

I realize the difficulty of persuading the B.C.R.A. that this threefold capacity is a usable product; although they would be wrong.

As I see it, then, there is only one possible method.

It is that I should go to France to work for Ph. and you – since you are good enough to say that I could help you. But that it should be arranged for me to be in contact with the sabotage organizations, against the day when they may need to win some objective at the cost of a life.

It seems to me this request is reasonable and moderate and it would be unjust to refuse it.

Ph. took me on, apparently, because he thought me capable of producing ideas which he could use. If what I am now writing does not cause him to change his mind when he reads it – as may easily happen – he will have to put me in a place where ideas can germinate in a mind like mine: in contact with the object.

The work I am doing here will be arrested before long by a triple limit. First, a moral limit; because the ever increasing pain of feeling that I am not in my right place will end in spite of myself, I fear, by crippling my thought. Second, an intellectual limit; obviously my

[1] Bureau Central de Renseignement et d'Action: a commando and sabotage organization of France Libre.

thought will be arrested when it tries to grasp the concrete, for lack of an object. Third, a physical limit; because my fatigue is growing.

When the limit is reached, I shall report that I have nothing more to contribute.

If I am kept in this country, I shall ask to be allowed to disappear in the obscurity of physical labour. Not only because of a certain impulse in that direction, but also because of an obligation. I cannot eat the bread of the English without taking part in their war effort.

The limit of fatigue is further removed, I believe, in physical than in creative intellectual labour. One can grit one's teeth and drive oneself on.

If I am allowed to make the journey I wish, it would be a sufficient stimulus, I believe, to banish all fatigue – unless the delay were very long.

I confess that I can hardly bear to contemplate the thought of not being allowed to go.

And there is still something more, in addition to the reasons I have given you.

Leaving aside anything I may be allowed to do for the good of other people, life for me means nothing, and never has meant anything, really, except as a threshold to the revelation of truth.

I feel an ever increasing sense of devastation, both in my intellect and in the centre of my heart, at my inability to think with truth at the same time about the affliction of men, the perfection of God, and the link between the two.

I have the inner certainty that this truth, if it is ever granted to me, will only be revealed when I myself am physically in affliction, and in one of the extreme forms in which it exists at present.

I am afraid it may not happen. Even as a child and when I thought myself an atheist and a materialist, I always had the fear of failing, not in my life, but in my death. This fear has never ceased to grow more and more intense.

An unbeliever might say that my desire is selfish, because truth revealed at the last moment can be of no use to anything or anybody.

But a Christian cannot think this. A Christian knows that a single thought of love, lifted up to God in truthfulness, even though mute and without echo, is more useful even for this world than the most splendid action.

To Maurice Schumann 1943 (?)

I am outside the truth; no human agency can bring me to it; and I am inwardly certain that God will not bring me to it except in that way. It is a certainty of the same kind as the one which is the basis of what is called a religious vocation.

That is why I cannot help being shameless, indiscreet, importunate like a beggar. Like a beggar, I have no argument except to cry my needs.

There is always Talleyrand's terrible reply: 'I don't see the need.' But you, you at any rate, will not give me that reply.

It is hard to depend on other people. But that is in the nature of the case. If affliction meant simply pain and death it would have been easy for me, while I was in France, to fall into the enemy's hands. But affliction means first of all necessity. It is only suffered by accident or by obligation. And an obligation is nothing without an occasion for fulfilling it. It was to find such an occasion that I came to London. I calculated badly. Or is it that the coward in me calculated too well? For my nature is cowardly. I am frightened of everything painful and dangerous. It is too easy to face the extremest dangers on paper, when there is no reason to suppose that anything real will come of it. Nothing is more contemptible. How can I help despising myself?

I think at last I have finished all I needed to say to you. I hope I shall really not need to return to such an uninteresting subject; and I don't know how to excuse myself for having dwelt on it so long. I wouldn't have done it unless compelled by necessity.

In my necessity, you are the only person I can look to for help.

I don't know what you can do for me. But at least you allow me to tell you my needs, and for that I am infinitely grateful.

Best wishes
S.W.

54 To her parents

1 February

Darlings,

I have had your letter of 21 December. Letters do get through, but slowly. One hardly has the courage to write, when one thinks how long these things take. To be sure of being to the point, one ought to write only about eternal subjects. About Krishna, for example....

Dear M.[1], if it's curious how you like to be happy, it's also curious

---
[1] Simone Weil's mother.

how I like you to be happy. I'm just as incorrigible in this matter. I passionately want the New York air to be sunny and intoxicating, the *Branch*° of the *Public Library*° to have some really good things, everyday life to produce some diverting little incidents, and some of your relations with neighbours to be pleasant and interesting (cultivate some with the evangelists next door, if they're still there). I was going to add a few worth-while films or plays, but I am too much afraid of colds. As for the Sunday morning services in Harlem, you don't appreciate them....

In my last letter I suggested you should apply to the Belgians about coming here. I will make further inquiries to see if you can come without a job, but I should be very surprised. There are none here, although the need exists. But it is impossible to try to get any new organization started. Personal contacts are very rare here, although the offices are all in the same quarter.

I like London more and more. But I don't get about much. I haven't the time. I told you I had found a room in the Notting Hill district? I could have betted on it! I was idiotic not to have looked there in the first place (address: c/o Mrs. Francis, 31 Portland Road, Holland Park, London, W.11). It is very pretty, at the top of a little house, with branches full of birds, and stars at night, just outside the window.

It's weird what a difference there is between the *pubs*° (don't worry, I go very seldom) and our bistros.

– The police in England is something really delightful.

Materially speaking, I manage very well. I eat well, sleep well, etc., and everyone is very nice. C. (with whom I work) is a very good comrade.

So you see, if you are happy, everything is all right....

Fondest love°

S.W.

New text of *Violetta*, definitive now, I think.

P.S. – I saw *Twelfth Night* here. To see that in London is something worth while. There's no break in continuity between Shakespeare's drinking scenes and the atmosphere of London *pubs* today, and that explains a lot (I don't mean by this that people get drunk in the *pubs*, because it is not so).

55 To the same

1 March

Darlings,

I received the letter addressed to Mme R.'s. I am so glad you say you are happy, although I daren't believe it.... The spring is here, and there are trees of pink blossom in the London squares. London is full of delicious little squares. But I don't see much of London, because the work absorbs me. Not that I am overworking at all. I am automatically stopped from time to time by fatigue, which forces me to rest until my energy revives; but I don't go out much at those times either. You say you are certain that my work is successful; but the truth is, I haven't the slightest idea if what I am doing is likely to be effective. That depends upon far too many unknown factors. But I cannot go into details. My companions are still as nice as possible. You can tell A. that some of the things I was told, when I was with you, about the groups here were completely untrue.

[....]

Up to now I have not had the opportunity or, above all, the time to see much of any English circles, and I greatly regret it. I continue to be enchanted by the altogether special atmosphere of the pubs in working-class districts. On Sundays I spend hours in Hyde Park watching the people who listen to the orators. I suppose that is the last remaining trace in any white country, and perhaps in the world, of the discussions in the Athenian Agora which Socrates frequented. I have a cheap room in a poor quarter (though it's perfectly satisfactory, and properly furnished). The atmosphere of the house, and especially the landlady – a teacher's widow who found herself alone in the world ten years ago, with no profession and no resources except the house, and a boy of four and a baby in arms – the whole thing is the purest Dickens. One sees that he put the humble people of England into his books precisely as they are. And the most surprising thing is that it is just the sentimental side of his books, which sounds so false, which exactly corresponds to the reality. It makes me perceive once again that this is the rule for all whose genius does not equal Homer's: when they portray reality faithfully, it sounds false.

I have seen Jacques. He said you were well, but in rather poor spirits, and that you are bored. I can understand being unhappy, but how can one be bored? Can't you think about Krishna? But I hope the spring will give you the chance of lots of country excursions. Do, I beg you, enjoy the country, the spring, the intoxicating blue sky over New York, and everything – enjoy it all to the full. Don't be ungrateful for things of beauty. Enjoy them with the thought that in every moment in which you enjoy them to the full, I am there with you.

The agreement about stars and sunsets is still in force.

The moonlight is sometimes marvellous in the London black-out.

I have still not found anyone who can tell me for certain where Stonehenge is.

I hope you keep on scouring the *Branch Public Library* for good and exciting books. And have you been to the *Branch* in Harlem, which Blanche told me about and where I'm sorry I didn't go, to look for literature about the negroes? You might make some discoveries which would be very useful to me later on.

Because my own little personal ideas and my own little conception of the world have continued in some measure, since I've been here, to show signs of cancerous proliferation. My work doesn't hinder the process; on the contrary, because it intersects with it. And my solitary life is very favourable to it.

Did you receive the new version of the *Violetta* poem? I have sent you two versions. Don't give my verses to K. to publish, because I have made one or two little improvements in almost every poem. I would gladly send them to you, but the posts are too uncertain.

I have great need of the article about the Romans. Could you get it sent as quickly as possible via the Delegation to M.Sch.?

[. . . .]

Would you write to Antonio?[1] I daren't do it.

Fondest kisses, my darlings,°

S.W.

[In April 1943 Simone Weil entered the Middlesex Hospital, to be moved later to the Grosvenor Sanatorium near Ashford, in Kent, where she died on 24 August of tuberculosis and voluntary undernourishment. It will be remembered that she had written to Maurice Schumann: 'I cannot eat the bread of the English without taking part in their war effort.' As the following letters show, she kept her parents in complete ignorance of her illness. She continued to put on the envelopes the address of her London lodgings.]

---

[1] A Spanish Anarchist peasant, interned at the camp of Le Vernet, and later at the camp of Djelfa in Algeria, by the Vichy government.

56 To the same

17 April '43

Darlings,

It is some time since I had any news of you . . . . I greatly fear you're in low spirits, if not worse. And yet, if the spring is as marvellous in New York as it is here, this would be the moment for a trip up the Hudson towards Albany. I wonder if there are any big forests not too far from New York. On the boat coming here I read an excellent book – authentic American humour – about the imaginary animals that are supposed to inhabit the forests of America. They were invented by the old 'lumbermen'° to pull the legs of the young ones, but they became a tradition, so that now the appearance, habits, etc., of each fictitious animal are permanently established.

The sky must be very blue over New York. The spring here is wonderful. London is full of pink and white blossoming trees.

If you see D. will you tell him that in view of his character (choose other words . . .) and his outlook it is not at all my opinion, but not at all, that he would feel better here than in New York.

As for me, I am much better here. But I regret every day more and more bitterly and excruciatingly that I followed A.'s advice last year. Apart from that I am perfectly all right. I am working, though without any notion of whether it will ever be of any use; but in complete freedom. My companions, especially Sch. and the C.'s, are kind to the point of absurdity. Mme C. is a remarkable woman; and he too is a man of great value. And one couldn't dream of a better comrade than Sch.

Unfortunately I have only seen the B.'s once, because I have been so absorbed in work.

I see the R.'s regularly; they are not far from my office. Mme R. speaks of you in the most touching terms.

Hyde Park is marvellous just now.

As for the house where I live (and where I have a tree just outside my window with all its leaves coming out), I think I told you that it is pure Dickens. Well, it is getting more and more so.

My landlady would be very glad if B.[1] could come and attend her little boys. I diagnosed thyroid troubles in the younger one and took him to our headquarters hospital, where the diagnosis was confirmed. It happened to be the consulting day of an English doctor who comes

---

[1] Simone Weil's father, who was a doctor.

there once a month and who is a *King's Physician*.° When my landlady heard this her heart nearly stopped, and the little boy asked if he was having the same medicine as the king.

– If you are both well and not short of money, I do so hope you are able to enjoy, really and completely, the blue sky and the rising and setting sun and the stars, the fields and the growing flowers and leaves, and the baby. Wherever there is anything beautiful, think that I am there with you.

I wonder if there are nightingales in America?

Fondest love, my two darlings,°

Simone

P.S. – My poems must not be published in America, definitely; I have changed another word or two in almost all of them.
P.S. for M. – Don't forget Krishna . . . .

57 To André Weil

17 April 1943

My dear brother,

I have not written before because it is really difficult to know what to say to you, and discouraging to think of the time between the sending and receiving of the letter.

M. having spoken about you to C., I thought I had better give him your complete biography. Result: if you were to adhere to France Combattante – by writing to R. for example, in due form – they would be very pleased . . . .

In principle, as I see it, to adhere implies no more than the affirmation that it was right and good, in June 1940, to proclaim that France would remain in the war; which I for my part have never doubted.

This information is unfortunately all I have to offer. Think it over (trying to allow for effects of distance) and act for the best.

I have told our parents that I love London; but the truth is only that I would love it passionately if the state of the world allowed me any freedom of mind. As things are, I cannot enjoy anything.

Every day, I am more and more cruelly torn by regret and remorse for having been so weak as to follow your advice last year.

As for you, if you now had favourable conditions for mathematical work I would certainly advise you to devote yourself entirely to mathematics, for good and all if possible, until the day of your death.

Take good note, however, that I myself feel thankful every day for having crossed the sea again.

But in the event of your coming over to us, in the moral sense, I have no idea at all what they would do with you. Not make you a soldier, certainly, as things are; or more exactly, a soldier with special duties. But what? I don't know. And where? I've no idea . . . .

The B.'s are charming. Unfortunately I have only seen them once.

I have work and, as usual, I am too tired to go about. The journey from my room to the office and back is enough. (*N.B.* – Better not let your parents read this, although it's their custom. So take precautions.)

Love to Eveline, Alain, and my niece. I hope she still goes into peals of laughter.

Salut,
S.W.

58 To her parents

10 May

Darlings,

I have just received a cable. I should be so glad if I could really believe your 'very happy'° is literally true . . . . I hope at least that Sylvie makes you happy when you see her, and that her peals of laughter are still the same.

Have the American papers said that the spring here is the best in living memory? The flowers of spring and early summer are all coming out together, and fruit blossom of every kind is full out. On Sundays the whole of London overflows into the parks. The sky is a pale, profound, delicious blue.

And you – I hope you are taking trips on the Hudson and that you sometimes make an hour's journey to be in the country. I beg you to do it. Have you enough money? Should I send you some? I easily could, I think.

I have not yet received the typed copies. But darling M., I didn't tell you to do it yourself. I said get the Delegation to do it.

[. . . .]

The few comrades I have here are still as kind as ever. But otherwise

I hardly see anybody. Unfortunately I have still not had time to mix at all in English circles.

I was very glad to hear that Mme C. is Sylvie's godmother.

Good-bye, darlings, God bless you.°

Fondest love,°

Simone

No doubt you will have seen in the papers that one of my good trade union comrades, G., has arrived here.

P.S. – I wish I could give you details of my work, etc. – But really it is better to wait until I can tell you all about it by word of mouth. I will tell you now, though, that I have no practical responsibilities. And I prefer it that way.

59 To the same

22 May '43

Darlings,

It seems a long time since I had any news . . . true there was a cable (to which I replied) a fortnight ago, saying 'very happy' (which is good to hear even if one only half believes it). But the last letter was dated 15 March . . . . What a lot of letters the Atlantic sharks must be eating! I wonder if they find ours digestible? I hope they get nourishment from them for their aesthetic faculties, etc., and learn to appreciate the submarine landscapes much better.

Everything still goes well for me here. C., who was away from London for a time, has just come back. I am glad, because he is a real comrade; and you know what those words mean to me. It's a piece of luck for me to be working with him. (I scarcely ever see A.Ph.)

For the rest, I have really had no dealings with anybody so far – except for occasional jobs to relieve the pressure on C., which interrupt the course of my ordinary work.

The latter is on a purely theoretical level. I have done another 'magnum opus',[1] or rather I am doing one, because it is not finished yet.

When it is finished, I really wonder what they can do with me? Such

---

[1] Probably the text which was posthumously published as *L'Enracinement* and has appeared in English as *The Need for Roots*.

SW O *

aptitudes as I possess (which amount to almost nothing, in my opinion) are still restricted in all sorts of ways....

Naturally, I don't think there is the slightest reason to suppose that what I am writing will ever have any effect.... But, as you can guess, that doesn't stop me from writing. Perhaps, darling M., one day you will type these things for me too (no news yet of the manuscripts).

All this strictly confidential.

As to what is being done now, whether it is good, bad, or doubtful, I have no part or responsibility in any of it, as I have told you. I scold my colleagues occasionally, but very seldom because one has so little time for talking. And they are such good comrades.... Apart from them I see almost nobody.

London is as hot as in summer. The parks are green. There are happy crowds in them after working hours. You be happy too, darlings. Get all the joys you can, and savour them. Next time you see Sylvie give her a nice smile from me. *And for you, my two darlings, fondest love and kisses°,*

Simone

P.S. – Darling M., have you read the *Shropshire Lad*? (By A. E. Housman, first published 1896.) If not, get it from our *Branch* of the *Public Library*. I have just re-read it and I like it more and more. It is in the 125th Street *Branch*.

P.P.S. – Just received your letter of 3 April, which sounds a bit depressed. What is this job? Are you short of money?

60 To the same

31 May

Darlings,

Just as I was finishing my last letter (a week ago) I received yours of April, by ordinary mail.

It seemed to me very gloomy. I hope that events since then have raised your morale.

Do you expect to see José[1] soon and make the acquaintance of her second little boy? Can it be arranged?

[....]

[1] A friend who lived in Morocco. This sentence evidently means: Have you any chance of being able to go to North Africa soon?

It seems to me that you would be so much better there, so far as human wisdom can discern better and worse. . . .

Darling M., perhaps you would see Antonio – if he is still alive . . . – and then he wouldn't think any more about me.

Here, we know nothing officially about our final establishment – whether we shall stay here or leave. But I think that by the force of events everything will gradually converge upon the same place.

Latterly everybody here (I mean the French) has been in a state of extreme nervous tension, from the uncertainty and delays.

Abnormally hot spring weather here, mixed with rain. They say fruit is already beginning to show . . . . Alas! Except for the almond trees in London I have not seen any flowering trees. Have you? I hope so.

My impression is that you haven't enough money to indulge in the smallest pleasure. Is it so? Do please tell me the truth. A little pleasure is as necessary in this world as water and bread (or coca-cola and corn-flakes°).

Thanks ever so much for the papers. I've got them.

I hope you have had my last letter in which I told you in detail about my work (if it deserves the name).

Nothing of interest here in the theatre for a long time. But soon, I'm told, they are going to do *As you like it* in the open air in a park. I hope not to miss that.

Keep a little joy in your hearts if you can, darlings.

Fondest love°
Simone

61 To the same

9 June '43

Darlings,

You must have been surprised, a little more than a month ago, to receive the same cable at New York and Bethlehem at almost the same time. There was a muddle which would take too long to explain, but a word will enlighten you: to save myself a journey to the post, I was rash enough to accept the services of S.D. That excellent child not only complicates everything in her own mind but creates comic opera in all her surroundings.

I have started doing a few lines of Sanskrit again every day, in the *Gita*. How it does one good, the language of Krishna!

To her parents 1943

What are your prospects? Mobile or stationary? I know nothing of mine.

You inquire about my *breakfast*°. I have no fixed rules, but by far the most convenient are the *tea-shops*°, of which there are always one or two just outside the tube stations (and I have a tube straight from my room to the office). These are the A.B.C.'s and Lyons.

I have been agreeably surprised by the cooking here (in view of what everyone said): some of the traditional dishes are remarkable, especially the *roast lamb with mint sauce*°. The *roast pork with apple sauce*° is also highly honourable. It must date back at least two thousand years (you follow my reasoning).

And it has been another surprise to see how much – and since long before the war, I believe – taste here has been influenced by the part of the world where you are. People have developed a taste for adulterations, especially chemical mixtures. This is particularly noticeable with drinks, but also with food (gelatine *jellies*°, chemical sauces, etc.).

I asked an Englishwoman here whether *apple sauce*° is eaten only with fowl or pork, or sometimes as a sweet also. She said: 'Rarely, or if so, mixed with jam.'

In my view, a change in dietary habits is an event of prime importance for the progress or decadence of real culture.

The pure taste of the apple is as much a contact with the beauty of the universe as the contemplation of a picture by Cézanne. (Darling M., do you remember the sonnet in which Rilke tries to express something like that?) And more people are capable of savouring a compote of apple than of contemplating Cézanne.

At least, so one would think. But today in great cities it is rather the other way round.

You won't be complaining, today, that I say nothing about food.... As regards *stout*°, there is a difficulty. Several of the places where I eat do not provide alcoholic drinks; and in the *pubs* one doesn't eat. That is how it is here. And I am incapable of swallowing a great glass of *stout* without eating anything.

Did I ever tell you that a *pub* and a bistro, side by side, would show more eloquently than many big volumes the difference between the two peoples – their history, their temperament, and the way the social question presents itself for each of them?

A *public-house*° is a place with compartments, separated by (literal) partitions, which open on to the same counter but which are almost completely shut off from one another's view. The personnel move from one part of the counter to another, being separated by the counter from the public in the two compartments. One of the compartments is entitled *public bar*°: in it there are one or two benches, sometimes a table, a darts board; the people in it are nearly all standing up, conversing in groups, each with a great glass of beer in his hand or within reach. They are very happy. Another compartment is entitled *saloon*°; it is more like our cafés. There are little tables and upholstered chairs. The drinks are exactly the same. People seem less happy. As a rule, this one is frequented by people of more position.

Sometimes there are one or two other compartments.

There is a symbol here; and when one considers it, a symbol of something very beautiful. Not as regards the people of position, obviously; but as regards the others.

These people – who have a great deal of dignity – are without the refractory spirit that my mother once used to have, and I respect them the more for it . . .

Well, it's time to part; au revoir, darlings. And darling M., enjoy the fine days and think of Krishna. And think of me only in thinking of each joy and each pleasure which I would enjoy if I was with you at the same time as being here, and enjoy it for me. May you both feel glad to be alive.

Fondest love,°

Simone

I have had your letter in which you say you are going to read *Erewhon* aloud. It gave me infinite pleasure.

62 To the same

15 June

Darlings,

I have just received your letter of 8 May. How happy it made me! Before they disappeared, I hope you filled your eyes and your hearts with the pink and white flowers of the trees on Riverside Drive. All that is ancient history here. What one sees now is cherries, strawberries, ripe peaches.

The roses have been early and abundant this year, like everything

To her parents 1943

else. Long before their usual date, I believe, they were out in profusion in the parks.

I am glad that B. no longer thinks of coming here. First, because there was never the slightest possibility. And second, because he would be very unhappy here. It is extremely easy to be so, if one has that sort of character; and as you know, he has it in a high degree.

You know too that I am very differently made.

[....]

The B.'s are away from London on holiday. I saw Mme B. just before they left. She is very nice – but a bit insular (I am thinking of something she said about the malnutrition of children on the Continent). She was going to write to A.

I also see Mme R. from time to time. She speaks of you both in the most touching terms. She's another one who would like to have her doctor again.

As to my landlady's little boy's thyroid, I carefully refrained from saying that I had made a diagnosis. I didn't want a repetition of the story of my appendicitis, do you remember? (No doubt, you remember better than I do!)

I am pleased by what you said about A.'s good mood while he was in New York. I feared he might have fallen into a state of permanent gloom. Perhaps he is beginning to work again a little?

Antigone has gone through a few bad patches, it's true. But they didn't last. It's all far away now.

I wonder if you really have a chance of a job in North Africa?

How uncertain and unpredictable everything is at the present time .... One can only live from day to day. At least, darling M., you ought not to be bored.

Listen – I forbid you to kill yourself with your pearl bags. Do just enough to keep yourself amused, and stop as soon as you are bored. I want, when I see you again, to find you as fresh and young as ever, and still looking like my younger sister ....

Don't worry at all. Neither about my food – I give you my word I eat regular meals which you yourselves would consider perfectly all right; nor about my clothes – I don't lack for anything.

It is true that between the hot days here there are some others when it would be very imprudent to go out in summer clothes. I am told it is the same in July and August.

Darlings°, I hope you are finding some good things in the *Public Library*°. Darling M., do you know that Meredith wrote some very nice poetry? I discovered that recently.

I do wish I could suggest some books so that we could feel together while you were reading them. But since I've been here I have hardly read anything. I have covered paper with ink....

My colleagues are a long way off. They don't know their luck in escaping the rough side of my tongue; without knowing anything, I still have little doubt that they richly deserve it (like all the others...). If you see B., be sure to tell him that I did not have, do not have, and, I hope, never will have (I'd rather sleep under bridges) any responsibility for anything – either for good or evil.

Did you not get my *Iliad* essay back from K. with the rest? He ought to have a copy.

I don't know whether the article about the Romans has arrived or not. The others are here. Thank you.

Greetings to A. Congratulate him from me on his first Communion (if he has made it). Ever so much love to Sylvie – and the same to you to the *n*th power.

Simone

P.S. – Might B.[1] not enjoy Jane Austen?

63 To the same

25 June

Darlings,

I held this letter back, making the usual mistake of waiting for one from you....

C. is back in London, but I haven't seen him yet. Although he is a comrade, or rather just because he is such a good comrade, I await this interview with some apprehension. There will certainly be some 'divergences of sociological outlook'. The allusion, if you remember, is to Dona Aurora[2]... But don't be uneasy. C. does not behave like that.

I am so fed up with all this inextricable absurdity that there are

---

[1] Simone Weil's father.
[2] The allusion is to a trial in Spain, about 1934. Dona Aurora, having killed her daughter whom she adored, was said to have accounted for her act by 'divergences of sociological outlook'.

times (and pretty often) when the only thing that interests me is to know whether you will get to North Africa.

[. . . .]

They say the Spaniards have been released from the camps. But who knows if Antonio is still alive?

I met here some time ago (did I tell you?) the son of Br., the man for whom you typed that letter, darling M. He was leaving the next day. Strange youth – very nice in some ways, it would seem. I had the impression that he was very annoyed with me for a long time because I did not reply to his father's letter ('Who are you'?).[1]

Life seems monotonous here just now. An oppressive lull of waiting for something.

As to theatres, etc., nothing of interest. The cinemas (I've not been to any) persist in showing films of the 'thriller' type, set in contemporary Europe (the Continent), about the struggle against the Gestapo.

They say that the public – especially the men and women in the Forces – instinctively protests and rushes to see any film, however dud, which has nothing to do with the war.

The roses are [2] nearly over. There are marvellous sweet-peas. The raw carrots served in salads are rather hard now (which does not, of course, prevent my eating them). The spring is already long past, and the summer, no doubt, will be brief. Really, one doesn't need many light clothes.

There is no question for me of a play, or poetry, or a theory of religions, or folklore, etc. But on the third point, I sometimes have the impression – true or false – that somewhere in the back of what I use for a brain something has arrived which might perhaps, later on, when I have some time, become an idea . . . .

In any case, all these buds of ideas always grow in the same direction. . . .

Well, au revoir, darlings, I embrace you both again and again and again.

Simone

Received your letter of 9 June, written at Bethlehem. Will do all I can. I, too, would be delighted.

---

[1] This refers to an article by S. W. in a magazine, about which the father, who did not know her, wrote her a letter of congratulation beginning with the words: 'Mademoiselle – Who are you?'

[2] One or more words deleted by the censor.

P.S. Saw C. Divergences less than I feared. But I can speak only for him personally.

64 To the same

5 July 1943

Darlings,
   The last letter I've had from you was dated 9 June. I could not tell from it whether you base your hopes of North Africa simply on the general situation or whether you have had definite and personal assurances. From here, I still cannot form any opinion as to your chances. Anyway, I have put in my word for you, with the most persuasive arguments I could think of. It's all I can do. Unfortunately, it does not depend directly upon Ph.

A little time ago, I made the acquaintance of a 'Blimp'. It is an interesting type to observe. He said he had suffered so much during the first three months of the war (i.e. 1939), having realised that in any case it was the end of everything, that something died in him and the disasters of war can no longer touch him. The cause of this frightful suffering was the first, very unsystematic, measures of State control and the appointment of a number of Leftist politicians to important jobs . . . . After that, how could any further disasters affect one!

Of course, this kind of thing is non-existent among the young, or so I am told.

For several days (and nights) the heat has been stifling. But don't be anxious, I am able to dress accordingly.

The spring certainly seems far away. It will soon be harvest, and a splendid one, they say. The strawberries are over. In their place one sees, first, 'loganberries', a sort of wild raspberry with quite a raspberry taste but very rough and sometimes very tart; and then proper raspberries. Apart from fruit and pudding, the sweet course is nearly always with gelatine. I'm told this fashion for gelatine dates from long before the war . . . . See one of my previous letters.

Before long – in an hour perhaps, or tomorrow, or the day after – there will be a wind and a little rain, and it will be almost cold. Or at least it is probable; and all London is waiting for it in a sort of suffocating torpor. This weather must be a trial for the people in factories. But for me, who don't have to move about, it is not intolerable.

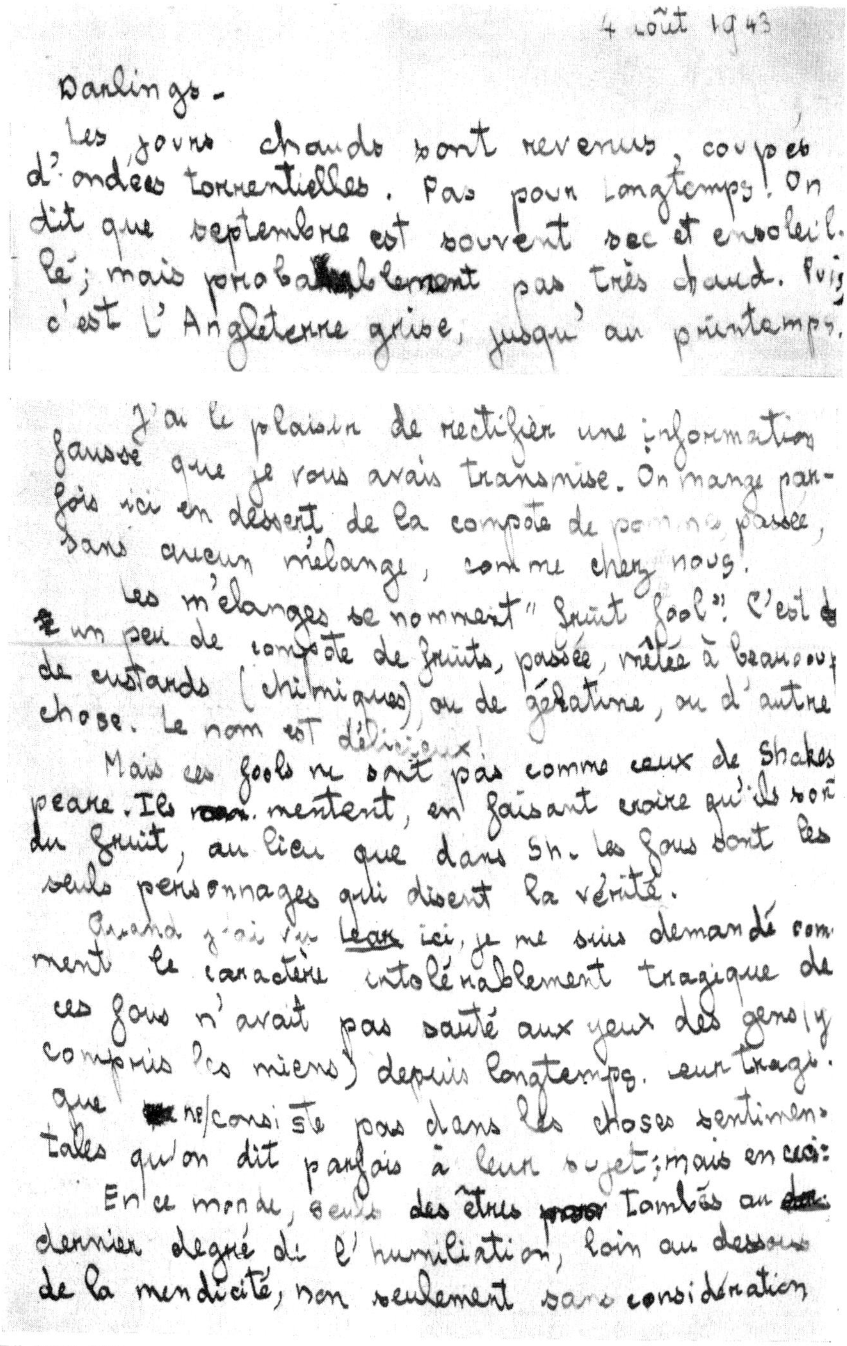

4 août 1943

Darlings –

Les jours chauds sont revenus, coupés d'ondées torrentielles. Pas pour longtemps! On dit que septembre est souvent sec et ensoleillé; mais probablement pas très chaud. Puis c'est l'Angleterre grise, jusqu'au printemps.

J'ai le plaisir de rectifier une information fausse que je vous avais transmise. On mange parfois ici en dessert de la compote de pommes passée, sans aucun mélange, comme chez nous.

Les mélanges se nomment "fruit fool". C'est un peu de compote de fruits, passée, mêlée à beaucoup de custards (chimiques) ou de gélatine, ou d'autre chose. Le nom est délicieux!

Mais ces fools ne sont pas comme ceux de Shakespeare. Ils mentent, en faisant croire qu'ils sont du fruit, au lieu que dans Sh. les fous sont les seuls personnages qui disent la vérité.

Quand j'ai vu leurs ici, je me suis demandé comment le caractère intolérablement tragique de ces fous n'avait pas sauté aux yeux des gens (y compris les miens) depuis longtemps. Leur tragique ne consiste pas dans les choses sentimentales qu'on dit parfois à leur sujet; mais en ceci:

En ce monde, seuls des êtres tombés au dernier degré de l'humiliation, loin au dessous de la mendicité, non seulement sans considération

PLATE III

The opening, and a later portion, of Simone Weil's letter to her parents, 4 August 1943 (No. 68 in this book, pp. 199, 200) (Continued overleaf)

sociale, mais regardés par tous comme dépourvus de la première dignité humaine, la raison — seuls ceux-là ont en fait la possibilité de dire la vérité. Tous les autres mentent.

Dans Lear, c'est frappant. Même Kent et Cordélia atténuent, mitigent, adoucissent, voilent la vérité, louvoient avec elle, tant qu'ils ne sont pas forcés ou de la dire ou de mentir carrément.

Je ne sais pas ce qu'il en est des autres pièces, que je n'ai ni vues ni relues ici (sauf 12th Night). Darling M., si tu relisais un peu Sh. avec cette pensée, tu y verrais peut-être des aspects nouveaux.

L'extrême du tragique est que, les fous n'ayant ni titre de professeur ni mitre d'évêque, personne n'étant prévenu qu'il faille accorder quelque attention au sens de leurs paroles — chacun étant d'avance sûr du contraire, puisque ce sont des fous — leur expression de la vérité n'est même pas entendue. Personne, y compris les lecteurs et spectateurs de Sh. depuis 4 siècles, ne sait qu'ils disent la vérité. Non des vérités satiriques ou humoristiques, mais la vérité tout court. Des vérités pures, sans mélange, lumineuses, profondes, essentielles.

Est-ce aussi le secret des fous de Velasquez ? La tristesse dans leurs yeux est-elle l'amertume de posséder de la vérité, d'avoir, au prix d'une dégradation sans nom, la possibilité de la dire, et de n'être entendus par personne ? (sauf Velasquez.) Cela vaudrait la peine de les revoir avec cette question.

Darling M., sens-tu l'affinité, l'analogie essentielle entre ces fous et moi — malgré l'École, l'agrégation et les éloges de mon "intelligence" ? Ceci est encore une réponse sûre que j'ai à donner.

PLATE IV

Continuation of Simone Weil's letter to her parents, 4 August 1943 (No. 68 in this book, p. 200)

To her parents 1943

Your descriptions of Sylvie are a delight to me. It must be lovely to be in a park with her. When you are, think that I am there with you. . . . At least you will have known the joy of being grandparents.

Tell me what you are reading now.

Au revoir, darlings. I hug you both again and again.

Simone

65 To the same

12 July 43

Darlings,

I have just received your cable. I hope you will see Antonio.[1] I am still without any information in the matter.

Have had a long, very nice, letter from Blanche. Will you thank her and say that I will write as soon as I am able and have the time to tell her a lot of interesting things?

(That, I should imagine, will be when pigs fly in formation.)

I think all the time about Sylvie and her sunny laughter. But whatever nostalgia I also feel for the yolk of eggs and vegetables and fruit which I didn't eat at five months and which would have imparted today such an accelerated rhythm to my work of covering sheets of paper which no one will ever look at (except you, perhaps, some day . . . .), I would rather have had a mother like mine (not to mention the father), in spite of the inadequate milk . . . . As Mme D. would have sententiously put it, there is more than one kind of milk.

I hope she isn't given gelatine.

Tell A. that I have on my desk the Education Report he speaks of. At first sight it does not seem very inspiring; but I have not had time to read it. I don't know if I shall be able to get it sent to him.

Nothing of interest here. People (I mean our compatriots) get more and more tense. Mental phenomena of exile. I keep more and more out of things. (Which doesn't imply the slightest discord with my colleagues.) It is much better that way.

Have got to know a few English girls, very young and very nice. It is interesting. But the opportunities to see people and converse at leisure are very, very limited. It is the same everywhere today.

Au revoir, darlings. Thousands of kisses.

Simone

[1] That is to say: I hope you will soon get to Algiers.

66 To the same

18 July 43

Darlings,

Your description in your last letter of your stay at Bethlehem gave me a lot of pain and pleasure at the same time. A lot of pain, because of the heat and other discomforts, and I do so want you to have nothing but well-being in every way! At the same time I am very glad you don't put on rose-coloured spectacles when you write. If the colours are mixed one knows one is getting the truth and letters can bring you really close.

Naturally, it was the parts about Sylvie that gave me pleasure. You can never tell me too much about her; I am insatiable. You cannot imagine what it is for me. It makes me happy both to think of her and to think of the brief but unalloyed happiness she has given you. I only wish she had somewhere to walk where there are no crocodiles of little schoolgirls.

There seems to be nothing in her circumstances at present which could make her grow up as a 'Mary in tar'.[1]

I am delighted, too, that the A.'s and the Reverends[2] are nice and sympathetic neighbours. Remember me to all. And tell the young one that I think of her and do not forget her, and that I very fervently hope the spiritual good she desires will come to her one day *authentically*.

Darling M. you think that I have something to give. That is the wrong way to put it. But I too have a sort of growing inner certainty that there is within me a deposit of pure gold which must be handed on. Only I become more and more convinced, by experience and by observing my contemporaries, that there is no one to receive it.

It is indivisible, and whatever is added to it becomes part of it. And as it grows it becomes more compact. I cannot distribute it piecemeal.

To receive it calls for an effort. And effort is so fatiguing!

Some people feel in a confused way that there is something. But once they have made a few polite remarks about my intelligence their conscience is clear. After which, they listen to me or read me with the same hurried attention which they give to everything, making up their minds definitely about each separate little hint of an idea as soon as it appears: 'I agree with this', 'I don't agree with that', 'this is marvel-

---

[1] Presumably a reference to the Grimm story 'Mother Holle'.
[2] An American clergyman and his wife who lived on the same floor as S.W.'s parents.

lous', 'that is completely idiotic' (the latter antithesis comes from my chief). In the end they say: 'Very interesting', and pass on to something else. They have avoided fatigue.

What else can one expect? I am convinced that the most fervent Christians among them don't concentrate their attention much more when they are praying or reading the Gospel.

Why imagine it is better elsewhere? I have seen some of those elsewheres.

As for posterity, before there is a generation with muscle and power of thought the books and manuscripts of our day will surely have disappeared.

This does not distress me at all. The mine of gold is inexhaustible.

As for the practical uselessness of my writing effort – since they refused to give me the job I wanted, that or something ... (but I cannot conceive the possibility for myself of anything else).

There it is.

The chance of your seeing Antonio[1] is what chiefly interests me now. But don't count on it too much, for fear of disappointment. I am still without any information on the subject.

Au revoir, darlings. A thousand kisses.

Simone

67 To the same

28 July 1943

Darlings,

I have just received two letters (7 and 14 July). That makes it easier to talk.

There's been a misunderstanding. There's no change for me, and none in prospect, so far. I still live quietly in my room, with my books distributed between it and the office.

If you are successful – once it is actually settled – I'll tell my colleagues, who will understand what they have to do. And I'll back them up. I'll say that from the point of view of my capacity for work, and so on ....

Actually, I have already explained all that to them, as an argument on your behalf.

From the French side, I don't think there will be any difficulties as far as I am concerned. I can't see any possible obstacle.

[1] See note on p. 195.

But once the thing is authorized in writing, there may still be very long delays (or short – everything depends upon the situation at the time).

André (the one here) thinks there may be similar delays for you.

I have seen C., and spoke to him again about you. He spoke to André, who was passing through. André sees no objections and thinks there won't be any difficulty. [He thinks] that as regards the French authorities it's very easy. (This is very hopeful, but wait... perhaps it doesn't depend solely on him. Don't rejoice too soon!)

But André warns, etc. (See above.)

If I were you, I should go at once to see the paternal old gentleman with white hair, if you remember, and ask what the position is.

But, from another point of view, what is much more important still is to go and see those very useful people at the extreme south of Manhattan. (Or have you done so already?) If I were you, unless the French officials have become extremely efficient, I should try – with the help of M.'s irresistible smile – to expedite matters with those people. Reminding them of your previous visits with me.

Speaking of Manhattan, I read somewhere that Walt Whitman was born in Brooklyn, died in New Jersey, and – except for a journey to New Orleans when he was about thirty, and several years during the civil war at Washington, where he was employed in an office and devoted his spare time to *welfare work*° in military hospitals – he spent his whole life in New York.

I never knew that! (Check whether it's true)

[....]

... For me it is as difficult to do what is called 'pulling strings' as to climb Mount Everest. A similar kind of incapacity.

... I expect to see Sch. very soon. I will explain the position to him. He will do something if he can, and if he chooses (it is very difficult just now to foretell people's reactions).

[....]

Sch., unlike me, has never thought of collecting odds and ends of knowledge which didn't concern him, so his ignorance of science is total; and in consequence he has an infatuated admiration for everything scientific. He is much more right-minded than me. And is infinitely younger. And very, very nice.

Unfortunately, it is not only about science that I am heretical. One of these days I shall cause him pain. It would have happened already, no doubt, only I haven't seen him for two months.

[. . . .]

C. has promised to do something about you without delay as soon as he has gone to join the other André. If the affair moves too slowly you should get the Delegation to telegraph about you to the latter. But only at a time when C. will be with him. Then I would telegraph to C. at the same time, informing you by cable if necessary.

Don't hope too much!

A thousand kisses for you both, *my darlings*.

Simone

68 To the same

Darlings,

4 August 1943

The hot weather is back, mixed with torrential rain. But not for long. They say September is often dry and sunny, but probably not very hot. After that it is the English greyness until the spring.

In the evenings people dance in the open air in the parks. The more frivolous little *cockney*° girls go every evening to the *parks*° and the *pubs*° with *boys*° whom they pick up on the way – to the great distress of their mothers, who cannot persuade them to go to church instead. They don't see the point of it.

Of course, I am writing in the plural when I mean the singular. I am thinking of a little girl of nineteen, fresh, wholesome, pretty, very nice, who comes here to do the housework. I sometimes have little talks with her, in spite of the language barrier. She often tells me long stories of which I can't catch a word, and then asks my opinion; I vigorously approve, and it makes me tremble to think what blasphemies or immoral notions I may have endorsed! I believe, though, that she does take care of herself with the boys, as she puts it. Most of her free time, apart from boys, goes to the hairdresser. She hasn't got two ideas in her head, or rather, not one. Family pure *cockney*. District; the City. Father: tobacco worker; goes to *pub* on Sunday mornings (but without drinking to excess, it appears). Mother: very pious Methodist. Six children, including two boys, aged between 19 and 9. The nine-year-old girl spends the whole of Sunday at church (Methodist), and with her mother is the only one to do so. She likes it very much. It seems the father is the only one in the family who reads a newspaper. The eldest daughter (the one I know) thinks of the war simply as the risk of a bomb falling on her. She hasn't the faintest idea of what is going on.

I am glad to be able to correct some false information I gave you. As with us, strained apple compote *is* sometimes eaten here as a sweet by itself.

Mixtures are known as 'fruit fool'°; they consist of a compote of fruit, strained, and mixed with a lot of (chemical) custard or gelatine or suchlike. The name is delightful!

But these *fools*° are not like the ones in Shakespeare. They are liars, in pretending to be fruit, whereas in Sh. the fools are the only people who tell the truth.

When I saw *Lear* here, I asked myself how it was possible that the unbearably tragic character of these fools had not been obvious long ago to everyone, including myself. The tragedy is not the sentimental one it is sometimes thought to be; it is this:

There is a class of people in this world who have fallen into the lowest degree of humiliation, far below beggary, and who are deprived not only of all social consideration but also, in everybody's opinion, of the specific human dignity, reason itself – and these are the only people who, in fact, are able to tell the truth. All the others lie.

In *Lear* it is striking. Even Kent and Cordelia attenuate, mitigate, soften, and veil the truth; and unless they are forced to choose between telling it and telling a downright lie, they manoeuvre to evade it.

I do not know if it is the same in the other plays, which I have neither seen nor re-read here (except *Twelfth Night*). Darling M., if you were to re-read a bit of Sh[akespeare] with this in mind, perhaps it would reveal some new aspects.

What makes the tragedy extreme is the fact that because the fools possess no academic titles or episcopal dignities and because no one is aware that their sayings deserve the slightest attention – everybody being convinced *a priori* of the contrary, since they are fools – their expression of the truth is not even listened to. Everybody, including Sh.'s readers and audiences for four centuries, is unaware that what they say is true. And not satirically or humorously true, but simply the truth. Pure unadulterated truth – luminous, profound, and essential.

Is this also the secret of Velasquez's fools? Are their eyes so sad because of the bitterness of possessing the truth and having won at the price of nameless degradation, the power to utter it and then being listened to by nobody (except Velasquez)? It would be worth while to look at them again with this idea in mind.

Darling M., do you feel the affinity, the essential analogy between these fools and me – in spite of the École and the examination successes and the eulogies of my 'intelligence'?

This is another reply on 'what I have to give'.

In my case, the École, etc., are just another irony.

Everyone knows that a high intelligence is often paradoxical and sometimes a bit wild....

The eulogies of my intelligence are positively *intended* to evade the question: 'Is what she says true?' And my reputation for 'intelligence' is practically equivalent to the label of 'fool' for those fools. How much I would prefer their label!

Nothing new about your prospects since my last letter (of 28 July; let me know by cable if you don't receive it). Nor about mine.

[....]

A thousand kisses, darlings. Hope, but with moderation. Be happy. I hug you both again and again.

Simone

69 To the same

16 August 1943

Darlings,

Very little time or inspiration for letters now. They will be short, erratic, and far between. But you have another source of consolation.

By the time you get this (unless it arrives quickly) perhaps you will also have the awaited cable. (But nothing is certain!...)

[....]

Au revoir, darlings. Heaps and heaps of love.

Simone

INDEX

INDEX

(References are to pages)

Aeschylus, 103, 123, 125, 129
Alain, *see* Chartier
Algebra, xiii, 3, 113, 117
Alsthom (Paris factory), 1, 6, 10 n., 55
American Red Cross, 153
Analogy, Method of, 3, 5
Anaximander, 159
Annam, *see* Indo-China
Annunzio, Gabriele d', 83
Antigone, 49, 50, 51, 91, 161
Anti-Semitism, 95, 99, 144
Apollonius, 113
Arabs, the, 101, 111
Archimedes, 74, 118, 133
Archytas, 114, 115
Aristotle, 120
Assisi, 85, 86
Assyrians, the, 160
Attente de Dieu, xii
Austen, Jane, 192
Autran, Charles, 118
Auxerre, 1

B., Monsieur (Manager of factory near Bourges), x, 1, 30
Babylon, Babylonians, 112-19, 160
Bach, J. S., 82, 87, 93; Andante of 4th Brandenburg Concerto: 73, 83, 93
Barcelona, 106, 108
Bernanos, Georges, x, xiii, 166
Bhagavad-Gita, the, 135, 159, 188
'Blimp', A, 194
Boétie, Estienne de la, 92
Bologna, 77, 79
'Bourbaki', 88
Bourges, 20, 23, 43
Bousquet, Joë, 145
Bramante, 80
Broglie, L.-V. de, 88, 90
Brunelleschi, 75, 81
Buddhism, 159

Catharism, xii, xiii, 129-31, 143, 159
Catholicism, xiii, 23, 105, 126, 155, 159, 171, 172
Cellini, Benvenuto, 75, 77
Cézanne, Paul, 189
Chaplin, Charles, 44

Chartier, Emile-Auguste, (Alain), 3, 44
Christ, Christianity, xii, xiii, 23, 44, 75, 80, 103, 105, 122, 125, 129, 130, 140, 141, 155, 159, 160, 161, 171, 172, 175, 176, 178, 197
Cicero, 128
Class feeling, 24, 25, 41
Communism, Communists, xi, 7, 33, 53, 59, 61, 94, 99
Condition ouvrière, La, x, xi
Czecho-Slovakia, 94, 96, 100

Daladier, Edouard, 95
Dante, 75, 78, 83
Descartes, 3, 88
Detœuf, Auguste (Director of Alsthom), x, 1, 10, 61, 64, 91
Dickens, Charles, 181, 183
Diogenes, 123
Dionysius the Areopagite, 160
Dionysus, 122, 123, 160
Diophantus, xiii, 113, 117
Donatello, 75
Donizetti, 79

École Normale Supérieure, 9, 13, 110 n., 155 n., 201
Écrits historiques et politiques, x, 71
Egypt, Egyptians, 112, 116, 117, 124, 128, 130, 160
England, 96, 97, 100, 128, 132, 143, 145, 162, 163, ('Potato Fair') 165, (Police) 180
English cooking, 189, (Gelatine) 195, 200
Entretiens au bord de la mer, 5
Epictetus, 129
Erewhon, 190
Euclid, 115, 121
Eudoxus, 2, 88, 91, 115, 116, 121
Existentialism, 161; 'Dasein', 159

Farrington, Benjamin, xiii
Fascism, Fascist, xii, xiii, 7, 40, 53, 81, 127; (Casa del Fascio at Florence) 84
Ferrara, 77
Flandin, P.-E., 6, 94, 102
Florence, 72, 73, 74-75, 77-78, 81, 83, 85, 88
Forges de Basse-Indre (Paris factory), 1, 17
Francis, St., 78-79, 85, 86, 123, 126, 129

Francis, Mrs., 166, 180, 181, 191
Fresnel, 89
Front-line Nurses, Plan for an organization of, 136, 145-53

Galileo, 75, 83, 126
Geometry, 2, 13, 112, 113, 116, 121, 160
Germany, 7, 71, 94-95, 96, 97, 99-101, 106, 152, 158
Ghiberti, 75
Giambologna, 75
Gide, André, 12
Giorgione, 77, 81, 83, 93
Giotto, 75, 83, 85, 88, 93, 126
Gracchi, the, 128
Giraudoux, Jean, xi, 91
Goethe, xii, 72, 76, 85
Goya, 93

Ham, Hamitic, 160
Harlem, *see* New York
Hebrews, the, xi, 122, 129, 160
Hegel, 6
Heraclitus, 159
Herbert, George, 142 n.
Herodotus, 122
History, 9, 10, 13
Hitler, Adolf, 97, 98, 100, 148, 149, 151, 152, 158, 161
Homer, 93, 103, 118, 181
Horace, 77
Housman, A. E., 187
Huyghens, Christian, 89

Iliad, the, 49, 92, 93, 103, 192
Indian thought, 119
Indo-China, 101, 110-11
Isaiah, 160, 170
Italy, xi, xii, 71, 72, 88, 91, 92, 106, 127

Japan, 7
Jews, *see* Hebrews
Job, 160
John of the Cross, St., 135, 159
'Journal d'Espagne' (*Écrits historiques et politiques*), x, 71
'Journal d'usine' (*La Condition ouvrière*), x, xi

King Lear, 102-4, 200
Krishna, 179, 181, 184, 188, 190

Lagrange, 135
Lawrence, D. H., x, 93
Lawrence, T. E., 93, 163

Lenin, 15
Le Puy, 1
London, 143, 144, 145, 155, 156, 157, 161, 162, 165, 180, 183, 184, 185, 187, 188; ('the City') 97; (Notting Hill), 180
Lorenzo de'Medici, 75, 83
Louis XIV, 94
Lucretius, 73

Machiavelli, 75, 83
Manichaeism, xiii, 130, 159
Marcus Aurelius, 85, 129, 140
Marseilles, 71, 132, 133, 143, 157
Marxism, 6
Masaccio, 83, 93
Mathematics, 2, 8, 112-21, 133, 135, 184
Maurras, Charles, 160
Menaechmus, 114, 115
Meredith, George, 192
Meunier, Mario, 87
Michelangelo, 74, 75, 78, 80, 81, 83, 87
Middlesex Hospital, 169, 182
Milan, 72, 73, 75, 76, 79, 85
Modern Times (film), 44, 58
Montaigne, Michel de, 91
Monteverdi, 78, 82, 83, 93; *Incoronazione di Poppaea*: 82, 88
Moses, 160, 172
Moulins, 6
Mozart, 78, 82; (*Figaro*) 83
Mussolini, B., 73, 91
Musset, A. de, 74

Napoleon, 94
Nebuchadnezzar, 160
Neugebauer, Otto, 134
New York, 143, 144, 145, 157, 169, 181, 183, 190, 198; Harlem: 180, 182
Nietzsche, F. W., 122, 123
Noah, 160, 161
Nouveaux Cahiers, Les, 61, 64, 91

Odyssey, the, 79, 92, 126
Orphism, 117, 124, 125
Osiris, 122, 160

Pacifism, xi (passive defence exercises) 8, 158
Pallanza (Lake Maggiore), 72, 73
Pascal, 89
Péguy, Charles, 97
Perrin, Father J.-M., x, 71
Persia, 115, 128, 130
Pétain, Marshal, 158
Petrarch, 75, 83

Index

Pherekydes, 159
Physics, 2, 4, 5, 13, 89-90, 134-5
Planck, Max, 88, 90, 134, 135
Plato, Platonism, xiii, 86-87, 91, 114, 116, 117, 123, 125, 126, 130, 131, 135, 159; *Gorgias*, 86, 125; *Phaedrus*, 73, 78; *Philebus*, 123-4; *Republic*, 84-85, 86, 88, *Theaetetus*, 86, 121; *Epinomis*, 121
Plutarch, 92
Popper, Karl, xiii
Prometheus, 124, 160
Public Houses, 180, 189, 190, 199
Pythagoras, Pythagoreans, 2, 76, 112, 113, 114, 115, 116, 117, 118, 119, 120, 121, 124, 125, 131, 137, 159

Raphael, 82
Ravenna, 77
Rembrandt, 76, 93
Renault (Paris factory), 1, 6, 56, 58, 59, 61, 62, 156
Retz, Cardinal de, 36
Reynaud, Paul, 158
Roanne, 1
Roman Empire, 113, 115, 119, 130, 137, 152, 161; S.W.'s essay on, 182
Rome, 78, 79-82, 85, 87; Roman Law, 128
Rossini, 79, 83
Russell, Bertrand, xiii
Russia, Russians, xii, 7, 8, 10, 62, 63, 67, 101, 149, 152

St. Etienne (Lycée at), 14
St. Quentin (Lycée at), 71
Shakespeare, 102-4, 180, 200
Socialism, Socialists, 7, 40
Socrates, xiii, 87, 120, 121, 125, 181

Sophocles, 49, 51, 91, 93, 102, 103, 129
Spain, x, xii, 71, 76, 105-9
Spartans, the, 160
Spinoza, 87
Stay-in strikes, 52, 57-61
Stendhal, 73
Stévin, 135
Stoicism, xiii, 38, 50, 125, 140, 159
Sumerians, the, 112, 160

Tacitus, 75
Taoism, xii, 159
Témoignage Chrétien, Cahiers du, 144, 154, 155
Teresa, St., 123
Thales, 2, 113, 159
Thibon, Gustave, x, 71
Thorez, Maurice, 59
Titian, 77
Toscanini, Arturo, 85, 86
Trotsky, L., 15
Toulouse, 130

Upanishads, the, xiii, 159

Valéry, Paul, 92
Velasquez, 200, 201
Venice, 72, 77
Venise sauvée, 168n.
Verdi, G., 73, 78, 79
Verrocchio, 75
Vichy, 32, 157, 159
Vinci, Leonardo da, 75, 76, 81, 93, 126

Wagner, R., 78, 80, 87, 122
Walter, Bruno, 78, 82
Whitman, Walt, 198

Made in United States
Orlando, FL
07 August 2023